CURRENT PROSE

A COLLEGE READER

by

Robert J. Geist

Michigan State College

and

Thomas A. Bledsoe

Formerly, University of Illinois

Rinehart & Company, Incorporated

Publishers in New York and Toronto

Second Printing, July, 1954

**Copyright, 1953, by
Robert J. Geist and Thomas A. Bledsoe**
Printed in the United States of America
Library of Congress Catalog Card Number: 53-6819

NOTE TO THE TEACHER

IN CURRENT PROSE we have tried to assemble a rather brief collection of interesting and teachable essays which reflect the kind of reading the average student is likely to do after college. And we have tried to choose essays which, either as models or as departure points, can lead, in a college course in composition, to the kind of writing he will need to do.

We have assumed that the kind of reading the student is likely to do is good, clear, contemporary, and generally informal exposition. Accordingly, the book is, as the title suggests, current: most of these pieces have been written since the end of World War II, and our two selections from the nineteenth century, a letter by Macaulay and a chapter from *Life on the Mississippi,* we chose for their contemporary relevance.

We have gone to a great many sources, some of them frequently represented in anthologies, some of them not. We have drawn rather heavily on the better newspapers, for example. Most of these selections are from columnists and feature writers, but we have included a news story and an editorial. We have gone to a number of magazines of various sorts; we have excerpted from a number of recent books. In short, we have tried to make CURRENT PROSE a fair cross sample of the kind of reading the college student and graduate will encounter while getting on with the business of being alive in America in the 1950's.

As a result, most of the selections in this book have not been previously anthologized. However, we have not made a fetish of newness. We have included a number of frequently reprinted pieces, like Thurber's "University Days," classics of their kind. We have tried to make our mixture a stimulating blend of the familiar and the new.

The selections encompass a wide variety of subject matter. We have avoided categories or the attempt to cover areas of anything whatever; in our reading we looked for the kind of writing we wanted to represent, with no preconceived notions of what topics should be covered. Of course, in the process of collecting more than seventy essays, kinds of patterns inevitably emerge, and we have arranged them in a series of loose clusters that seem to us to frequently illuminate through juxtaposition. We have used no labels. If the student is sometimes provoked by one essay to read on to another related one, our arrangement will succeed.

Avoiding categories, however, does not mean avoiding ideas. CURRENT PROSE would be a poor reflection of good contemporary writing if it were not lively and provocative. The content, the scope, the approach of these essays varies widely; we believe their level of interest is consistently high. Most of the important issues of our time, and many of the basic problems of the human condition, are considered in one essay or another—considered, we believe, in terms the student can and should be expected to comprehend.

We have deliberately varied the length, range, and complexity of these pieces. We have used a number of quite short essays, things of the length the student himself may frequently be called on to write. These are balanced by a similar number of fairly long essays (five to seven thousand words); the majority of the selections are of medium length, bulky enough for a class hour, but not too long for careful analysis. We do not believe there is anything here the student should not be expected to master; but within this framework we have ranged

Note to the Teacher vii

from things which can be quickly assimilated to those which will stretch him a little. We believe there is stimulation here for the quickest, and clarity for all.

All these essays are intended to lead to writing. Many of them can serve as models, the others as springboards. Because we believe that reading in a composition course should lead to writing, and also that many writing difficulties begin as reading difficulties, we have emphasized both reading and writing in our Suggestions for Study. Many of the questions concern rhetoric and structure; some concern content and ideas. With a few exceptions, the Suggestions for Study end with a question on vocabulary (questions on vocabulary in context, which occasionally contain some jokers) and a suggested writing assignment. Most of the time we have concentrated on questions which we hope will lead to other questions, and which will get the student into the reading as a piece of writing. In the beginning of the book we have rather consistently begun by asking for the main idea; in later sections, to make room for other questions, we have frequently omitted this. Obviously, however, our whole approach in these questions requires that the student make a start by deciding what the essay is all about.

In place of introductory analyses we have provided brief leads of the sort the student will find in most contemporary magazines. We did this partly because these are a familiar device in the reading he is likely to do on his own, but more out of a desire not to intervene between the student and the essay or the teacher and the student. As every teacher knows, and as the anthologist is painfully reminded, the problem of what to do—or not to do—with apparatus in a book of readings is one that never gets satisfactorily answered. We have tried to make our apparatus useful but not obtrusive, serviceable but not gaudy.

We have confined this book to exposition,[1] in the belief that exposition is what the student is learning to write and is what he is most in need of learning how to read. The classic types are all represented, and identification of these methods

---

[1] The teacher who wishes to supplement this collection of contemporary exposition with fiction, poetry, or older essays is referred to three inexpensive Rinehart Editions: *The Rinehart Book of Short Stories*, *The Rinehart Book of Verse*, and *Great English and American Essays*.

viii *Note to the Teacher*

is found in the Suggestions for Study. There is no narrative *per se,* but there is a good deal of expository narrative, a method the student frequently finds compatible and uses well. Questions on these pieces point up the expository intent. There are several examples of the extended use of description to develop an expository idea.

Our fundamental premise, besides a belief in the interrelation of reading and writing and in the importance of the student's becoming well acquainted with modern informal prose, is that—keeping in mind the teacher's interests and the student's frame of reference—both want material that fits and neither wants to be bored. We hope we have satisfied both needs.

Our indebtedness to the authors, newspapers, magazines, and publishers for permission to reprint is recorded at the bottom of the opening page of each essay. Without them there would have been no anthology. We are further indebted to many of our colleagues and friends for suggestions and criticisms, and especially to Frank Norvish, of Northeastern University, for a warm and thoughtful reading, and to William Hackett, William Pate, and John Pickering for belief, help, encouragement. To Esther Gist, Jeanne Magee, Al Margolies, and Ceil Neville, our thanks for cooperation well beyond the call of duty in getting the book out properly—and on time. And to our wives, not only for useful suggestions and criticisms, but for tolerating the kind of isolation anthologizing demands, this book is affectionately dedicated.

Lansing, Michigan R. J. G.
Port Washington, New York T. A. B.
February, 1953

TABLE OF CONTENTS

....

The Dark Side of Mercury   **1**
    by JOHN CROSBY

The Grammarian   **2**
    by RICHARD LOCKRIDGE

University Days   **8**
    by JAMES THURBER

Athletes   **15**
    by DAVID MURRAY

Too Much Football   **17**
    by ALLEN JACKSON

Heartache on the Campus   **36**
    by MRS. GLENN FRANK

x   Contents

I Sent My Wife to Vassar　46
　　　by VANCE PACKARD

from *Kon-tiki*　60
　　　by THOR HEYERDAHL

from *The Sea Around Us*　67
　　　by RACHEL CARSON

The Spaceship　71
　　　by ARTHUR C. CLARKE

Nature's Utmosts　76
　　　by ALAN DEVOE

The Wind That Means Life to India　83
　　　by SANTHA RAMA RAU

The Window in St. Martin's Stomach　88
　　　by RICHARD MATCH

Science Can Be Silly　97
　　　by ANTHONY STANDEN

Academic Upheaval　102
　　　by JOHN T. COX, JR.

Career at Y-12　105
　　　by DANIEL LANG

On War　118
　　　by RUTH BENEDICT

Contents   xi

Journey into Fear   **121**
     by WILLIAM D. BLAIR, JR.

War and the Lady Correspondent   **128**
     by WALTER BERNSTEIN

New American Language   **133**
     by JOHN CROSBY

The Acid Test   **136**
     by ROSCOE FLEMING

American English   **138**
     by IVOR BROWN

Maine Speech   **141**
     by E. B. WHITE

But Me No Shoulder Butts   **144**
     by H. I. B.

Fony and Fantom   **146**
     by WILLIAM CHAPMAN WHITE

Haywire   **149**
     by JOHN ALLAN MAY

Retroactive Weather   **151**
     by JOHN CROSBY

"When Your Mother Is Hung"   **153**
     by CATHERINE DRINKER BOWEN

Contents

How to Write a Letter by CAMERON SHIPP	154
An Entirely New Book by E. J. KAHN, JR.	159
Birth of the St. Louis Blues by W. C. HANDY	171
Swing Music by JAMES A. POLING	177
Down with Sense by FRED LOUNSBERRY	179
In Defense of Sense by RICHARD RODGERS	183
We Were Sixteen by THOMAS SANCTON	187
from *My Story* by MARY ROBERTS RINEHART	193
I Love Nelly by JIMMY SAVO	198
A Miserable, Merry Christmas by LINCOLN STEFFENS	203
Coon Hunt by E. B. WHITE	209

A Cub-Pilot's Experience	215
by SAMUEL L. CLEMENS	
The Campers Are Coming	223
by WILLIAM CHAPMAN WHITE	
Maine Guide	225
by LOUISE DICKINSON RICH	
Clucks and Quacks	229
by JOHN GOULD	
Jersey Fair	232
by BERNARD PEYTON, JR.	
Souvenir Shopping	234
by BERNARD KALB	
The Murdered TV Set	238
an editorial from the New York Herald Tribune	
Salt of the Earth	239
by MABEL SLACK SHELTON	
In Praise of Salt Pork	243
by WILLIAM CHAPMAN WHITE	
The Cocktail Party	246
by ART BUCHWALD	

xiv   Contents

I Admire the Human Race   249
  by ROGER WILLIAM RIIS

A Letter to Will Durant   252
  by H. L. MENCKEN

Co-educational Soap Worship   256
  by RED SMITH

On Not Conforming   260
  by RUTH BENEDICT

They Didn't Conform   263
  by PEG SONENFELDT

The Strangest Place in Chicago   266
  by JOHN BARTLOW MARTIN

A Letter to an American   280
  by THOMAS BABINGTON MACAULAY

It's Hideously True   284
  by AL CAPP

Confession of a Confederate   293
  by NUNNALLY JOHNSON

An Englishman Views the Republican Convention   297
  by JOHN ALLAN MAY

from *The Making of an Insurgent*   301
  by FIORELLO H. LA GUARDIA

Bosses and Machines   313
    by EDWARD J. FLYNN

Is It Anyone We Know?   317
    by AGNES ROGERS

The Wife Problem   328
    by WILLIAM H. WHYTE, JR.

Lend an Ear to Old Case   346
    by CLAY FELKER *and* ERNEST HAVEMANN

"There But for the Grace of God"   358
    by MILTON GROSS

The Champ Is Gone, but...   361
    by JOE CUMMISKEY

This I Believe   364
    by DAVID E. LILIENTHAL

CURRENT PROSE

A College Reader

If education, like charity, begins at home, it is more and more likely, these days, to begin in front of the television set. Here a well-known columnist considers television's influence in educating the young.

THE DARK SIDE OF MERCURY
by John Crosby

SCIENCE FICTION WRITERS are plagued by a lot of small vexations. They have to learn how to cuss in outer space lingo ("Blast me for a Martian mouse!"). They have to get acclimated to the fact that "Tennis, anyone?" is not quite the proper line for a space cadet on Jupiter. Lately, the writers have been assaulted by a vicious new menace, namely small fry who know too much for their own good.

Just recently Tom Corbett, Space Cadet, took a terrible scolding from an 11-year-old, to wit: "A short time ago, you had an adventure on Mercury's dark side. I noticed two things wrong. First, when you were there you forgot to put weights on you, because Mercury's gravitational pull is very little. Second, when you were hunting for the mail robber, you were talking with Capt. Peterson and you didn't use communicators, even though you were next to him he couldn't have heard you because Mercury's atmosphere is all gone so sound waves cannot travel there unless you were talking into the ground and Capt. Peterson's ear was on the ground he could not have heard you. So I hope in the future your program will be more accurately.

"Your friend

Copyright, 1952, New York Herald Tribune Inc .

2   *Current Prose*

"Michael Kascia, age 11."

Michael Kascia, you get out of the cosmos this minute and straight back to your grammar lessons! "Your program will be more accurately," indeed! Where were you raised—in a planetarium?

SUGGESTIONS FOR STUDY:

1. What is the purpose of the first paragraph?
2. How is this paragraph developed?
3. What mistakes can you point out in the letter?
4. Do these mistakes make reading difficult?
5. Does the last paragraph make specific what Crosby means by "small fry who know too much for their own good?"
6. What tone does Crosby assume in the last paragraph?
7. Write a short anecdote in which you (or a friend) knew too much for your (or his) own good.

....

A former student recalls a slave-driving teacher and, in summing her up, sees her in a new perspective.

THE GRAMMARIAN
by Richard Lockridge

I HEARD only recently that Miss Fox, after a few years of retirement, had died in California, where the laxity of the climate probably disagreed with her. It was a little startling to learn that her death had happened so recently, because I had somehow fallen to thinking of her, as I did
....
Reprinted by permission. Copyright 1937, The New Yorker Magazine, Inc.

rather often, and usually with a feeling of guilt, as a historical character. It was difficult to realize that she came so close to the contemporary. She was a little woman, and made, I suspect, of flint, and when I was in high school she taught me English.

She seemed to be rather old even then, and that was a fairly long time ago. She was a little stooped, and gave the impression of being done almost entirely in gray, in spite of her black dresses, which had high collars held up with stays, and the little flutter of her white W.C.T.U. ribbon. But you never thought of her as frail; after you had been in her class for a while, you got to thinking of yourself as frail, but never of her. She walked two miles to the school every day and two miles back again, carrying a great load of papers to correct, and her own inflexibility. So far as I know, she never had a first name, and if she had had, I do not think anyone would ever have thought of calling her by it.

It is odd to think that for many years after I passed through the disinfection of her class, she kept on hitting boys and girls over the head with grammar and working herself and them to a frazzle in a dour, uncompromising search for perfection. It is also a little odd to think that she is no longer doing this, but possibly she is giving the angels a few lessons and fighting grimly against a certain grammatical looseness which she has probably found where she is now. I wouldn't put it past her to go above the angels, either; she would snip away at bad grammar wherever she found it.

She found a lot of it, of course, in second-year English, which was what she taught. We drifted up to her vaguely, I realize now, our English a boneless thing in spite of all the diagrams of sentences we had made on blackboards, and if we thought of English letters at all, it was with a kind of yeasty sentiment. Miss Fox took all that out of us. She was not sentimental about English letters; she didn't, I suspect, even like them very well, and considered that a good bit of laxity had crept into them from time to time. She was beautifully free from that expansive desire, which one found in some of the other instructors, to help us see the beauty of literature, and she had no thought of making us love it.

It is this method, I gather from rumors which trickle from the educative fields, which is in vogue just now, and even then there were a few instructors who took the larger view. I had one or two of them; one particularly I remember. He was an odd, impassioned gentleman, and he used to act out the beauties of literature for us on occasion. One of the grimmest memories of my youth concerns an afternoon when we all came to his classroom and found the shades drawn, so that the room was an unhealthy, yellow murk—the shades were a rather tired yellow. He was sitting at his desk, with his gray hair pulled down, and was staring in a rather awful way at a bottle of ink. We crept in, silenced and a little frightened, and nobody said anything for several minutes. We just sat there, troubled. Then, with no warning, the instructor let out a little shriek. We all jumped and wished we could get out. In another minute, I think, we would have got out, but then the instructor spoke.

"Is this a dagger which I see before me?" he screamed, in tones of anguish. We all settled back then, of course, and quieted down, although he grew noisier and noisier. After a while it began to seem, in a rather unpleasant way, a little funny, and it still does.

Miss Fox never did anything like that, and never gave, I am sure, a rap whether we appreciated the beauties of the English speech or not, so long as we learned its grammar. There was a certain amount of literature to be got through, naturally, and we went through Milton, a little grimly. I don't think Miss Fox really cared much for Milton's, or anybody else's, poetry, and she lightened up the ordeal with curious little side trips to visit the horrors of alcohol and tobacco. In the middle of "Comus," there was one such bitter little excursion to the subject of General Grant, who had, it seemed, died because he insisted on smoking a lot. But even if her heart was not entirely in it, she took us resolutely through Milton, with only a few mishaps. One of the more arresting of the mishaps was mine.

We had been told to pick a passage—a good, long passage—and memorize it. The only stipulation was about the length. Aside from that, we could pick any passage which, by its beauty, appealed to us: (Miss Fox always uttered the word "beauty" in a flat, disapproving tone.) In alphabetical order, the next day we recited what we had learned, and as the turn came down toward me, I began to have serious misgivings. Everybody else, or almost everybody, had picked a pleasant, idyllic passage about, as I recall it, birds and clouds, and it came over me that I had made a mistake. But it was the only passage I had learned, so there was nothing to do but give it, and I did. I've forgotten most of it, but it concerned the amorous gambols of a couple of Miltonian immortals, and the lines which loomed up when I came to them were those which described how the male immortal had, on beds of something or other:

> Fill'd her with thee, a daughter fair,
> So buxom, blithe, and debonair.

I think it was not until I saw the expression on Miss Fox's face that I realized the full enormity of this couplet. Miss Fox's face turned slightly grayer and all the sharp bones stood out in it, and the white W.C.T.U. ribbon quivered on what would, under happier circumstances, have been her breast. Quite unintentionally I had put her in a spot; she was torn between the conviction that I had committed this offence by intention, and should have something dire befall me, and the realization that anything she did would only make matters worse. Finally she just said "Well!" in a tone which I hope never to hear again from human lips, and called the name of the next student.

Probably it was the lurking danger that things like that might come up in literature which made Miss Fox suspect it; and there was always, too, the likelihood that the classics had been written by loose persons who smoked and drank and, hence, were likely to abuse grammar. And English grammar was the god before which Miss Fox burned the sharp, acrid, but infinitely penetrating incense of her devotion. The prohibition of alcohol, tobacco, and the hanging participle—this was the goal toward which she strove with a valiance and disregard of self which, even now, a little frighten me. She made us work hard, but she herself worked many times as hard; she must, indeed, have put in almost as much labor on each member of her rather large class as each student she was trying to save did on himself.

Miss Fox kept us writing almost constantly about literature and allied subjects, such as the evils of alcohol. We found it a good idea to put in a few licks against liquor and cigarettes when the occasion arose, and to make it arise if possible, but even this did not soften Miss Fox's harsh integrity if your grammar slipped. She was ruthlessly fair; I got in rather bad by writing, in conscious perversity this time, an essay mildly questioning the toxic qualities of nicotine, but this merely made her dislike me and didn't affect my grades one way or the other.

Miss Fox took home all the papers from all the boys and girls and went over them with a blue pencil, marking in the margins the existence of grammatical errors. She did not correct the errors; she did not even specify them. She merely, with the cold distaste of a housewife in the presence of an untoward insect, noted the presence of sin. It was up to the student to find the sin out and correct it. It was up to him then to write the paper over, correcting all the errors and not making any new ones, and have the result "checked." A paper was checked when not even Miss Fox could find an infraction of the least of grammar's formalities. Usually a paper went back three or four times before it was checked, and you went back with it, during "seventh hour." There were six regular periods in a day, and overtime, almost all the overtime being devoted to Miss Fox.

Out of those sessions, boys and girls used to go white with weariness and vexation, their hands shaking from copying essays and their minds reeling with grammar. As dusk crept on, and after the slowest of them had gone, little Miss Fox would trot out smartly, her round black hat bobbing, and walk rapidly the two miles home, clutching the bundle of that day's papers. She must have sat up most of the night with them, her blue pencil and her black eyes flashing coldly, and her mouth set hard against error. Now and then, perhaps, her expression would soften a little as some wily pupil took a slash at the cigarette evil, but it would harden again at the next paragraph as an infinitive split wide open.

You came out of all this with, surprisingly enough, a good deal of precisely what Miss Fox was determined to give you—respect for the hard, bare bones on which the language hangs. If you went on to one of the nearby state universities, you were astonished, and gratified, to learn that if you had survived Miss Fox, you did not need to take Freshman Rhetoric. Perhaps they thought that exemption was as little as they could give you in recompense. If, years afterward—ten years, at any rate—you began to write letters to your closer friends in a style slightly more colloquial than Miss Fox would have approved, it was always with some sense of guilt and a fleeting, absurd thought that Miss Fox might find you out and make you come back to seventh hour and be checked.

She was a hard, uncompromising little woman, our Miss Fox of Kansas City, and I shudder to think what her blue pencil would do to what I have written about her. I would not please her, I know; I never did. But she was the best teacher I ever had.

SUGGESTIONS FOR STUDY:

1. Does the last sentence express the main idea of this character sketch, or is it a part of the main idea?
2. Do you find the essay organized in three main sections—her attitude, her methods, her results?
3. Why is Miss Fox suspicious of literature and devoted to grammar?
4. Does Lockridge portray her in action? Does he have her speak? Can you justify the small amount of speech?
5. Is the transition between paragraphs regularly as definite as that between paragraphs 1 and 2 (*when I was in high school . . . even then*)?
6. What is Lockridge's attitude toward Miss Fox? Does he share her prejudices? Does he really mean she is the best teacher he ever had, even though he shudders to think what her blue pencil would do to the present essay? Cite specific details.
7. Can you cite any detail which subtly prepares the reader for the final sentence?

8   Current Prose

8. Does Lockridge make use of contrast, repetition of key notions, narrative examples? Where?
9. What is the meaning of *yeasty sentiment, amorous gambols, hanging participle, style slightly more colloquial?*
10. Write a theme on the best—or the worst—teacher you ever had.

A classic story of confusion on the campus by one of America's greatest living humorists.

UNIVERSITY DAYS
by James Thurber

I PASSED all the other courses that I took at my University, but I could never pass botany. This was because all botany students had to spend several hours a week in a laboratory looking through a microscope at plant cells, and I could never see through a microscope. I never once saw a cell through a microscope. This used to enrage my instructor. He would wander around the laboratory pleased with the progress all the students were making in drawing the involved and, so I am told, interesting structure of flower cells, until he came to me. I would just be standing there. "I can't see anything," I would say. He would begin patiently enough, explaining how anybody can see through a microscope, but would always end up in a fury, claiming that I could *too* see through a microscope but just pretended that I couldn't. "It takes away from the beauty of flowers anyway," I used to tell him. "We are not concerned with beauty in this course," he

Reprinted by permission. Copyright 1933, The New Yorker Magazine, Inc.

would say. "We are concerned solely with what I may call the *mechanics* of flars." "Well," I'd say, "I can't see anything." "Try it just once again," he'd say, and I would put my eye to the microscope and see nothing at all, except now and again a nebulous milky substance—a phenomenon of maladjustment. You were supposed to see a vivid, restless clockwork of sharply defined plant cells. "I see what looks like a lot of milk," I would tell him. This, he claimed, was the result of my not having adjusted the microscope properly, so he would readjust it for me, or rather, for himself. And I would look again and see milk.

I finally took a deferred pass, as they called it, and waited a year and tried again. (You had to pass one of the biological sciences or you couldn't graduate.) The professor had come back from vacation brown as a berry, bright-eyed, and eager to explain cell-structure again to his classes. "Well," he said to me, cheerily, when we met in the first laboratory hour of the semester, "we're going to see cells this time, aren't we?" "Yes, sir," I said. Students to right of me and to left of me and in front of me were seeing cells; what's more, they were quietly drawing pictures of them in their notebooks. Of course, I didn't see anything.

"We'll try it," the professor said to me, grimly, "with every adjustment of the microscope known to man. As God is my witness, I'll arrange this glass so that you see cells through it or I'll give up teaching. In twenty-two years of botany, I—" He cut off abruptly for he was beginning to quiver all over, like Lionel Barrymore, and he genuinely wished to hold onto his temper; his scenes with me had taken a great deal out of him.

So we tried it with every adjustment of the microscope known to man. With only one of them did I see anything but blackness or the familiar lacteal opacity, and that time I saw, to my pleasure and amazement, a variegated constellation of flecks, specks, and dots. These I hastily drew. The instructor, noting my activity, came back from an adjoining desk, a smile on his lips and his eyebrows high in hope. He looked at my cell drawing. "What's that?" he demanded, with a hint of a squeal in his voice. "That's what I saw," I said.

"You didn't, you didn't, you *did*n't!" he screamed, losing control of his temper instantly, and he bent over and squinted into the microscope. His head snapped up. "That's your eye!" he shouted. "You've fixed the lens so that it reflects! You've drawn your eye!"

Another course that I didn't like, but somehow managed to pass, was economics. I went to that class straight from the botany class, which didn't help me any in understanding either subject. I used to get them mixed up. But not as mixed up as another student in my economics class who came there direct from a physics laboratory. He was a tackle on the football team, named Bolenciecwcz. At that time Ohio State University had one of the best football teams in the country, and Bolenciecwcz was one of its outstanding stars. In order to be eligible to play it was necessary for him to keep up in his studies, a very difficult matter, for while he was not dumber than an ox he was not any smarter. Most of his professors were lenient and helped him along. None gave him more hints, in answering questions, or asked him simpler ones than the economics professor, a thin, timid man named Bassum. One day when we were on the subject of transportation and distribution, it came Bolenciecwcz's turn to answer a question. "Name one means of transportation," the professor said to him. No light came into the big tackle's eyes. "Just any means of transportation," said the professor. Bolenciecwcz sat staring at him. "That is," pursued the professor, "any medium, agency, or method of going from one place to another." Bolenciecwcz had the look of a man who is being led into a trap. "You may choose among steam, horse-drawn, or electrically propelled vehicles," said the instructor. "I might suggest the one which we commonly take in making long journeys across land." There was a profound silence in which everybody stirred uneasily, including Bolenciecwcz and Mr. Bassum. Mr. Bassum abruptly broke this silence in an amazing manner. "Choo-choo-choo," he said, in a low voice, and turned instantly scarlet. He glanced appealingly around the room. All of us, of course, shared Mr. Bassum's desire that Bolenciecwcz should stay abreast of the class in economics, for the Illinois game, one of the hardest and most important of the season, was only a week off. "Toot, toot, tootoooooot!" some student with a deep voice moaned, and we all looked encouragingly at Bolenciecwcz. Somebody else gave a fine imitation of a locomotive letting off steam. Mr. Bassum himself rounded off the little show. "Ding, dong, ding, dong," he said hopefully. Bolenciecwcz was staring at the floor now, trying to think, his great brow furrowed, his huge hands rubbing together, his face red.

"How did you come to college this year, Mr. Bolenciecwcz?" asked the professor. *"Chuf* fa Chuffa, *Chuf* fa chuffa."

"M'father sent me," said the football player.

"What on?" asked Bassum.

"I git an 'lowance," said the tackle, in a low, husky voice, obviously embarrassed.

"No, no," said Bassum. "Name a means of transportation. What did you *ride* here on?"

"Train," said Bolenciecwcz.

"Quite right," said the professor. "Now, Mr. Nugent, will you tell us—"

If I went through anguish in botany and economics—for different reasons—gymnasium work was even worse. I don't even like to think about it. They wouldn't let you play games or join in the exercises with your glasses on and I couldn't see with mine off. I bumped into professors, horizontal bars, agricultural students, and swinging iron rings. Not being able to see, I could take it but I couldn't dish it out. Also, in order to pass gymnasium (and you had to pass it to graduate) you had to learn to swim if you didn't know how. I didn't like the swimming pool, I didn't like swimming, and I didn't like the swimming instructor, and after all these years I still don't. I never swam but I passed my gym work anyway, by having another student give my gymnasium number (978) and swim across the pool in my place. He was a quiet, amiable blonde youth, number 473, and he would have seen through a microscope for me if we could have got away with it, but we couldn't get away with it. Another thing I didn't like about gymnasium work was that they made you strip the day you registered. It is impossible for me to be happy when I am stripped and being asked a lot of questions. Still, I did better than a lanky agricultural student who was cross-examined just before I was. They asked each student what college he was in—that is, whether Arts, Engineering, Commerce, or Agriculture. "What college are you in?" the instructor snapped at the youth in front of me. "Ohio State University," he said promptly.

It wasn't that agricultural student but it was another a whole lot like him who decided to take up journalism, possibly on the ground that when farming went to hell he could fall back on newspaper work. He didn't realize, of course, that that would be very much like falling back full-length on a kit of carpenter's tools. Haskins didn't seem cut out for journalism, being too embarrassed to talk to anybody and unable to use a typewriter, but the editor of the college paper assigned him to the cow barns, the sheep house, the horse pavilion, and the animal husbandry department generally. This was a genuinely big "beat," for it took up five times as much ground and got ten times as great a legislative appropriation as the College of Liberal Arts. The agricultural student knew animals, but nevertheless his stories were dull and colorlessly written. He took all afternoon on each of them, on account of having to hunt for each letter on the typewriter. Once in a while he had to ask somebody to help him hunt. "C" and "L," in particular, were hard letters for him to find. His editor finally got pretty much annoyed at the farmer-journalist because his pieces were so uninteresting. "See here, Haskins," he snapped at him one day. "Why is it we never have anything hot from you on the horse pavilion? Here we have two hundred head of horses on this campus—more than any other university in the Western Conference except Purdue—and yet you never get any real lowdown on them. Now shoot over to the horse barns and dig up something lively." Haskins shambled out and came back in about an hour; he said he had something. "Well, start it off snappily," said the editor. "Something people will read." Haskins set to work and in a couple of hours brought a sheet of typewritten paper to the desk; it was a two-hundred-word story about some disease that had broken out among the horses. Its opening sentence was simple but arresting. It read: "Who has noticed the sores on the tops of the horses in the animal husbandry building?"

Ohio State was a land grant university and therefore two years of military drill was compulsory. We drilled with old Springfield rifles and studied the tactics of the Civil War even though the World War was going on at the time. At 11 o'clock each morning thousands of freshmen and sophomores used to deploy over the campus, moodily creeping up on the old chemistry building. It was good training for the kind of warfare that was waged at Shiloh but it had no connection with what was going on in Europe. Some people used to think there was German money behind it, but they didn't dare say so or they would have been thrown in jail as German spies. It was a period of muddy thought and marked, I believe, the decline of higher education in the Middle West.

As a soldier I was never any good at all. Most of the cadets were glumly indifferent soldiers, but I was no good at all. Once General Littlefield, who was commandant of the cadet corps, popped up in front of me during regimental drill and snapped, "You are the main trouble with this university!" I think he meant that my type was the main trouble with the university but he may have meant me individually. I was mediocre at drill, certainly—that is, until my senior year. By that time I had drilled longer than anybody else in the Western Conference, having failed at military at the end of each preceding year so that I had to do it all over again. I was the only senior still in uniform. The uniform which, when new, had made me look like an interurban railway conductor, now that it had become faded and too tight, made me look like Bert Williams in his bellboy act. This had a definitely bad effect on my morale. Even so, I had become by sheer practise little short of wonderful at squad manoeuvres.

One day General Littlefield picked our company out of the whole regiment and tried to get it mixed up by putting it through one movement after another as fast as we could execute them: squads right, squads left, squads on right into line, squads right about, squads left front into line, etc. In about three minutes one hundred and nine men were marching in one direction and I was marching away from them at an angle of forty degrees, all alone. "Company, halt!" shouted

General Littlefield. "That man is the only man who has it right!" I was made a corporal for my achievement.

The next day General Littlefield summoned me to his office. He was swatting flies when I went in. I was silent and he was silent too, for a long time. I don't think he remembered me or why he had sent for me, but he didn't want to admit it. He swatted some more flies, keeping his eyes on them narrowly before he let go with the swatter. "Button up your coat!" he snapped. Looking back on it now I can see that he meant me although he was looking at a fly, but I just stood there. Another fly came to rest on a paper in front of the general and began rubbing its hind legs together. The general lifted the swatter cautiously. I moved restlessly and the fly flew away. "You startled him!" barked General Littlefield, looking at me severely. I said I was sorry. "That won't help the situation!" snapped the general, with cold military logic. I didn't see what I could do except offer to chase some more flies toward his desk, but I didn't say anything. He stared out the window at the faraway figures of co-eds crossing the campus toward the library. Finally, he told me I could go. So I went. He either didn't know which cadet I was or else he forgot what he wanted to see me about. It may have been that he wished to apologize for having called me the main trouble with the university; or maybe he had decided to compliment me on my brilliant drilling of the day before and then at the last minute decided not to. I don't know. I don't think about it much any more.

SUGGESTIONS FOR STUDY:

1. Does Thurber express his main idea in any one sentence?
2. What are the main divisions of the essay?
3. If you have difficulty deciding whether the agricultural student in journalism is a main division, what does this suggest about Thurber's attitude toward closely knit organization? Does this attitude fit his total purpose in the essay?
4. Does Thurber use transitions between paragraphs?
5. Does Thurber have a sense of climax in the several parts of the essay? Does he use the end of the paragraph purposefully?
6. Does Thurber use dialog effectively? Cite examples.

7. What is the basis of the humor in Thurber's describing the botany professor as "brown as a berry, bright-eyed, and eager to explain" or in his attitude toward General Littlefield?
8. What is the basis of the humor in *lacteal opacity* and *variegated constellation?*
9. What is Thurber's purpose in numbering swimmers 978 and 473? Where else does he use this method of exposition?
10. Describe a bit of confusion from your own school experience, or an incident in which an underling makes shrewd observations about his superior.

A student views the campus hero with something less than enthusiasm.

ATHLETES
by David Murray

NOAH WEBSTER defines an athlete as "One trained to contend in feats of physical prowess; one possessed of great physical strength." The definition is all right, but it doesn't go into the matter deeply enough; it certainly doesn't give a single one of my reasons for not liking athletes, and I certainly don't like them.

The first reason is that they're always perfectly healthy. They should count that as a blessing and be properly humble and grateful, remembering the many weaknesses to which the flesh falls heir. But no, they must brag about their cold showers and training-table diet. They must make statements

―――――――――――
Reprinted by permission from The Green Caldron, A Magazine of Student Writing, the University of Illinois.

about being able to whip a large number of wildcats barehanded. When they get up in the morning, they have to stand in front of open windows and breathe with a sound accompaniment. They're always going around pounding their chests and slapping other people on the back. They manage to give an impression of being made from a special brand of protoplasm. Some of them come right out and say that I am in line for a life of sickness and an unpleasant early death.

I can pass over physical superiority with recollection of mastodons and the extinct larger varieties of dinosaur, but the athletes insist that their brands of morals, sportsmanship, and character are above average too. They try to tell me, for example, that violent contact on a football field with eleven other muscular morons results in a finer nature. I once knew some golfers, and all that they ever got from golf was a great irreverence and a wonderful vocabulary. How should the fact that a man indulges in great exertion give him a road map to the better spiritual life?

I can't really believe that athletes have no brains. They must have to have invented their language. One says to another, "He parried in sept, so I retreated five, lunged in carte with an out wrist, got good contact, and filled the box," and they both make sense from it. No athlete ever looked as if he were ashamed of what he had done, but he hides every mention of it in gibberish. The sports writers talk that way too. The other day I read about a man who made a spectacular slide for home on his digestive distillery. I think such language is a perverted form of vanity.

Insofar as I'm concerned, athletes can be healthy, turn into moral masterpieces, and talk nonsense until they drop. I might even find some excuse for their actions. That is, if they would stop stealing my girls. They've stolen every one of them, and there were some very nice numbers in the collection. I go out and get myself a nice blonde to have and to hold so that a mutton-headed basketball center can take her to the big dance. It makes me feel like a bird-dog—you know, an animal that scares up pheasants and guinea hens all day for a Ken-l-ration supper. I'll be thrice terrorized with eternal damnation before I like athletes.

SUGGESTIONS FOR STUDY:

1. What is the main idea and where is it stated?
2. Is the arrangement of the main divisions of the essay haphazard or purposeful?
3. Does Murray use topic sentences for his paragraphs?
4. Does he make clear transitions from one paragraph to the next?
5. Are his words well chosen for the tone Murray desires? For example?
6. "He parried in sept, so I retreated five, lunged in carte with an out wrist, and filled the box." What sport is this jargon taken from? Is it accurate? How would you find out?
7. Write a theme following the plan used here—the statement of an opinion in the first paragraph, a reason supporting this opinion in each of several subsequent paragraphs.

The student writer of the preceding selection humorously describes college football as "violent contact on a football field with eleven other muscular morons." But how does the intelligent athlete feel about the sport? Here a former University of Michigan guard who lettered on three championship teams and played in the Rose Bowl offers his considered opinion.

TOO MUCH FOOTBALL
by Allen Jackson

FOOTBALL is a complicated game, and the intense competition fostered by the business practices of big-time college football causes this complication to be increased. The

Reprinted by permission. Copyright, 1951, The Atlantic Monthly.

result is that the players, if they wish to play the game at all, must spend more time on the gridiron than they bargained for. However, any spectator will tell you there are certain benefits connected with playing college football, such as being part of a school's football tradition, learning fair play, having one's character built, traveling to different parts of the country, and being glorious. All of these compensate the athlete for the loss of school time. But after having played four years at guard for the University of Michigan, which possesses the largest college football stadium in the world, I can see that the supposed benefits of big-time football are either grossly exaggerated or completely imaginary, and it seems to me that most of the enormous amount of time I spent on the gridiron was wasted.

One of the most harmful aspects of the highly organized and regimented athleticism which is the result of a college sport having become "big time" is that the spontaneity has been taken out of the sport. In professional athletics the individual player expects to devote his whole person to his game because his livelihood depends upon consistent, "professional" performance. But the college athlete is primarily a student, not a professional, and when he is forced into the overorganization and overperfection which the big-time game demands, he can no longer decide for himself whether he should study or play football on a particular day.

Probably few of the freshmen who try out for the team realize how much of their time will eventually be exacted by football. I remember discovering with dismay, as a freshman, that if I were to keep up with the rest of the men who were competing for positions on the varsity I would have to report for spring practice. Practicing football for six weeks during the warm and budding spring did not strike me as being either a glorious or a worth-while occupation, but I needed to do it during both my freshman and sophomore years if I was to get in the line-up. I was engaged in actual practice on the field for about twenty hours a week during the spring semester, and during the fall my working week was boosted to about twenty-eight hours. Of course this includes only the time actually spent on the field, and does not include such things as evening movies of the next week's opponent, study time wasted because of fatigue, extra time demanded by game trips to other schools, and time spent in whirlpools and under heat lamps in the training room.

The four-year total actually spent on the field, counting three extra weeks of Rose Bowl practice, comes to about 1350 hours. Although it was hard for me to realize it at the sophomoric height of my athletic zeal, my reason now tells me that football is only a single, minor, and unacademic part of a college education, and that it should not be more important than other single parts of college—such as, for example, the study of history. At Michigan I took six courses in history, each of them meeting three times a week for fifteen weeks, and each requiring an average of two hours of study for each hour in class. The total number of hours here is 810, about half of the time that I spent on the gridiron.

Of course many of the men on the Michigan team receive excellent grades despite their football playing. Last year the team average was higher than the school average, and the two players with the highest grades were an engineer and a premedical student. But these very men have agreed with me that high grades do not mean satisfactory learning, and that football interferes with learning. Besides demanding that the student forego concerts, visiting lecturers, and outside reading during the football semester, big-time football also requires students with heavy loads to take part of their courses in summer school, and to skimp and cram their way through the fall semester as best they can.

A significant little adage which circulates in Michigan athletic circles says in effect that there are three aspects of college life at Michigan—intellectual, social, and athletic—but that the student has time for only two. This idea can circulate only where athletics have become, or are thought to have become, as important as the academic work of the University. The student who plays football is expected to sacrifice his studies for the sake of the game, and he is very darkly frowned upon if he misses practice for the sake of his studies. When after one Saturday game I limped off the field with a twisted ankle, I knew that I would be expected to spend a good deal of Sunday in the training room taking treatment for the injury. But since Sunday was the only time that I was able to study for a coming examination, I stayed away from the training room. As a result the ankle stiffened and on the practice field I was made to feel guilty for the rest of the week. The coaches are aware that in theory studies come first, but they are also aware that, in a big-time league, if studies actually come first, second-rate teams are likely to be the result.

One of my teammates, a philosophy student who at the time played fourth string, possessed a scholarship which would have enabled him to study in Europe. However, if he made use of this scholarship he would be unable to return in time to play football the following season. He asked the coaches' advice on this, hoping that they would tell him to go to Europe by all means, and come back and play for them when he was ready. But instead it was hinted that if he stayed he might well get to the "top" the next season, whereas if he took the scholarship it was quite possible that someone else would have his place when he got back. These suggestions were further implemented by numerous long-distance telephone calls from alumni who were amazed that anyone should consider taking a trip to Europe when there was a chance he might make the Michigan team. So he stayed, and the next season played third string.

Another teammate of mine decided during his junior year to use his GI Bill to cultivate a long-standing desire to study the piano. He had already earned a varsity letter as a sophomore center on Michigan's '48 National Championship team, and was looking forward to playing first string in his senior year, inasmuch as the man ahead of him was graduating. But during the following spring semester he became so engrossed in his piano playing that, although he still intended to play football in the autumn, he decided not to turn out for spring practice. Consequently, when he returned for practice in the fall of his senior year he was promptly and without explanation assigned to the fifth string. He was replaced by men who had practiced the previous spring and who because of this were evidently considered better gambles toward a winning combination.

The reasonable and sensible thing to do in such a situation would be to quit football because it was now obvious that he had fallen from favor and would never make the first team. But it is impossible to be sensible in the midst of people who are afflicted with football. Making what the fanatic football alumnus would call a courageous display of determination, he decided to try to win back his position, a decision which he now thinks foolish and wasteful. The result of his efforts was that by the end of the season he was still nothing more than a third-string center; and with the exception of two non-conference games and the waning, reserve-flooded minutes of the other games, he spent most of his time sitting on the bench.

2

While examining the nature of big-time football it will be necessary for me at times to criticize the position of the coaches. I wish to make the point here that it is not the individual but the position with which I find fault, and that this position must be criticized because it is one of the major means through which big-time football accomplishes its distortion of the sporting spirit.

One of the ideas most thoroughly drummed into the heads of young Michigan football players is that it is a very valuable thing to be associated with Michigan football tradition. These men talk about Michigan's record, the fine men who have played for Michigan, in a manner almost liturgical, and the implication is that such things happen only at Michigan. Although much of this talk is sincere it is nevertheless misguided; it ignores the fact that Michigan tradition means basically that Michigan has always won more games than it has lost, and it means to keep on doing so.

At Michigan to win is of utmost importance; fair play and sportsmanship are fine, but to win is of utmost importance. Judging from the loud noises I have heard from chauvinistic, unathletic alumni from other big football schools, the Michigan people are not unique in proclaiming a "We're the best" athletic philosophy. But thanks to Fielding H. Yost and his point-a-minute teams of 1901 through 1905, the Michigan alumni have a better record to boast of than do the alumni of most other schools.

Yost was one of the first coaches to begin the custom of ensuring a winning record by encouraging large men to come to Michigan primarily to play football—a custom which is still zealously fostered. He was so successful in obtaining skillful players that between 1901 and 1905 his teams won 55 games in a row, and each year averaged 548 points to the opponents' 8 points. Most of the old-time Michigan alums will tell you that Fielding Yost was successful because he was ahead of his time as a coach, and this is certainly true. In pioneering player-recruitment and in consciously or unconsciously promoting a public acceptance of the idea that winning, and winning by a big score, is an end in itself, Yost acted in strict accordance with some of the most basic elements in modern football.

I do not quarrel with Yost's winning record as such, but I do quarrel with the tendency in modern football to *emphasize* winning as an end in itself, and the tendency toward a "kick him when he's down" attitude which such an emphasis fosters. Such an attitude, it seems to me, was more evident than the good sportsman's attitude when Yost's teams consistently ran up scores like 128 to 0, 88 to 0, and 130 to 0 against little schools without recruiting systems, such as Buffalo, West Virginia, and Ferris Institute. Such records, of course, are possible only when the public gives prestige to those who trample weak competition.

Whether big-time football distorts the values of the football-following public by its win emphasis or whether the public makes possible such emphasis by giving prestige to the teams which trample weak competition is a problem similar to the chicken and egg question. But whatever the cause, the result is that teams which feel the need of strengthening their reputation do so by keeping their reserves on the bench and running up the score on the first weak opponent encountered.

When the 1947 Michigan team went to the Rose Bowl there

was a difference of opinion, among football experts, over whether Michigan or Notre Dame had the greatest team in the world. This controversy probably had much to do with the fact that most of the Michigan first team was kept in the Rose Bowl game until the latter part of the fourth quarter, by which time it had run up a score of 49 to 0 on the weaker Southern California team. But even with this large accumulation of points there was almost a full team of Michigan reserve players who did not get into the game or who played for only a few seconds—the reason being, clearly, that if Southern Cal was prevented from scoring, the record would look much more impressive, and it would be obvious to the football experts that Michigan undoubtedly had the greatest team in the world.

3

The prestige which the college football business has succeeded in gaining for schools with winning records often produces an unsavory bigotry which goes beyond ordinary pride among both the players and students from a big football school. At Michigan one of those bigotry-fostering, tradition-conscious pre-game speeches which were impressive to sophomores but tiresome to seniors was to this effect: The men whom we were about to play would be battling *Michigan;* they would as a result be intimidated; and we should take advantage of this fine opportunity to dominate them. As a psychological device this idea was probably useful in giving confidence to sophomore players—but whether it worked or not, the point is that good sportsmen do not emphasize the use of their grandfathers' reputations to intimidate an opponent.

"When Michigan loses, someone has to pay." I heard the first of many repetitions of this illogical idea in 1949 when Michigan's 25-game winning streak was decisively broken by Army. Since then I have heard it repeated with dogged monotony by the coaches after each Michigan loss, including Michigan's loss to Michigan State last fall. During the practice week following this game I personally counted forty-three repetitions of the slogan. This one slogan symbolizes to me the perversion of the sporting spirit which has been produced by big-time football. The slogan not only implies that Michigan *shouldn't* have lost, but it also suggests that the loss was caused by something wrong somewhere—perhaps something shady on the part of the other team.

The point of view suggested by this slogan becomes positively unchristian in its implication that revenge will be sought at the expense of next week's opponent. This desire for revenge is doubly evil in that it cannot be directed at the people who seem to have inflicted the injury but must be spent upon the first innocent victim who happens along. But the brass-tack meaning of "When Michigan loses, someone has to pay" is simply that since Michigan prestige and Michigan gate receipts depend upon a spectacular winning record, a lost game must be counteracted, if possible, with a larger than usual winning score the following Saturday. And the slogan is successful in arousing these attitudes. Many of the players continue to deify the coaches long after they should have outgrown this, and to them everything said on the field is gospel. Those who do not care for much of what goes on are in the game too deep to get out, and if they wish to stay on the team they must close their minds to reason and allow themselves to be directed.

I do not wish to imply that the players are actually taught unfair tactics at Michigan: this is certainly not true. But the Michigan coaches find it necessary to emphasize winning to a much greater degree than is natural or reasonable, and in a game like football this sort of emphasis is bound to lead to unsportsmanlike conduct. Indeed, the feeling that it is terribly necessary to win is so strong, and the resultant feeling of relief after having won a game is so pronounced, that if any questionable tactics have been used by Michigan men during the game they are merely laughed off.

Virtually all of my teammates on last year's squad were very clean players, but the atmosphere of big football often turned team spirit into mob spirit when the group as a whole accepted actions which to the individual would seem unsportsmanlike. One of the key players on last year's team was noted for his feats in the boxing ring and for his quick temper.

When on Monday afternoons the team would watch movies of the preceding Saturday's game, this player would occasionally be seen landing a seemingly accidental left-hook on an opposing player's chin. Of course the movies of any football game are likely to show up actions which appear to be underhanded; but the point here is that such actions—especially by the hotheaded boxer—would invariably strike the coaches as funny, and they would run the play over again in slow motion so that everyone could see and laugh.

The assembled players took their cues from the coaches and also laughed heartily to see such fun. Then, a few plays later on the screen, the coaches would solemnly draw our attention to the fact that the other team was "gang tackling," and that we would have to look for just "this sort of thing" from our next week's opponent because it was *that* kind of team. Michigan's maize and blue players are not encouraged to "gang tackle" of course; they are simply ordered to cover the opposing ball-carrier with "a blanket of blue."

4

Another bromide which the big-time football votaries like to administer to promising young athletes is that there is something wonderful about being part of the "team spirit" found in big-name teams. Human beings have long since proved themselves social animals, and it seems reasonable that they should enjoy team games. But big football has perverted the team spirit as well as the sporting spirit.

In the first place the competition for individual positions on big teams is altogether too stiff, and this does more to break down than to build up team spirit. The bigness of the game, the publicity and prestige which go along with a first-team position, and the large number of grim and intense young athletes who are drawn to the gridiron by these abnormalities cause a spirit of internecine conflict to be as much in evidence as *esprit de corps*.

Besides this, the increasing specialization demanded by big-time football does nothing toward engendering social cohesion on the team. The compulsion to win generated by the game's big-business aspect demands that the individual players become precise and accurate in their various specialties to a degree unnatural in college athletics. On the Michigan practice field the ends, backs, and linemen all spend much of their time in separate corners of the field, performing their various specialties with monotonous repetition. During the week there are only one or two hour-long scrimmages, on the average, and the rest of the time is devoted to various forms of dummy practice, running of signals, and practicing specialties. All of this is necessary to produce a winning team in a big-time league, but it is not much fun. Any sport which requires a week's practice of specialties for each sixty-minute game has become too mechanized to allow the spontaneous sort of team spirit which would seem to be the special value of college football.

Everyone has seen football teams gather in the center of the field just before the opening kickoff for a last-minute handshake, and this sight, plus the stock sport page photographs of men on the bench who are "trying just as hard as the men in the game," seems to indicate that team spirit is an actual and worth-while reality in big-time football. I should like to state plainly and emphatically that much of the huddled handshaking and bench emotion is artificial. The players know that in order to win it is necessary to get "worked up" for the game, whether they feel like it or not. Also, the bigness and complexity of modern football produces a decrease in team homogeneity and a corresponding decrease in spontaneity. The players sense that they will be less effective without such homogeneity, and they attempt to regain this feeling on the practice field and in the big game by an artificial emphasis upon such devices as the pre-game handshake and the bench chatter.

My first experience with the automaton spirit which big-time coaches often find it necessary to enforce in order to make their teams efficient winning machines was when, as a freshman, I was used as a human dummy to test the proficiency of the '47 Rose Bowl varsity. Occasionally, when one of my freshman or reserve teammates would be laid out by the businesslike efficiency of the varsity, in such a way that play could not be resumed until the field was cleared, the coaches would promote big-time football's party-line attitude toward such a situation by reciting this slogan: "Well, move the ball or move the body." The varsity players, tickled by such wit, would then move the ball to an uncluttered part of the field and resume play.

When I became a varsity player I began to notice other evidences that big-time football cannot afford to depend upon spontaneous team spirit. At the training table on the Friday night before a game the Michigan players were expected to show that they were in the process of "storing it up" for the next day's contest by eating their meal with a quiet intensity which precluded laughter or any evidence of high spirits. Probably there were a few players who actually felt a sort of judgment-day taciturnity, but for many of the players it was an artificially imposed atmosphere, and bad for the digestion. If, as often happened, some of the lighter hearts would forget for a moment that they were supposed to be grim on Friday evenings, there would be ominous and foreboding looks from the coaches' table—and if the unwholesome gaiety persisted, the coaches would silence it by uttering with gloomy irony, "We hope you'll all be this happy tomorrow night."

Another instance in which the Michigan players had an attitude externally imposed upon them will serve also to exemplify the pernicious effect which big-time football has had upon the reputations of schools which sponsor big-name teams. A few days before we started on our Rose Bowl journey we were summoned for an orientation lecture, a surprising amount of which was devoted to our table manners and general deportment while in Pasadena. It seemed that many of the teams which had in the past gone to the Rose Bowl had been guilty of ungentlemanly conduct—one team, we were told, had been fond of throwing bread rolls the length of a table in the hotel dining room and flipping squares of butter against the ceiling, where they stuck. But Michigan, we were told, did not do that sort of thing. Although it was good to hear that Michigan did not do that sort of thing, neither I nor my teammates had ever been in the habit of throwing butter at the ceilings of plush hotels, and we wondered why we were being so energetically told to act in a normal manner.

The reason was that the big-time football system has unconsciously superimposed a mercenary stereotype upon the college football player, and people often *expect* a visiting football team to be rowdy; because of this, the coaches were at pains to impress us with lurid examples, of questionable authenticity, of how not to act. In Pasadena we conducted ourselves with a normal amount of gentility—neither better nor worse than the average of the teams which preceded us, a waitress told me. But the Michigan players heard themselves complimented profusely on their conduct.

The point of all this is that when an entire athletic group, like college football players, has such a reputation that players who conduct themselves with ordinary grace are looked upon as above average, there is something wrong with the system. Moreover, schools which sponsor big-name teams, and so associate themselves with this bad reputation, subtly lose prestige in the eyes of the general public. Big-time football has promoted a syllogism something like this: football players are something less than students; therefore, universities which sponsor big football teams, though famous, are something less than universities.

5

In order to exhibit one of big-time football's most unscrupulous practices, I shall have to explain the nature and function of the "red shirts," as they are called at Michigan. The generally used term is "cannon fodder." Because modern football is such a complicated game, the head coaches are able to attend to only the first two or three teams, called "blues" at Michigan. However, it is necessary to have at least two more teams, the red shirts, against whom the blues can scrimmage, or who can hold the dummies for the blues to block. The blues do not play amongst themselves because they are likely to hurt one another and be lost for the big game on Saturday. Also it is necessary for the varsity blues to feel their power and be able to march up and down the field through the weaker red shirts.

A few of the red shirts know that they will never rise in the varsity hierarchy, and they are still content to come out for practice season after season to be used by the blues. But there are not enough of these men. The rest of the red shirts are players who dream of making at least the third-string varsity one day, but whom the coaches are reasonably sure will never make the grade. Instead of telling these men that their chances of making the varsity are extremely small, the coaches, because they need men on whom their varsity can sharpen its claws, encourage the red shirts to return each year to try again. Of course all this is a matter of subtle suggestion; it is impossible to prove actual misrepresentation of facts, but I have spoken to and played against a number of disenchanted red shirts who for four years held dummies and waited their turn to be mashed by the blues, only because it was hinted that they might make it one day.

To a young boy who is fresh out of high school—where he was a big man because of his football playing—the slightest hint by a big college coach that he might make the varsity is enough to set the home town buzzing and to increase the player's illusion of prestige. When he fails to make the varsity team, it seems one of life's most terrible tragedies.

Two years ago, such a player came to Michigan. As a great high school star and a holder of state records in track he was looked upon by his friends and home-town supporters as a potential All-American, and when the Michigan coaches watched him operate on the freshman team they seemed to agree. The following season—last fall—the player's picture was in every sporting magazine in the country, and since such publicity could occur only with the coaches' sanction, it was assumed that he would do great things. Then the football season began, and game after game the highly publicized player was left sitting on the bench. Although he dressed for all the games, and made all the trips, for some reason unknown to himself or to his teammates he was never allowed to play, except for a few seconds in one game, and by the end of the season it was apparent that he would not make a varsity letter. When Michigan prepared to make its second trip to the Rose Bowl, a trip on which ten more than the usual number of players were taken, so that even some of the red shirts went along, the coaches refused to take him, and in so doing as much as told him that he would never play for Michigan.

To a boy who had been heralded as a second Tom Harmon this was a crushing blow, especially since any reasonable person would assume that the football system, after publicizing the player with such vigor, would feel honor-bound to take him along on the Rose Bowl trip. What happened to this boy represents in concentrated form what happens to most of the students who play big-time football. They are first deluded into thinking that they are great and that football is great; then they are used by the system and finally discarded with at best nothing to show but a scrapbook full of redundant and inaccurate clippings.

Of course such build-up and subsequent disappointment occurs elsewhere in life, particularly in a professional sport like baseball. But this is all part of the professional scene, and it has no place in college athletics. College football should have all the benefits of a strictly amateur sport; but it is losing these and acquiring the undesirable aspects of a professional sport.

6

Any accusation that football leaves the player with nothing but a scrapbook full of clippings will move the defenders of the game immediately to demand that some mention be made of the "character building" upon which football seems to have a priority. Aside from the probability that the coaches who direct uncommercialized college sports, such as track, wrestling, and gymnastics, could present good arguments showing these sports to be just as effective builders of character as football, it seems to me that anyone who assumes that athletics are an extraordinary factor in the development of an individual's character is guilty of ignoring the many forces which contribute to such development.

But in the football world there is great emphasis placed upon character development; and if, in the coaches' not infallible judgment, an individual player's character does not seem to be developing in the manner prescribed by the big-time football system, his position on the team will be endangered. Because all big-time football players and coaches have grown up with the idea that it is necessary to give your all for the alma mater, anyone who does not seem willing to do this is looked upon as a coward.

The importance of winning in big-time football makes it absolutely necessary to field the best team possible on important Saturdays, regardless of injuries. When the modern compulsion to win is superimposed upon the old give-your-all idea, the pressure on an injured player to play despite his injury is immense. No matter how many times a player proves himself in battle, the first time he decides that an injury should keep him off the playing field he is given the raised eyebrow and accusing stare by the coaches, trainer, and even some of his teammates. This subtle accusation is caused by the team's collective dread of weakening the winning combination, and it is especially acute if the injury is not obvious and the coming game is expected to be close.

Near the end of my junior year, when I was a first-string, battle-scarred veteran of many games, I received what I considered to be a very serious knee injury a week before Michigan was to play Ohio State for the conference championship. The knee was badly swollen, and it was impossible for the doctor who looked at it to make a valid diagnosis until the swelling subsided. But, since I could not walk, and since it was necessary for me to spend two days in the hospital, I assumed that I would not be expected to play in the big game.

However, the man who substituted for me lacked both my weight and experience. So I found to my dismay that as soon as I could walk I was expected to "gut it out," as the Michigan training-room slogan would describe it, by reporting to the practice field, having my knee trussed up with tape, and preparing to give my all for Michigan. Although I could feel loose things inside my knee, I was so intimidated by this frightening preoccupation with guts that I hobbled dutifully out onto the practice field.

On the field I found that my obvious inability to play was looked upon with suspicion, and I began to hear remarks that I was allowing the knee to get the better of me. Instead of being ordered back to my hospital bed for a thorough examination, I was merely told that whether I played or not was entirely up to me. At this point it was clear that I was expected to play, and if I did not I would be dubbed a quitter. Like everyone else, I think there are certain things for which it is worth while to give my all, but I decided then that the primitive alma-materism of an obsolete generation of college playboys was not one of them, and I did not play.

About a week later the knee became locked in a rigid position, and it was necessary for me to return to the hospital. It was now possible to see that a piece of cartilage had been torn in such a way that there was little chance of its growing back together, and an operation would be required. The operation did more than fix my knee, because now the coaches knew that I had not been faking and that I could once more be depended upon to give my all for Michigan. But the point had been made: big-time football has no respect for either the individual's word or his body.

7

A word must be said about the rabid football alumni and the overzealous football fans. I find no fault with anyone who has a normal interest in athletics, but the perverted bigness of football produces people with a perverted interest in sport. Although the number of the most adhesive of these hangers-on to the football scene is not large, their presence is distressing because they are undoubtedly the articulate representatives of a much larger group whose interest in and attitude toward bigtime football allow the unhealthy and prolonged hysteria which permeates the college football scene each fall.

Except for a fawning and familiar interest in a few backfield stars, many of the football alumni whom I met had no real interest in the players as individuals; indeed their interest in the stars was usually based only upon athletic reputation and seldom upon character. Many of the football alumni who help destitute athletes through school, from my observation, do this because of a selfish interest in the perpetuation of the school's winning record, with which they have identified themselves, and not because of a personal interest in the welfare of the particular athlete. It is this sort of person who exerts the pressure which fires coaches when the team has not won enough games to satisfy the alumni's collective ego. These are the men who are influential in promoting among young boys a distorted idea of what it really means to play big football; and these are the ones who think that other people's judgments of men are as superficial as their own when they say that football players will have no trouble finding jobs, because everyone is glad to hire a football player.

Concerning the finding of jobs, it would be my guess that largely because of *very* widespread recruiting practices, the term football player has become synonymous with ape, and because of this it is often better for the job applicant to save mention of his gridiron record until after he has become acquainted with a prospective employer. Concerning the meaty subsidization question, I am glad to say that the University does none of it. A few of the players receive help from alumni, but a school with Michigan's prestige and record can usually get all the football material it needs without such aid.

During my four years at Michigan I played in games which took me from New York to California, but I was never given the opportunity to meet or speak to an opposing player. If there is any value in having an intercollegiate schedule, it would seem that such value would come from the opportunity which game trips afford to become acquainted with men from other schools and other parts of the country. But big football has no time for palaver. Indeed, on almost every trip we took, we were cautioned to keep to ourselves—because, and this is another slogan that I unfortunately know by heart, "We are here for only one purpose, and that is to win."

Often during a game I would develop a genuine fondness for some of the players with whom I was exchanging blows, and I would have valued a friendly glass of beer with them after the game. But the visiting team was always whisked off to its train with businesslike alacrity; about the only thing

I learned from traveling to other schools was that in every college stadium the grass is more or less green.

Nor did I learn anything from making the Rose Bowl trip—I merely verified my suspicion that of all the farces connected with big-time football, the Rose Bowl is the biggest. The so-called honor and glory of playing in the Rose Bowl is transient and meaningless, as is any glory and honor which is nothing more than the product of a publicity man's imagination; the three-week extra practice is not justified by the benefits of the game; and the trip to the coast is crowded and regimented. But the visiting team does at least get a trip out of it, and this is more than the host team gets. Of course I had no opportunity to speak to any of the California players, but it is impossible for me to understand how they, as Rose Bowl participants, could think of themselves as anything but extremely unlucky. For them there is no send-off, no cross-country trip, and no guided tours—nothing but three more weeks of drudgery under a southern California sun.

So, after four years of seeing everything there is to see in big-time college football—victories, defeats, publicity, hospitals, championships, and bowls—of being known as a "football player" rather than a human being, of seeing myself and my teammates misrepresented and misquoted by sportswriters who seldom attempted to know the players personally, of playing in a 97,000-seat stadium in which my nonpaying student friends were forced to sit in the end zone, of having my natural desire for physical exercise corrupted and commercialized, of giving up pleasant afternoons in favor of kicking and rolling in the dust and muck of the practice field—I have decided that big-time football is a poor bargain for the boys who play the game.

SUGGESTIONS FOR STUDY:

1. What is the topic of each numbered division?
2. Does Jackson use topic sentences regularly or only occasionally? Is transition between paragraphs clear?
3. In the opening paragraph of section 2, what does Jackson gain by limiting his attack? Does he limit it anywhere else? Where?

Too Much Football 35

4. What does Jackson consider Yost's great contributions to the game? Is this heresy?
5. Is Jackson justified in his interpretation of the slogan: "When Michigan loses, someone has to pay"?
6. What is the difference between "a gang tackle" and "covering an opposing ball-carrier with a blanket of blue"?
7. Do you agree with the statement that "schools which sponsor big-name teams . . . subtly lose prestige in the eyes of the general public"?
8. What tone does Jackson intend when he speaks of the "primitive alma materism of an obsolete generation of college playboys" or of the fact that he has learned the grass is more or less green in every college stadium? Can you cite other examples?
9. What is the meaning of an *adage, spontaneity, liturgical* manner, *chauvinistic* alumni, *unsavory bigotry, intimidated,* to *deify, virtually* all, *bromide, votaries, internecine* conflict, *esprit de corps, engendering* social *cohesion, homogeneity, automaton, taciturnity, mercenary stereotype, lurid* example, questionable *authenticity,* complimented *profusely, syllogism,* varsity *hierarchy, illusion* of *prestige,* coaches' *sanction, infallible* judgment, frightening *preoccupation, articulate* representative, *destitute* athletes, *perpetuation* of a record, businesslike *alacrity, transient* honor?
10. Write a theme in which you use personal experience to develop an opinion on any controversial subject.

From freshman girl to wife of a former president of the University of Wisconsin, Mrs. Frank has observed fraternities and sororities in considerable detail and from various points of view. She finds them a cause of . . .

HEARTACHE ON THE CAMPUS
by Mrs. Glenn Frank

A FEW weeks ago at a large middle-western university I talked with a student who had recently been discharged from the army for poor health. The boy said he liked the school, his courses and his professors. There was one thing, however, which he did not like. He had come to the university as a legacy to one of the leading fraternities, but after looking him over the fraternity brothers had not invited him to become a member.

"I guess the war had made me too old," he said, grinning, but for all his nonchalance I could see the hurt in his eyes. He had been cruelly snubbed. Right at the start of his college career he had discovered that the very democracy for which he had fought didn't exist at this great university.

His discovery is not unique. Reports of friction between returning veterans and the Greek-letter societies come from many other colleges and universities supported by taxpayers' money. Young men who have been matured in the hard school of war are finding themselves the victims of a ridiculous and

---

Woman's Home Companion, April 1945 issue. Copyright 1945, The Crowell-Collier Publishing Company.

juvenile caste system which is totally un-American. This should not be. It is time for the legislatures of this country to enact stringent laws abolishing both college and high school fraternities and sororities from coast to coast.

To some people that may sound like a strong remedy for a comparatively minor evil in our educational system. But I do not consider it minor.

For more than a quarter of a century, as a sorority woman myself and as the wife of the president of one of our largest state universities, I have had a close-up view of the operations of the Greek-letter societies. What I have seen has convinced me that any good which these societies accomplish is far outweighed by the unhappiness and heartbreak which they inflict upon thousands of young people every year, and by the class-consciousness, religious bigotry and race prejudice which they foment right in those institutions which should be the most liberal. They have no more place in our public educational system than a Hitler youth movement.

Yes, you may say, but if fraternities and sororities should be abolished, wouldn't students organize other cliques and clubs? I admit that they would, but such groups would be formed in a normal natural way. Students would be judged on their merits and find their own level. A boy or girl would not be relegated to a fixed position in campus society during the first days of school, as is provided under smug Panhellenic rules, merely because of the prestige or bank account of his parents, or because of the way he flipped a cigarette or handled a cup of tea.

Only the other day I heard of the case of a dull and unattractive youth who was taken into an exclusive fraternity merely because his father, a rich alumnus, had presented the chapter house with a pine-paneled library; and I know of another case, just as recent, where a brilliant and beautiful girl was kept out of a sorority because her father happened to be a railroad engineer.

"What a pity God couldn't have made him a doctor or a lawyer instead," one of the sorority members said, but, imbued with the snobbery of her group, she voted against the girl just the same.

Such discrimination is the rule rather than the exception and just as often students are casually black-balled because of some trivial or imagined flaw in their appearance, dress or manners. Over and over again I have known of a boy's being rejected by a fraternity because he failed to dance well or wear the latest cut of collar, or of a girl who was made to feel a campus outcast because she was a bit overweight, perhaps, or made the fatal mistake of cutting her lettuce with a knife.

The high school fraternities and sororities are, if anything, even more brutal than the college societies which they imitate because they are unsupervised and they victimize students of an even more impressionable age. Many needless tears are shed and many hearts are broken every year where they flourish. I even know of one adolescent girl who committed suicide because her high school sorority refused to admit her sister to membership.

I realize that in certain places where high school fraternities and sororities have been suppressed by law they have sprung up again in the form of subrosa organizations, but this can be prevented by requiring students to sign pledges against joining secret societies as is now done in the Milwaukee schools. Our main objective, however, should be the college fraternities and sororities. Once they are eradicated, their high school offshoots will wither and die quickly.

The appalling injustice and cruelty of the method by which students are rushed and pledged to fraternities and sororities was first brought home to me through personal experience.

The men of my father's family had for generations attended distinguished colleges and some of them had made distinguished records. My father felt that it was high time that the girls of the family should receive real educations too, and since there wasn't enough money to send me to Vassar, he decided to send me to the university of my home State, Missouri.

Before I left home, two of my mother's best friends said that since they had been Pi Phi's at Missouri they hoped I might become one too, and that they intended to write to the chapter recommending me. This conversation made me a bit apprehensive, but Mother brushed it aside. After all, I was going to the university to get an education, she said, not to become a Pi Phi. What difference did it make whether the sorority asked me or not?

But during my first hours at the university I was made to feel that sororities were the only thing that did matter. Although they represented only a minority of the women students, they had apparently taken over the campus. They were giving teas, luncheons and dinners. They were helping some freshmen to matriculate and escorting others around town in stylish carriages, but only those freshmen, of course, about whom they had received letters. The YWCA was arranging parties for all girls, but no one wanted to go to them.

The big event of the Pi Phi rushing program was an evening party at the chapter house where candidates for pledging were given a final once-over by the members. I shall never forget that party. While stunning girls, gorgeously gowned, looked us over critically, I felt the way a person must feel on his way to the gallows. My pink-dotted mull dress and hair tied with a ribbon were all wrong, I felt, and I knew that one false move, such as spilling my coffee, would bar me forever from Pi Phi. I was frightened and homesick and my throat was parched.

When I got back to my room that night, I wrote to Mother begging her to let me come home. I pleaded homesickness, not daring to tell her that I was a failure—that there was no use in staying on, no use getting an education or anything else, because the Pi Phi's hadn't asked me and apparently weren't going to ask me. Never before or since have I felt so rejected, so hopelessly unattractive.

I started packing, but one afternoon there was a call from the Pi Phi house. Would I come over? I was so excited that I thought my quaking knees would not carry me the several blocks. When I got there, one of the members pinned the Pi Phi's colors on my jumper dress. I was in!

It is impossible for me to put into words the relief which I experienced at that moment. It was like a reprieve from death. If I live to be a hundred, I shall never forget, either, the deep sense of inferiority which I felt during the period when

I thought I was not going to be pledged. Life for me simply wasn't worth living.

All this happened a long time ago, but the heartless and undemocratic methods used in rushing and selecting pledges have not been changed one iota. In 1925, when my husband started his long term of office as president of the University of Wisconsin, I thought I might find conditions there different, because Wisconsin had a reputation for liberality. But I discovered the system there was just as brutal as at Missouri, and it still is.

Every autumn at Wisconsin, as at many colleges, there would come a Sunday which always seemed to me the saddest day of the year. It was the Sunday on which the sororities sent out their invitations. It might be a beautiful fall day, but in boarding houses all over Madison, I knew, hundreds of teen-age girls would be waiting tensely for bids which would never come. As dusk fell all hope would die in their hearts and many, many of those youngsters would cry themselves to sleep that night.

I know, moreover, that the injury which is inflicted upon a young student's pride and self-respect when he is turned down by a Greek-letter society is, all too often, a permanent injury.

Not long ago I had a chat with a woman who failed to make a sorority during her stay at Wisconsin and who now lives in a fashionable suburb of Chicago. She has a successful husband, a lovely home and devoted children, but she confessed to me that if a guest in her house mentions colleges she gets up and leaves the room for fear she may be asked what sorority she belongs to.

Yes, and there is the case of Zona Gale. A short time before her death she told me how, more than thirty years before when she was a student at Wisconsin, she had wistfully watched the Delta Gammas starting off on picnics and had wished they would ask her to go with them.

Think of it—Zona Gale! Wisconsin's most famous daughter! Possessed of beauty, character, genius. Winner of the Pulitzer prize and holder of the highest honorary degrees which the university could confer. Yet the old cut of being ignored by the sororities had never healed. It was not vanity. Zona Gale had the least vanity of any woman I have ever known. It was just plain hurt—hurt inflicted by a system which doesn't make sense.

The scars which fraternities and sororities deal out gratuitously to the thousands of students whom they turn down every year are reason enough alone, it seems to me, to condemn them to extinction, but they are guilty of other gross crimes against democracy.

Recently a pretty sorority girl told me that she had been invited to a glee club concert by a brilliant nonfraternity man whom she really liked. Did she accept him? No indeed. Her sorority sisters might have made remarks. Instead, she went to the concert with a nitwit whom she didn't like. He didn't have an idea in his head, but he belonged to a good fraternity and her choice was highly approved.

Once in a sorority or fraternity, a student is compelled to conform to a caste system whether he approves it or not. If he doesn't join one, on the other hand, he is apt to find himself excluded from leadership in many college activities. Greek-letter students are a minority on most campuses but are so tightly knit and politically organized that they generally control elections.

At Wisconsin, for example, which is typical of most state universities, the highest social honor obtainable is that of being chosen king or queen of the junior prom, but only once since 1925 has a nonfraternity man been elected prom king, and there has been only one prom queen who was not in a sorority.

Some defenders of the fraternity and sorority system contend that this condition is proof positive that nonfraternity and nonsorority students lack inherent aggressiveness and leadership. That is utter bosh.

The most brilliant boy in my class at Missouri, a man who is now known throughout America, was rejected by the fraternities because he was considered countrified, and just a few months ago middle-western newspapers carried long obituaries about another nonfraternity man whom I knew years later. He wasn't considered good enough to enter a fraternity because his mother was guilty of the heinous crime of working for a living. He was good enough, though, to become a well-known lawyer in his state within a few years after leaving college, and to give his life for his country while serving with our air forces in the South Pacific.

No, under the present Panhellenic system, even Abraham Lincoln wouldn't possess leadership enough to make a fraternity, but a brief study of *Who's Who in America* proves that fraternities have no monopoly on ability. Just as many non-Greeks as Greeks make names for themselves after college.

Even more sinister than the other forms of snobbery is the religious bigotry and race prejudice which fraternities and sororities foster in the minds of the young.

The dean of women at one of our large universities told me only the other day that Catholic girls were admitted to sororities there under a quota system which permitted only a limited number of Catholics to be pledged each year. This quota does not in any way compare with the percentage of Catholic girls at the university. The same system prevails, I know, whether it is admitted or not, at many other colleges and universities.

As for Jewish students, they are excluded generally by leading fraternities and sororities. A few weeks ago I heard of a group of liberal-minded youths in one fraternity at an eastern college who rebelled against this taboo. By threatening to resign all at once the group forced this chapter to pledge a popular Jewish student. That was splendid, but I regret to say it is the only case of the kind I have ever heard of. In most houses, anti-Semitism is almost a part of the ritual.

In self-defense the Jews have formed their own fraternities and sororities, but they have been brutally snubbed year after year by a stuffy faction in Panhellenic which has refused to grant them national charters.

Now why, in a nation which is pouring out its substance to provide equal rights for all people, do we permit a cruel caste system to flourish in our public schools?

One of the reasons, I think, is the attitude of parents.

I knew a woman in Madison who devoted sixteen years of

her life, from the time her daughter was born until the child was of college age, to making social contacts which would enable her to get her daughter into an exclusive sorority, and that kind of thing is not uncommon. At a cocktail party recently, I talked with a number of mothers of teen-age children. Almost without exception they were much more concerned about getting their sons and daughters into fraternities and sororities than getting them an education.

Those women were not hopeless snobs. Most of them agreed that fraternities and sororities are unkind and undemocratic. Others deplored the added expense to which they are put—a sorority girl has to be equipped with a wardrobe comparable to that of a society debutante—but, well, since these organizations existed, they naturally wanted their children to belong to the best ones.

This same viewpoint is too often found among college faculty members. Not long ago I received a letter from a professor, famed for his liberal views, in which he asked me to help him get his daughter into a certain sorority. Since the fraternity and sorority system is deeply entrenched, he and many other professors who personally don't approve of it seem to feel that we must have it with us always, like death and taxes.

Such an attitude, it seems to me, is lazy and un-American. This country of ours has had many other deeply entrenched evils in its day, including slavery and inhuman child labor conditions, but we found ways of getting rid of them.

Among the most ardent exponents of the Greek-letter societies are the professional alumni—I've noticed they are often people who have not been very successful since leaving college—who maintain that fraternities and sororities bestow a kind of magical polish upon the boys and girls who belong to them.

That is mostly pure nonsense. During twenty-five years around college, I have never observed that the Greek-letter students acquired any better manners than the others, but if they did it would be a petty gain indeed compared to the dangerous caste ideas they are likely to absorb at the same time.

The only valid argument which the defenders of the system can muster is that the abolition of fraternities and sororities would create a housing shortage at many schools. True, but the problem isn't unsolvable. Why shouldn't state universities buy chapter houses outright and convert them into dormitories run under college management? The total value of chapter houses at both public and private colleges is about $100,000,000. A sizable sum, yes, but less than we were spending every day to fight a war for democracy. It would be a cheap price to pay for the democratization of education.

The time for this democratization is now. Because of the war, the fraternities are in a weaker position than they have been in a generation. Twenty per cent of all chapters are inactive, and most of the others are depleted in membership. More important, the war veterans who are entering our colleges are bringing with them a more adult point of view than the students of peace years. A man who has learned democracy in foxholes does not mold so easily to the fraternity pattern as a teen-age boy right out of high school.

Recently at one university I talked with a wounded veteran whose viewpoint, I believe, is typical of that of thousands of other servicemen. Because of his unusual heroism in a bloody action in the Pacific, three different fraternities tried to pledge him when he entered college a few months ago, but he turned them all down.

When I asked him why he did so, he said that he considered himself grown up and fraternities childish. Why should he, after what he had been through, scrub a sidewalk with a toothbrush during hell week because some upper classman ordered him to? Why should he let a lot of so-called brothers dictate what girls he might or might not go out with?

Yet we cannot depend upon this attitude of returning servicemen alone to end the fraternity and sorority evil. The Greek-letter societies cannot be laughed out of existence as they deserve to be. They are too deeply rooted. Concerted action by students, parents and educators will be needed before our legislatures can be expected to enact laws abolishing them.

I cannot repeat too often that this should be done right away. On foreign battlefields, a whole generation of American boys of college age jeopardized their lives, and many of them gave their lives, to safeguard democracy. Here at home, the most powerful agency for the preservation of democracy is the public school system from primary grade through university. To make that system wholly worthy of what our boys fought for, we must wipe out fraternities and sororities while the time is ripe!

SUGGESTIONS FOR STUDY:

1. What is Mrs. Frank's purpose in the first two paragraphs?
2. What is her purpose in the third paragraph? Where does she restate the substance of this paragraph?
3. What is the purpose of paragraph 5?
4. Does the fact that Mrs. Frank is herself a sorority member strengthen or weaken her argument?
5. How do paragraphs 4 and 6 make clear that Mrs. Frank is writing argument rather than mere exposition? Does she use the same technique elsewhere?
6. What is the longest narrative example Mrs. Frank uses? Is it effective?
7. Is your experience of Greek-letter societies similar to hers?
8. What, according to Mrs. Frank, are the evils of these societies? the causes of the evils? the cure?
9. What is the meaning of a *legacy, imbued with snobbery, deal out gratuitously, heinous crime, jeopardized their lives?*
10. Write a theme in which you discuss, in order, an evil, its cause, its cure.

Progressive education for children has been known more than once to create problems for un-progressively educated parents. As one father testifies, the problems may become even more complicated when the mother undertakes to become progressively educated too.

I SENT MY WIFE TO VASSAR
by Vance Packard

IF YOUR young son sticks his tongue out at you and calls you a nasty old stinkpot, don't slap him across the mouth. Instead, ignore the insult and rejoice secretly that you have such a fine, normal child! He is just channeling his aggressive, aggrieved feelings harmlessly by verbal projection.

I got that information straight out of the mouth of one of America's 116 most learned wives and mothers. I'm referring to my wife.

She became one of the 116 most learned wives and mothers by attending—along with 115 other wives from all parts of America—the Vassar College's unique Institute for Family Living at Poughkeepsie, N.Y., a few months ago. That's the special school held at Vassar, one of the world's leading women's colleges, where parents and their children can spend a month learning how to live a richer, more peaceable family life. On the teaching staff are some of America's leading child-guidance experts, educators, social workers, and homemaking and marriage experts.

Reprinted by permission from The American Magazine, February, 1951.

Director of the institute is the famed expert on family relations, Dr. Mary Fisher Langmuir. Some of the institute's teachers are men, but the majority are women.

Today, as a result of attending the institute, my wife is our neighborhood's expert on all problems of coping with children. Her opinions on the mysterious lore of child raising are eagerly sought by many of her neighbors. It is hard to realize that only a few weeks ago—before Vassar—she was a self-confessed flop as mother, homemaker, and wife. She was distressed by the fact that teachers were complaining about the brattiness of one of our children. . . . She felt that our household frequently seemed to be teetering on the edge of chaos. . . . And our marriage—well, it wasn't what she had been led to expect from reading *Little Colonel* and other idealized books for schoolgirls.

When she heard about this Vassar thing from a neighbor she would not rest until she had enrolled. With her, she enrolled our three youngsters: Vance, 8; Randall, 5; and Cindy, 2. They stayed in separate dormitories (with about 150 other children) under 24-hour guidance by attractive young experts (mostly female) on child rearing. All day long they romped in this Promised Land for Children, with its many play yards, nature cabins, swimming pool, and hundreds of acres of rolling lawns. Mrs. Packard saw the children only one hour each morning.

The rest of the time she was in this country-club atmosphere (golf links, tennis courts, luxurious dormitories) soaking up lectures on family living. She was instructed on how to cope with unruly husbands . . . how to handle children . . . how to live more abundantly on your husband's income . . . how to take the shine off his pants (use vinegar) . . . how to be a more scintillating, creative person. Furthermore, she had "new dimensions" added to her life as she engaged in Portuguese folk dancing, playwriting, wire sculpturing, speechmaking, and drum-making.

Well, the upshot is that I have on my hands a shimmering, transformed, confident woman who exudes patient understanding and knows all the answers. My three youngsters, likewise, are transformed almost beyond recognition. They are, I have to admit, more self-reliant, more friendly, more relaxed, and, for the most part, more civil to their daddy. I have overnight become the possessor of a more wonderful family than I would have imagined possible.

The rub is that I, the "master" of our household, am still pretty much the same gruff, reactionary old mossback. This has led to difficulties and awkward situations. My only consolation in my dilemma is that there are close to 115 other husbands around the country in the same fix. A few husbands were able to leave jobs long enough to be full-time students at the institute. (There is no law against husbands attending.) Most of us Vassar "daddies," however, visited only on week ends and were able to share our wives' rooms by paying $1.50 to have a cot moved in.

I got my first warning that something momentous was in ferment when I went up to Vassar after my family had been there a week. With me I was lugging several boxes full of extra stuff Virginia, my wife, had telephoned that she needed. I had assumed that she would be on hand to meet me. She wasn't, because my arrival coincided with a "basic seminar." It was a hot, sticky day. She strolled up 90 minutes later. I was in a black mood.

As is my custom in such situations I spoke my mind freely and loudly. I had assumed that she, as usual, would counterattack with blazing vigor. But an amazing thing happened: With an adroitness she had never displayed before, she hushed me up in about ten seconds by sweetly weathering my assault and calmly assuring me I certainly did have grounds for being angry. I found my mouth working, but no words coming out. (Vassar doesn't frown on loud verbal projections by husbands, but contends that most of it is pretty petty stuff.)

A couple of hours later Virginia disclosed that Vance, our oldest boy, had been acting boastfully and with a chip on his shoulder toward his new playmates. I replied matter-of-factly that I would fix that right away by taking him out in the woods (far from Vassar) and giving him a good whaling.

Very firmly she informed me, "I think we've been doing

too much of that sort of thing." The boy's obnoxious behavior, I was informed, was largely a defense mechanism that had manifested itself because he felt unsure of himself. A bullying daddy, she suggested diplomatically, would only aggravate the symptoms. What was needed from me was sympathetic affection to give him confidence.

That's the way it went all week end. At one point she said, "You know, we've been doing a lot of very foolish things." I've been hearing about these "foolish things" ever since.

The following week end she made the unsolicited remark that a father can be "detrimental" to his son. "What's that?" I demanded, suddenly taking notice. She tried to avoid repeating the ugly word "detrimental" but finally she explained. "If a father sets himself up as a model for a son and expects the boy to grow up just like him, the child is apt to get so frustrated trying to live up to expectations that he will become all mixed up emotionally."

Since Vassar I have been getting instruction on child rearing not only from my wife but from my children. The other morning Vance was shoveling his cereal into his mouth as if he were stoking a threshing machine. After a second reprimand I told him that if he didn't slow down and eat with his mouth closed he was going to get a licking.

His spoon poised in midair just long enough for him to explain, "Spanking is old-fashioned. Ha."

Frankly, I have been corrected so many times and have become so unsure of my old ways as a daddy that I count 10 before I open my mouth any more in front of my family. I have learned that I am not supposed to cuff Randall and state, "Get off that couch with your dirty shoes." Instead, I am supposed to ask him tactfully, "Randall, you wouldn't want to get the couch dirty, would you?"

My old habit of taking forthright action on behalf of my family is now frowned upon. I no longer feel free to announce on a Saturday afternoon: "All right, everybody. Get in the car! We're going to the museum." That, I'm told, is undemocratic authoritarianism. Instead, I now am expected to call a meeting and ask my children to help *plan* what we shall do during the afternoon. A vote is taken. The upshot is that we usually climb a mountain, instead.

The other day Randall asked, "Daddy, did you ever wrestle a live octopus?" I knew enough by now not to retort, "Go away, child, and stop asking silly questions." But what should I have said? I am not quite sure yet, so I patted him warily on the head and mumbled a plain, "No." But I am learning fast.

At the moment I am corresponding with some of the other husbands whose wives attended the institute to investigate the possibility of setting up a "Vassar Daddies Protective Association" for interchange of information.

While the institute was still in session I was relieved to find quite a few husbands becoming uneasy about the impact Vassar was likely to have on their home life. As I walked down a Vassar path with Mr. John Nickerson III, a broker from New Canaan, Conn., whose wife Nancy was attending the Vassar Institute, he shook his head grimly and said, "It will take Nancy two years to get over this."

One announced aim of the Vassar courses was to help the wives get "a new perspective" on their relationship with their husband. To some husbands that sounded ominous. They didn't want anyone to get a "new perspective" on them.

On a Saturday night before a square dance on the lawn, the husbands and wives were shown a movie about The Over-Dependent Husband. It dramatized a poor guy who had to be treated like a child by his wife. Afterward it was announced that there would be "a discussion of the movie for daddies only" in one of the lounges. I watched from a safe distance. Not a single daddy appeared at the lounge while I watched.

Since most of the wives were being transformed into glamorous creatures by the course on personal appearance it was thought wise to give the visiting week-end daddies a capsule, one-hour course. About 25 of us showed up to learn how to give ourselves "greater ocular impact." Immediately the teacher, Prof. Muriel Cox, gave us a lecturing.

"You fellows," she said, "want your wives to be neat and trim, and yet you develop bay windows. Come on, now; get your postures up."

There was an embarrassed sucking in of stomachs all down the row.

Apparently, even the little girls attending the Vassar children's school acquired a more confident attitude toward the male sex. Amid much tittering my wife told me about two 4-year-old girls who were overheard playing "Mummie and Baby." A little boy strolled up and asked to join in the play. (All Vassar-trained children ask "May I play with you?" before they butt into a game.)

The little girls told him he couldn't play because he was a boy.

"Let me be daddy," he suggested.

"We don't need a daddy."

"Everybody has a daddy," he replied.

"All right, then, be daddy," one girl said. "But you know what a daddy does, don't you? He goes to work. So you go over there in the next room and go to work!"

Almost every day since Vassar some incident has arisen which has given my wife an excuse to give me a tactful little indoctrinating lesson on family living. Last Tuesday I suggested that I could save her some lecturing if she would just let me read her notebooks. She professed that she couldn't find all of them and that she was a terrible note-taker. Finally she turned over two that she could "find." She did it grudgingly, and I can see why. Some of the notes weren't meant for my eyes.

Evidently, one of the lectures was on "The Eternal Feminine." It was a sort of pep talk on the theme that if women would just put their minds together they could change the world. There was a jotted notation that "women have more wisdom," and some stuff about women's wiles, softness, etc. Then, standing out, was this underscored admonition: *Brush Up on Technique.*

Now, every time Virginia puts her arms around my neck and says dreamily, "You are so wonderful to me," I see that line looming before me.

Near the end of the second notebook is this recommendation: "Make out list entitled *What I Want in Family Relationship by July, 1951,* and put it in sealed envelope."

Presumably hidden somewhere in my happy home is such a sealed envelope. So far, all I can say is that I know it is not in the living-room or the bedroom.

I confess that my first reaction to my Vassarized family was one of apprehension and bewilderment. Several times I wondered why on earth I had allowed myself to get into such a fix. At first, under pressure, I went along with my family against my better judgment. But as the months have passed since Vassar I have seen changes in my wife and children (and in my own behavior) that make me suspect that the whole experience has been very much worth while.

As I dope it, the essence of what my wife and the 115 other wives got at Vassar can be boiled down to a couple of key words:

For coping with a husband, the key word is *patience*.

For coping with children, the key word is *permissiveness*.

I kept coming across this magic word "permissiveness" all through Virginia's notebooks, and heard it night and day whenever I was visiting at Vassar. The ideal way to raise a child, I gather, is the permissive way.

What is permissiveness? I figure it is a 50-cent word meaning, "Let 'em do as they please as far as possible." When I asked a male visiting lecturer what the word meant he explained, "It means that if your child kicks you, you—being an adult—have acquired enough self-restraint and security not to kick him back."

A more official explanation is that permissiveness is "the ability to let children arrive childishly at their own truth."

The parent who is the extreme opposite of permissive is a *pressure* parent. *Pressure* is the ugliest word in the Vassar vocabulary. It did not take me long to discover that I have been a pressure papa of the worst sort.

Pressure, particularly by Daddy, is now taboo in our Silvermine, Conn., home. I cannot threaten, browbeat, push, isolate, slap, or even use sarcasm on our children. Such actions, I'm told, are "contrary to Vassar's basic philosophy."

Our children are now being raised on almost pure permissiveness. Mostly they do what their young hearts desire. Vance is just learning to ride a bike. Every day after school I find him careening wildly up and down the roads of Silvermine on his two-wheeler. In school, if he prefers doodling to arithmetic, that's all right with us—even if it may not be with his teacher. Under permissiveness, the theory goes, he'll soon love arithmetic if he is not pressed.

Cindy has a fondness for mopping the floor with one of my cast-off shirts, so she does that by the hour, undisturbed. When Randall was sick with the grippe and had a 102-degree temperature he was permitted to play out in the hallway with his trucks—because that is what he felt like doing.

One night at supper when Vance was in the middle of his fourth dessert, I started to protest, but Virginia signaled me to be calm. (All our children now eat only what they please, without wheedling or threatening from the Big Folks.)

After supper, obviously quoting some Vassar authority, my wife informed me, "All three of them (our children) will soon learn what they need in food, and eat it. If we butt in and try to dictate what, or how much, they should eat, we're just asking for trouble. For years, as you ought to know, they have balked at eating what we wanted them to just to punish us or to get attention."

How can you answer talk like that?

Under permissiveness you don't boss a child. You give him "nondirective guidance." The other day I announced—in my customary authoritarian voice—that the yard was a mess and needed to be picked up. Randall moaned and Vance immediately complained about his sore foot. Noticing my wife's frown, I suddenly remembered nondirective guidance and decided I had better give it a whirl.

In my most palsy-walsy, are-you-coming-fellows? voice I lured them out into the yard. "Let's see, now," I began, with elaborate casualness, "what do you think needs to be done?"

Silence.

So I began leading them around the yard. Just as we were in front of a heap of boards (the remains of an abandoned homemade jet propulsion launching platform), I asked Randall if he saw anything that needed picking up. With gratifying eagerness he asked, "This, Daddy?"

I agreed that was a fine idea. Soon Vance was seeing

things, wings of dismembered airplanes, a Roy Rogers comic book, candy wrappers. When we had canvassed the whole yard I asked—in my best nondirective-guidance style—"Well, how will we go about this?"

Vance instantly had a solution: "I'll shut my eyes and whirl. Where I'm pointing when I stop is where Randall will work." It wasn't a very practical idea, but I was stuck with it. So I said, "Fine, and you and I will divide up the rest." Thus the yard got cleaned.

Another type of permissiveness we're practicing in our home is letting our youngsters run their own lives just as fast as they can learn to do it. Vance (age 8) began making his own bed at Vassar, and is still doing it. He also washes out (enthusiastically) his own clothes on the scrubbing board. For these new habits Mrs. Packard and I will be eternally grateful to Vassar.

Perhaps we are imagining, but our impression is that he doesn't wallow in mud quite so much now that he washes his own clothes. Furthermore, since we've started giving him a clothing allowance and instructing him to buy his own clothes, he doesn't seem to come home quite so often with shirt sleeves ripped off.

In justifying putting children on their own financially, the Vassar homemaking expert, Gladys Jones, explained to my wife's class, "Sure, the youngster will buy crazy clothes, and toys that break in ten minutes, at first. But can you think of a cheaper way to teach him prudence?"

Our experience with Vance has been slightly different. He bought crazy toys and clothes galore for a few days, but now he has become a miser. He counts his money every night and hides it in secret caches. Now he refuses to waste his money on ice-cream cones, and even has lost his former passion for wanting to possess every new fire engine that comes on the market.

Although our home is now dedicated to permissiveness my wife insists that she (like all true Vassarites) does not believe in *extreme* permissiveness." In short, you can't let a child get away with murder. Just mayhem. There must always be clear limits set for the child's guidance, and he must know there will always be "consequences" to overstepping the limits.

What are the consequences if a child becomes so extremely obnoxious that something just has to be done? Even Vassar-trained youngsters, I found, can at times be little hellions. There are a lot of wrong ways to go about coping with an obstreperous child, I am told. For example, my way. The other day my wife informed me:

"Your trouble is that you are always issuing ultimatums. And you are more strict on discipline than you realize."

I was raised in a farm community in northern Pennsylvania where severe discipline was in fashion. It was believed that all boys are filled with foolishness until they get over "Fool's Hill." The best way to keep foolishness at a minimum was to administer frequent sound thrashings. I remember that my great ambition was to get over Fool's Hill. That came when you reached 16, which, oddly enough, was just about the age when a boy became husky enough to turn on his pa and take the stick away from him.

To a Vassarite, of course, such reliance on the stick is hopelessly old-fashioned and brutal. A few days ago I was having trouble trying to persuade Randall to move his building blocks back upstairs. He had them scattered all over the living-room. When he showed only the slightest signs of complying I was itching to start swinging. Mrs. Packard advised me to be firm but patient. Learnedly she advised me, "You can't *make* a child do anything. He'll always try to go you one better. The trick is to help him *want* to do it. Show him that he can help me keep the living-room straight."

Then she added, "Suppose you were a little shaver like Randall. How would you react if some giant of a parent who towered over you kept barking orders and threatening to beat you if you didn't obey him this instant?" (In his own exasperating good time Randall did move all the blocks. I had to remind him that two were under the sofa.)

While at Vassar, Virginia developed a schoolgirl crush on the director, Dr. Mary Fisher Langmuir, and is constantly quoting her to me. The favorite quotation she hauls out whenever I threaten to jump the traces on discipline is this one:

"It is pitiful the corners we drive children into, and the things they do to get out of them."

Even before Vassar I had, at my wife's insistence, stopped relying completely on the switch to obtain decent behavior from our children. She and I began trying out the slick modern psychology of offering them rewards for good behavior. In brief, we tried sugar instead of the whip. I proposed that we give a prize each week to the child who got the most gold stars for "Doing What You Are Told" each day. My wife approved, after amending it to read, "Doing What You Are Asked." Momentarily, at least, this system seemed to produce more order in the household.

Now, however, I learn that rewarding is frowned upon, too. My wife learned at Vassar that bribing is just as bad as bullying. The weakness of rewards, in the long run, psychologically, is that youngsters soon get wise and blackmail you into raising the ante. Come to think of it, I know that from experience. It cost us a rubber boat ($15) to get Vance to behave long enough in school to pass first grade. In the second grade, the price he demanded, and got, for passing was a bike ($42). At that rate of progression we would go bankrupt getting him out of 12th grade.

In offering rewards (bribes), my better half informs me, we fail to give the child the values he really seeks. More than anything he wants the parents' love and affection. And he wants appreciation and recognition *for what he already is*.

It is damaging enough to keep baiting children with rewards, but it is even worse to keep threatening to withhold money and rewards from them. They should be given an allowance from the family income as their just due, regardless of how they behave. My wife still finds it hard to adjust herself to the fact that she is not even supposed to threaten that Santa Claus won't come if the children don't behave. She has been using Santa as a club for years, and thinking how clever she was.

I had to pry for quite a while to get it out of her—she was afraid I might abuse the knowledge—but my wife finally acknowledged that Vassar actually endorses spankings in certain circumstances. You are supposed to try your very best to prevent head-on collisions from developing. But if they do develop, then "do what needs to be done."

Apparently, the experts have found that some children want to be spanked. When one child at Vassar was asked to reveal his three greatest wishes, one was to be spanked. Any child who wants a spanking feels a need for limits. He wants to be helped to stop.

The danger, I am advised, is not in the spanking itself but in the parent's attitude toward it. Daddies and mommies should not get caught in a who's-going-to-win contest . . . or have emotional hang-overs . . . or give the child any feeling whatever that he is being rejected.

One night, after I became exasperated by a tantrum Randall was throwing while Virginia and I were playing hide-and-seek with Cindy, Virginia informed me, "No child is ornery just to be ornery. Behind his orneriness are mean feelings, usually caused by some emotional hunger. What we need to do is help the child get these mean feelings off his chest, and we need to look behind his behavior to see *why* he acts that way."

For years we had been noticing Randall's fearfulness and his eagerness to comply and to be approved. Somewhere at Vassar, Virginia learned that the "middle child" in most American families is more neglected than a first or last child. The result is that he often tends to become a conformist to get approval. Randall, we suddenly realized, showed signs of fitting this middle-child pattern.

The middle child, in particular, needs to feel he is getting special attention and love from his parents and other adults around him. In Randall's case this has worked out vividly. Since Vassar he has blossomed out into a bolder, more assertive boy. Before he went to Vassar, for example, he was afraid of water and refused to go even into wading pools. Within a month after Vassar, he was romping in ocean surf.

With Vance the change that has taken place is even more startling. Once a sunny, exuberant child, he had become before Vassar, I confess, more and more of a supercharged smart aleck. He boasted like an Indian and was always automatically "ag'in'" almost everything that was suggested to him. If you asked if he was enjoying his own birthday party he would make a face and say "Nah-h-h-h."

School and Vance definitely did not mix. First, the complaint was that he was restless and always causing a commotion instead of doing his work. Later, a teacher complained that he was careless, lazy, rebellious. He was kept after school, licked at home. But nothing we tried seemed to do much good. A year ago we hired a rather stern nurse to watch the children while Virginia had an operation. The nurse quit after two days because of the way Vance defied and bedeviled her.

In his first few days at Vassar he ran true to form. I heard they were giving him a hearing test because he didn't answer when called. That made me laugh. I had discovered long ago that he heard only what he wanted to hear.

But gradually, under Vassar's permissiveness, we could see him relax and start to smile again. I asked him how he liked Vassar. He beamed and said "Fine!" In fact, he said he wished he could stay "a billion more months." Even the Vassar staff commented that his transformation and progress were "amazing." We were astonished when we were informed that he had become one of the most gifted and enthusiastic science pupils at the institute. (Now he is assembling his own "museum.")

On the last day Virginia and I asked Dr. Langmuir why Vance had been so careless and lazy before. She replied, "There is no such thing as a careless child. All children have a tremendous eagerness to learn." But sometimes they don't dare to show it. They are afraid of failing, and feel they are safe if they make it obvious they aren't trying. Often, as in Vance's case, they hide behind a wise-guy contrariness.

Why had Vance become afraid to try? One possible answer apparently was that his pressure papa was expecting too much of him. (That's a very common attitude of fathers toward first sons.)

My wife, I believe, also got real benefits out of Vassar. At Vassar she stopped fretting about her graying hair. At her "color analysis" the personal-appearance instructor told her that she can start wearing all the red she wants, now that her hair is becoming grayish. Virginia is crazy about red.

More important, she learned that the "perfect marriage" is a pretty dull thing. Now, instead of regarding me with sickened dismay when we get into an argument and I start hollering, she takes the calm Vassar view that tempests are an essential ingredient of really happy marriages. Vassar showed her that making up afterward can be a lot of fun.

Probably the basic idea she picked up at the institute is that an easy-does-it, take-life-as-it-comes attitude toward family life makes for richer, more rewarding living. This "insight" was drummed into her day after day for a month at Vassar, and I'm told that an insight is a very hard thing to forget. I noticed that one line in her notebook reads: "The things that worry us so much in children are part of the fun and excitement and strain and stress of growing up."

It has been an uncomfortable business being educated on family living by my own wife. But if I am going to be honest I must admit that I like practically everything the Vassar Summer Institute did to my family. In fact, I am delighted by most of it.

I just wish someone would invent a more painless method for initiating a daddy into a family that has been Vassarized. That would be handy information to have, because when the institute begins again in July with its 1951 session, there will probably be an even bigger crop of bewildered Vassar daddies. Where it will all end, nobody can tell.

SUGGESTIONS FOR STUDY:

1. Is the contrast in the first paragraph largely responsible for the humor?
2. Does Packard use contrast elsewhere?
3. What is Packard's main idea, and where does he express it?
4. Does a change in tone distinguish the second part of the essay from the first?
5. Considering, for example, the definition of permissiveness and the final paragraph, does Packard drop the bantering tone completely?
6. Is there a contradiction between Packard's describing himself

60   Current Prose

as "still pretty much the same gruff, reactionary old mossback" and the last part of the essay?
7. Do any of the direct quotations strike you as especially apt for their purpose? For example?
8. Is the Packard household better or worse after "Vassarizing"?
9. What is the meaning of *scintillating, obnoxious behavior, undemocratic authoritarianism, issuing ultimatums, ornery?*
10. Write a theme describing and evaluating a permissive or pressure parent, upbringing or experience; or write a theme about a decided change of attitude you have undergone.

••

To remove a serious objection to his theory about the migration of South Sea Islanders from South America to Polynesia, Thor Heyerdahl and five companions crossed the South Pacific on a balsa raft. One hundred days on a raft in the open sea gave Heyerdahl a unique opportunity to observe ocean creatures.

from KON-TIKI
by Thor Heyerdahl

THE SEA contains many surprises for him who has his floor on a level with the surface and drifts along slowly and noiselessly. A sportsman who breaks his way through the woods may come back and say that no wild life is to be seen. Another may sit down on a stump and wait, and often rustlings and cracklings will begin and curious eyes peer out. So it is on the sea, too. We usually plow across it with roaring
••••••••••••••••••

From: KON-TIKI: Across the Pacific by Raft, by Thor Heyerdahl. Copyright 1950 by Thor Heyerdahl. Published in the U. S. by Rand McNally & Company. In Canada by Allen & Unwin, Ltd.

engines and piston strokes, with the water foaming round our bow. Then we come back and say that there is nothing to see far out on the ocean.

Not a day passed but we, as we sat floating on the surface of the sea, were visited by inquisitive guests which wriggled and waggled about us, and a few of them, such as dolphins and pilot fish, grew so familiar that they accompanied the raft across the sea and kept round us day and night.

When night had fallen and the stars were twinkling in the dark tropical sky, a phosphorescence flashed around us in rivalry with the stars, and single glowing plankton resembled round live coals so vividly that we involuntarily drew in our bare legs when the glowing pellets were washed up round our feet at the raft's stern. When we caught them, we saw that they were little brightly shining species of shrimp. On such nights we were sometimes scared when two round shining eyes suddenly rose out of the sea right alongside the raft and glared at us with an unblinking hypnotic stare. The visitors were often big squids which came up and floated on the surface with their devilish green eyes shining in the dark like phosphorus. But sometimes the shining eyes were those of deep-water fish which came up only at night and lay staring, fascinated by the glimmer of light before them. Several times, when the sea was calm, the black water round the raft was suddenly full of round heads two or three feet in diameter, lying motionless and staring at us with great glowing eyes. On other nights balls of light three feet and more in diameter would be visible down in the water, flashing at irregular intervals like electric lights turned on for a moment.

We gradually grew accustomed to having these subterranean or submarine creatures under the floor, but nevertheless we were just as surprised every time a new species appeared. About two o'clock on a cloudy night, when the man at the helm had difficulty in distinguishing black water from black sky, he caught sight of a faint illumination down in the water which slowly took the shape of a large animal. It was impossible to say whether it was plankton shining on its body, or whether the animal itself had a phosphorescent surface, but the glimmer down in the black water gave the ghostly creature obscure, wavering outlines. Sometimes it was roundish, sometimes oval, or triangular, and suddenly it split into two parts which swam to and fro under the raft independently of each other. Finally there were three of these large shining phantoms wandering round in slow circles under us.

They were real monsters, for the visible parts alone were some five fathoms long, and we all quickly collected on deck and followed the ghost dance. It went on for hour after hour, following the course of the raft. Mysterious and noiseless, our shining companions kept a good way beneath the surface, mostly on the starboard side where the light was, but often they were right under the raft or appeared on the port side. The glimmer of light on their backs revealed that the beasts were bigger than elephants but they were not whales, for they never came up to breathe. Were they giant ray fish which changed shape when they turned over on their sides? They took no notice at all if we held the light right down on the surface to lure them up, so that we might see what kind of creatures they were. And, like all proper goblins and ghosts, they had sunk into the depths when the dawn began to break.

We never got a proper explanation of this nocturnal visit from the three shining monsters, unless the solution was afforded by another visit we received a day and a half later in the full midday sunshine. It was May 24, and we were lying drifting on a leisurely swell in exactly 95° west by 7° south. It was about noon, and we had thrown overboard the guts of two big dolphins we had caught earlier in the morning. I was having a refreshing plunge overboard at the bow, lying in the water but keeping a good lookout and hanging on to a rope end, when I caught sight of a thick brown fish, six feet long, which came swimming inquisitively toward me through the crystal-clear sea water. I hopped quickly up on to the edge of the raft and sat in the hot sun looking at the fish as it passed quietly, when I heard a wild war whoop from Knut, who was sitting aft behind the bamboo cabin. He bellowed "Shark!" till his voice cracked in a falsetto, and, as we had sharks swimming alongside the raft almost daily without creating such excitement, we all realized that this must be something extra-special and flocked astern to Knut's assistance.

Knut had been squatting there, washing his pants in the swell, and when he looked up for a moment he was staring straight into the biggest and ugliest face any of us had ever seen in the whole of our lives. It was the head of a veritable sea monster, so huge and so hideous that, if the Old Man of the Sea himself had come up, he could not have made such an impression on us. The head was broad and flat like a frog's, with two small eyes right at the sides, and a toadlike jaw which was four or five feet wide and had long fringes drooping from the corners of the mouth. Behind the head was an enormous body ending in a long thin tail with a pointed tail fin which stood straight up and showed that this sea monster was not any kind of whale. The body looked brownish under the water, but both head and body were thickly covered with small white spots.

The monster came quietly, lazily swimming after us from astern. It grinned like a bulldog and lashed gently with its tail. The large round dorsal fin projected clear of the water and sometimes the tail fin as well, and, when the creature was in the trough of the swell, the water flowed about the broad back as though washing round a submerged reef. In front of the broad jaws swam a whole crowd of zebra-striped pilot fish in fan formation, and large remora fish and other parasites sat firmly attached to the huge body and traveled with it through the water, so that the whole thing looked like a curious zoological collection crowded round something that resembled a floating deep-water reef.

A twenty-five-pound dolphin, attached to six of our largest fishhooks, was hanging behind the raft as bait for sharks, and a swarm of the pilot fish shot straight off, nosed the dolphin without touching it, and then hurried back to their lord and master, the sea king. Like a mechanical monster it set its machinery going and came gliding at leisure toward the dolphin which lay, a beggarly trifle, before its jaws. We tried to pull the dolphin in, and the sea monster followed slowly, right up to the side of the raft. It did not open its mouth but just let the dolphin bump against it, as if to throw open the whole door for such an insignificant scrap was not worth while. When the giant came close up to the raft, it rubbed its back against the heavy steering oar, which was just lifted up out of the water, and now we had ample opportunity of studying the monster at the closest quarters—at such close quarters that I thought we had all gone mad, for we roared stupidly with laughter and shouted overexcitedly at the completely fantastic sight we saw. Walt Disney himself, with all his powers of imagination, could not have created a more hair-raising sea monster than that which thus suddenly lay with its terrific jaws along the raft's side.

The monster was a whale shark, the largest shark and the largest fish known in the world today. It is exceedingly rare, but scattered specimens are observed here and there in the tropical oceans. The whale shark has an average length of fifty feet, and according to zoologists it weighs fifteen tons. It is said that large specimens can attain a length of sixty feet; one harpooned baby had a liver weighing six hundred pounds and a collection of three thousand teeth in each of its broad jaws.

Our monster was so large that, when it began to swim in circles round us and under the raft, its head was visible on one side while the whole of its tail stuck out on the other. And so incredibly grotesque, inert, and stupid did it appear when seen fullface that we could not help shouting with laughter, although we realized that it had strength enough in its tail to smash both balsa logs and ropes to pieces if it attacked us. Again and again it described narrower and narrower circles just under the raft, while all we could do was to wait and see what might happen. When it appeared on the other side, it glided amiably under the steering oar and lifted it up in the air, while the oar blade slid along the creature's back.

We stood round the raft with hand harpoons ready for action, but they seemed to us like toothpicks in relation to the mammoth beast we had to deal with. There was no indication that the whale shark ever thought of leaving us again; it circled round us and followed like a faithful dog, close up to the raft. None of us had ever experienced or thought we should experience anything like it; the whole adventure, with the sea monster swimming behind and under the raft, seemed to us so completely unnatural that we could not really take it seriously.

In reality the whale shark went on encircling us for barely an hour, but to us the visit seemed to last a whole day. At last it became too exciting for Erik, who was standing at a corner of the raft with an eight-foot hand harpoon, and, encouraged by ill-considered shouts, he raised the harpoon above his head. As the whale shark came gliding slowly toward him and its broad head moved right under the corner of the raft, Erik thrust the harpoon with all his giant strength down between his legs and deep into the whale shark's gristly head. It was a second or two before the giant understood properly what was happening. Then in a flash the placid half-wit was transformed into a mountain of steel muscles.

We heard a swishing noise as the harpoon line rushed over the edge of the raft and saw a cascade of water as the giant stood on its head and plunged down into the depths. The three men who were standing nearest were flung about the place, head over heels, and two of them were flayed and burned by the line as it rushed through the air. The thick line, strong enough to hold a boat, was caught up on the side of the raft but snapped at once like a piece of twine, and a few seconds later a broken-off harpoon shaft came up to the surface two hundred yards away. A shoal of frightened pilot fish shot off through the water in a desperate attempt to keep up with their old lord and master. We waited a long time for the monster to come racing back like an infuriated submarine, but we never saw anything more of him.

We were now in the South Equatorial Current and moving in a westerly direction just 400 sea miles south of the Galapagos. There was no longer any danger of drifting into the Galapagos currents, and the only contacts we had with this group of islands were greetings from big sea turtles which no doubt had strayed far out to sea from the islands. One day we saw a thumping turtle lying struggling with its head and one great fin above the surface of the water. As the swell rose, we saw a shimmer of green and blue and gold in the water under the turtle, and we discovered that it was engaged in a life-

and-death struggle with dolphins. The fight was apparently quite one-sided; it consisted in twelve to fifteen big-headed, brilliantly colored dolphins attacking the turtle's neck and fins and apparently trying to tire it out, for the turtle could not lie for days on end with its head and paddles drawn inside its shell.

When the turtle caught sight of the raft, it dived and made straight for us, pursued by the glittering fish. It came close up to the side of the raft and was showing signs of wanting to climb up on to the timber when it caught sight of us already standing there. If we had been more practiced, we could have captured it with ropes without difficulty as the huge carapace paddled quietly along the side of the raft. But we spent the time that mattered in staring, and when we had the lasso ready the giant turtle had already passed our bow. We flung the little rubber dinghy into the water, and Herman, Bengt, and Torstein went in pursuit of the turtle in the round nutshell, which was not a great deal bigger than what swam ahead of them. Bengt, as steward, saw in his mind's eye endless meat dishes and a most delicious turtle soup.

But the faster they rowed, the faster the turtle slipped through the water just below the surface, and they were not more than a hundred yards from the raft when the turtle suddenly disappeared without a trace. But they had done one good deed at any rate. For when the little yellow rubber dinghy came dancing back over the water, it had the whole glittering school of dolphins after it. They circled round the new turtle, and the boldest snapped at the oar blades which dipped into the water like fins; meanwhile, the peaceful turtle escaped successfully from all its ignoble persecutors.

SUGGESTIONS FOR STUDY:

1. What is the main idea? Is it directly stated? Where?
2. What are the main divisions?
3. Are the comparisons in the first paragraph helpful in clarifying Heyerdahl's point?
4. What words help create a sense of mystery about the nightly visitors?
5. What details dispel any sense of mystery about the whale shark?

6. How does the paragraph beginning, "The monster was a whale shark . . ." differ from those immediately before and after?
7. Do the reactions of the men on the raft make the descriptions of the sea creatures more vivid?
8. What do you learn about a remora fish from the selection?
9. What is the meaning of *phosphoresence, proper goblins, falsetto, dinghy?*
10. Write a theme with a unifying main idea concerning various creatures you know about; or write a theme questioning the validity of a popular notion. (See also "Science Can Be Silly," p. 97.)

This account, based on scientific research rather than personal observation, suggests further the interest and variety of life beneath the sea.

from THE SEA AROUND US
by Rachel Carson

THE EXISTENCE of an abundant deep-sea fauna was discovered, probably millions of years ago, by certain whales and also, it now appears, by seals. The ancestors of all whales, we know by fossil remains, were land mammals. They must have been predatory beasts, if we are to judge by their powerful jaws and teeth. Perhaps in their foragings about the deltas of great rivers or around the edges of shallow seas, they discovered the abundance of fish and other marine life and over the centuries formed the habit of following them farther and farther into the sea. Little by little their bodies took on a

---
From *The Sea Around Us* by Rachel L. Carson. Copyright 1950, 1951 by Rachel L. Carson.

form more suitable for aquatic life; their hind limbs were reduced to rudiments, which may be discovered in a modern whale by dissection, and the forelimbs were modified into organs for steering and balancing.

Eventually the whales, as though to divide the sea's food resources among them, became separated into three groups: the plankton-eaters, the fish-eaters, and the squid-eaters. The plankton-eating whales can exist only where there are dense masses of small shrimp or copepods to supply their enormous food requirements. This limits them, except for scattered areas, to arctic and antarctic waters and the high temperate latitudes. Fish-eating whales may find food over a somewhat wider range of ocean, but they are restricted to places where there are enormous populations of schooling fish. The blue water of the tropics and of the open ocean basins offers little to either of these groups. But that immense, square-headed, formidably toothed whale known as the cachalot or sperm whale discovered long ago what men have known for only a short time—that hundreds of fathoms below the almost untenanted surface waters of these regions there is an abundant animal life. The sperm whale has taken these deep waters for his hunting grounds; his quarry is the deep-water population of squids, including the giant squid Architeuthis, which lives pelagically at depths of 1500 feet or more. The head of the sperm whale is often marked with long stripes, which consist of a great number of circular scars made by the suckers of the squid. From this evidence we can imagine the battles that go on, in the darkness of the deep water, between these two huge creatures—the sperm whale with its 70-ton bulk, the squid with a body as long as 30 feet, and writhing, grasping arms extending the total length of the animal to perhaps 50 feet.

The greatest depth at which the giant squid lives is not definitely known, but there is one instructive piece of evidence about the depth to which sperm whales descend, presumably in search of the squids. In April 1932, the cable repair ship *All America* was investigating an apparent break in the submarine cable between Balboa in the Canal Zone and Esmeraldas, Ecuador. The cable was brought to the surface off the coast of Colombia. Entangled in it was a dead 45-foot male sperm whale. The submarine cable was twisted around the lower jaw and was wrapped around one flipper, the body, and the caudal flukes. The cable was raised from a depth of 540 fathoms, or 3240 feet.

Some of the seals also appear to have discovered the hidden food reserves of the deep ocean. It has long been something of a mystery where, and on what, the northern fur seals of the eastern Pacific feed during the winter, which they spend off the coast of North America from California to Alaska. There is no evidence that they are feeding to any great extent on sardines, mackerel, or other commercially important fishes. Presumably four million seals could not compete with commercial fishermen for the same species without the fact being known. But there is some evidence on the diet of the fur seals, and it is highly significant. Their stomachs have yielded the bones of a species of fish that has never been seen alive. Indeed, not even its remains have been found anywhere except in the stomachs of seals. Ichthyologists say that this "seal fish" belongs to a group that typically inhabits very deep water, off the edge of the continental shelf.

How either whales or seals endure the tremendous pressure changes involved in dives of several hundred fathoms is not definitely known. They are warm-blooded mammals like ourselves. Caisson disease, which is caused by the rapid accumulation of nitrogen bubbles in the blood with sudden release of pressure, kills human divers if they are brought up rapidly from depths of 200 feet or so. Yet, according to the testimony of whalers, a baleen whale, when harpooned, can dive straight down to a depth of half a mile, as measured by the amount of line carried out. From these depths, where it has sustained a pressure of half a ton on every inch of body, it returns almost immediately to the surface. The most plausible explanation is that the whale, unlike the diver, does not have air pumped to him while he is under water, and therefore has in his body only the limited supply he carries down. Therefore he does not have enough nitrogen in his blood to do serious harm. The plain truth is, however, that we really do not know, since it is obviously impossible to confine a whale and experiment on him, and almost as difficult to dissect a dead one satisfactorily.

SUGGESTIONS FOR STUDY:

1. What is the main idea? Is it directly stated? Where?
2. What are the main divisions of the selection?
3. Does Miss Carson use topic sentences for her paragraphs?
4. If she is more consistent in this than Heyerdahl was in the previous selection, does the kind of writing in each selection help to account for the difference?
5. Is there a notable difference in diction between the two selections? Which requires the greater acquaintance with biological vocabulary?
6. What do the following words mean: *fauna, predatory, delta, rudiment, modified, plankton, untenanted, pelagically, caudal, ichthyologist?*
7. Is there a difference in the kind of evidence the two authors use for their statements? What is it?
8. Is Miss Carson reasoning by cause-and-effect regarding the powerful jaws and teeth of the ancestral whales, the long stripes consisting of circular scars on the head of the sperm whale, the fish bones found only in seals' stomachs?
9. Make an outline of the second paragraph.
10. Write a theme about a subject of your choosing making use of the plan revealed in your answer to question 9.

Space ships aren't here yet, but they're a lot closer than being just the fantasies of science-fiction writers. Here a well-known British scientist, Chairman of the British Interplanetary Society, discusses a typically practical problem facing those who seriously plan the conquest of space.

THE SPACESHIP
by Arthur C. Clarke

THE PICTURE we now have of the various vehicles needed for interplanetary travel is a good deal more complex than has been suggested, for example, in the many works of fiction the subject has inspired. Yet, when one considers the matter, it would hardly be otherwise. Space-flight involves many different problems, varying greatly with different missions. One might therefore expect to find almost as many diverse types of spaceships as there have been types of aircraft —and one day, no doubt, there will be an equally bewildering variety of designs.

Some features, however, all spaceships will have to possess in common. They will have to provide a comfortable environment for their occupants, supplying them with air and maintaining them at the correct temperature, irrespective of surrounding conditions. Adequate food and water supplies will have to be carried in as compact a form as possible. Every ship, once it has been launched on its journey, will be a tiny self-contained world relying entirely on its own re-

---

From *The Exploration of Space* by Arthur Charles Clarke. Copyright, 1951, by Arthur Charles Clarke. Reprinted by permission of Harper & Brothers.

sources: those aboard it can expect no help from outside if anything has been forgotten or if there is a failure in the ship's mechanisms. Complete reliability and self-sufficiency will be the targets for which the spaceship designer must strive, once the minimum requirements of fuel and payload have been met.

Let us first consider the problem of the air supply. Here at sea level on the Earth, we are under an atmospheric pressure of about fifteen pounds per square inch, or almost a ton for every square foot of our bodies. We are not normally aware of this pressure, because it is equalised inside and out. Given time to adjust itself, the body can function over a considerable pressure range—down to a third of the normal atmospheric value, and up to four or five times this. The actual limits depend on the length of time the abnormal conditions last: clearly in a spaceship which might be travelling for weeks or months the pressure must be kept at a value comfortable and safe for the crew. There is no need, however, for it to be as high as the standard sea-level value of fifteen pounds per square inch, and indeed there are sound reasons why it should be as low as practicable.

The cabin of the spaceship has no equalising pressure outside it, being in a perfect vacuum, and so it must be strong enough to withstand the full internal pressure. To build a large container which will not burst when there is a force of one ton acting outwards on every square foot of its surface is not easy, particularly when weight is at a premium. The use of a lower pressure would simplify construction, and would also reduce the small air loss through the leaks which are inevitable in any pressurised system.

Fortunately, there is no difficulty in doing this. Our normal air is only one-fifth oxygen—the remaining four-fifths of nitrogen is simply "ballast" and plays no part in respiration. Thus the oxygen in the atmosphere contributes only three pounds to the total fifteen pounds of pressure—and if we used in the spaceship an atmosphere of *pure* oxygen at three pounds pressure our lungs would receive just as much of the gas as under normal conditions.

It is not yet certain if it is quite safe to live indefinitely in a pure oxygen atmosphere at three pounds per square inch —a fifth of normal pressure—but it is undoubtedly safe for prolonged periods. This fact is of great importance not only in the design of spaceship cabins but also of "space-suits," where the same problems have to be met, together with the additional requirement of flexibility.

Having decided to employ a pure oxygen atmosphere, we must provide the spaceship with some means of removing the carbon dioxide produced by respiration. Several chemicals are known which can perform this feat (e.g. sodium hydroxide and sodium peroxide), and the latter will not only remove the carbon dioxide but will replace it with fresh oxygen. In addition, supplies of pure oxygen can be carried in the liquid state in suitable storage flasks.

The amount of oxygen needed by a man under normal conditions is surprisingly small—just over three pounds a day if he is engaged in continuous moderate exertion. When resting or sleeping, the consumption is reduced to a third of this value, and as there would not be much physical activity inside the ship, an allowance of two pounds per man per day would appear to be ample.

It would also be necessary to remove excess water vapour from the air. This can be done by chemical means, but a simple and effective method is to pass the air through a chilled pipe and condense the water out of it.

On very long voyages, the chemicals needed for oxygen replenishment would weigh a considerable amount, and it has been seriously suggested that we might employ Nature's method of purifying the atmosphere—in other words suitable green plants should be carried in the spaceship! As is well known, plants absorb carbon dioxide (in the presence of sunlight) and, after converting it to starch, liberate oxygen. Although this idea is an attractive one at first sight, it loses some of its charm when one considers the additional complications and the weight of chemicals that would have to be taken along to feed the plants.

This scheme, or some variant of it, may, however, be used

in certain cases, for biological processes can often perform feats beyond the power of the chemist. No simple, direct way is known of converting carbon dioxide back into oxygen, yet this is a task performed by every blade of grass in the world. On space-stations, and in the bases we shall set up on the planets, the atmosphere may well be kept pure by the use of plants specially bred for this purpose.

At this point we might mention one curious result of the absence of gravity which has an unexpected effect on the air-conditioning problem in spaceships. The gases which we exhale, being considerably warmer and hence lighter than the surrounding air, normally rise upwards so that, even when we are sleeping or sitting still, the air around our nostrils is continually replenished. This effect is seen most clearly in the case of a candle flame, which has a steady current of fresh air flowing into it from below. Now this form of circulation, since it depends on differences in weight, cannot occur aboard a spaceship in its normal, free-orbit condition. It has, in fact, been shown experimentally (by filming candles in a freely falling chamber) that flames cannot burn in the absence of gravity: they quickly "suffocate" in their accumulated combustion products.

This implies that an efficient system of forced ventilation must be installed in a spaceship to sweep away the waste gases as soon as they are formed. It is also a warning that one must take nothing for granted in space, and a reminder that gravity may be an important factor even in processes that seem unconnected with it.

Next in priority to the air supply is the regulation of temperature. The "temperature of space" is a subject about which there is much confusion, the general idea being that it is extremely cold outside the atmosphere. In fact, the reverse is nearer the truth.

Consider the case of a solid body floating in space at the Earth's distance from the Sun. One side will be in shadow, the other in full sunlight. This side will become extremely hot—at least if it is darkened and so readily absorbs heat waves. In the extreme case of a completely black body, the temperature at the parts directly facing the Sun would be somewhat above that of boiling water. On the other hand, if the surface was white or silvered, it would reflect most of the heat and so be quite cool.

The dark (or night) side of the body would be cold in any case, since it is continually losing heat by radiation and has none coming in. However, if the body were a good conductor, the temperature extremes would be equalised to some extent. And if, as in practice would probably be the case, it were rotating even at quite a slow rate, the temperature over its whole surface would be practically uniform.

It must also be remembered that a considerable amount of heat would be generated inside the spaceship by the bodies of the passengers. A double-hulled ship in space would behave like a very efficient thermos flask, and it would often be more important to *lose* heat than to conserve it.

On a journey from Earth to Venus, the amount of heat received from the Sun would be twice as great at the end of the voyage as at the beginning. On the trip to Mars, the reverse would be the case. Moreover, when the ship was in the shadow of a planet—which would be for a considerable fraction of the time if it were circling in a close orbit—there would be no solar radiation at all. This last condition would also apply at night on an airless world such as the Moon. It appears, therefore, that the ship should have some simple but efficient means of regulating its heat-loss, and this might be done by the use of folding shutters which would expose blackened or silvered areas of the hull according to circumstances. An internal source of warmth would be needed during prolonged periods of darkness, and this could best be obtained by the combustion of fuel in a small heater.

In general, it can be said that temperature control does not present very great problems on the voyages which we will be undertaking during the first decades of space-travel. On journeys very near the Sun, or far beyond Mars, the situation will be different. However, by the time such feats as these are seriously contemplated, we should have plenty of power from nuclear sources to use either for heating or refrigeration.

76   *Current Prose*

SUGGESTIONS FOR STUDY:

1. What is Clarke's purpose in the first paragraph?
2. What sentence announces the subject of the selection?
3. What are the main divisions?
4. Does Clarke use definite "markers" for these divisions?
5. How many paragraphs are included in each division?
6. For what purpose does Clarke bring in a candle flame and a thermos bottle?
7. Is the vocabulary too technical for the general reader? Cite specific words.
8. Does the essay presuppose too great an acquaintance with processes like photosynthesis or air pressure?
9. In the light of your scientific vocabulary and knowledge, does Clarke convince you that he knows his subject and is writing factually and not fancifully? Why?
10. Write a theme in which you discuss a scientific problem solved or unsolved, or in which you discuss the factors required in a successful mechanism like a space ship or in a process like preparing for an examination.

The late Robert Ripley, creator of Believe It or Not, *would have been delighted by* . . .

NATURE'S UTMOSTS
by Alan Devoe

EVERY CREATURE in Nature, and every act and organ of every creature, is, of course, sufficiently astonishing to keep any thoughtful man open-mouthed for a lifetime. The

Reprinted from Nature Magazine, February 1950, by permission of Nature Magazine, the author, and The Reader's Digest.

world is one amazing marvel, in every part and particular. But every now and then Nature, as if gathering and concentrating all her powers to astound us, produces a prodigy that makes all the others pale to insignificance. Every now and then, so to speak, she does her utmost. The results are almost beyond belief—but they are real.

An eye is a fabulous mechanism, whether it is the kind of eye that you and I have in our heads, or the stalk-mounted eye of a land-crab, or the bulgingly curved eye that makes it possible for a rabbit literally to see what is happening behind its back. But all other kinds of eyes come to seem commonplace beside the eyes of the fish named *Anableps*. A denizen of tropical America, this species is given to swimming with the upper part of its head leveled. The top half of each of its eyes is above water, and the lower half beneath. Four eyes' visual problem is taken care of by its possessing two pupils in each eye. As the fish glides along, its upper pair of pupils scan the great outdoors overhead, while simultaneously its lower pupils, with a different refractive power, study the depths beneath—altogether a handy arrangement.

Nature has put many sorts of strange tongues into the heads of her creatures. There is the toad's tongue, rooted at the *front* of the mouth so it can be protruded an extra distance for nabbing prey. There is the gecko lizard's tongue, so long and agile that the lizard uses it to reach out and wash its eyes. But the tongue to end all tongues, the ultimate lingual whopper, has been achieved in the case of the anteater. Long as an anteater's head is, it is not long enough to contain the tremendous tongue wherewith it licks into ant-hills and secures its supper. The tamandua anteater's tongue is not rooted in its mouth or throat at all. It is fastened to the anteater's breastbone, most usefully, and fatally to the ants.

There is a natural association between tongues and teeth; and in some of her creatures Nature has combined the two. She has produced toothed tongues. A penguin's whole tongue is spiny, so its slippery prey cannot wriggle free, and a flamingo's tongue is spine-fringed to act as a strainer. The flamingo just grabs a whole beakful of muddy water, and then strains out everything except the sea food in it. In the combination of teeth and tongues, Nature's utmost creation is perhaps achieved in a common garden snail. The snail uses its toothed tongue to rasp at vegetation. Its mighty prowess in mangling our gardens is testimony to the wild lavishness of Nature's gift of teeth. A snail's tongue bears one hundred thirty-five rows of them. In each row there are one hundred and five teeth. As the snail goes champing through the flower bed, it is exercising fourteen thousand, one hundred seventy-five teeth, minute teeth, to be sure, but they are, nevertheless, teeth, and efficient ones.

Protective coloration is a familiar wonder of the natural world. It renders a speckled fawn invisible in the sun-dappled thicket, and makes the streaked neck of a bittern indistinguishable among the reeds. In some creatures Nature has produced still more astonishing protective colorations that can change with circumstances, enabling various insects and lizards to shift from the green of leaves to the brown of withered twigs, and dressing weasels and snowshoe rabbits in earth-brown coats for summer and snow-white coats for winter. But it is in the sea that Nature exhibits what is perhaps the utmost triumph of all her optical illusions. It is a quick-change that has to be seen to be believed. Its practitioners are squids. As the squid swims, its body shows wavering stripes of horizontal light and dark, giving exactly the effect of streaks of water in motion. As the squid comes to rest, these wavy horizontal streaks are extinguished. At a wave of Nature's wand, presto!, their place is taken by *vertical* bands, shimmering and undulating. The motionless squid has miraculously become, apparently, a bed of gently waving water weeds, difficult to detect.

Whenever Nature seems to have done her utmost to make one kind of creature astonishing, she has a way of capping the performance by mixing in the astonishingness of some wholly different sort of creature to make an incredible blend. Songbirds are surprising enough in their own right; underwater creatures in theirs. But in the common little bird called the water ouzel or dipper there has been achieved a mixture of opposites that has left many a bird-watcher rubbing his eyes. The ouzel likes water insects. But it does not merely dive for them. It leaps into a stream, goes straight to the bottom, and then walks about on the bottom as placidly as a robin foraging over a lawn in the open air. The ouzel's feathers are so thick that its body never gets wet. As an utmost in improbability, the ouzel even *flies* under water, using exactly the same technique that other songbirds use only for winging through the sky.

Many of Nature's creatures are speedsters, and feats of running can be seen everywhere in the outdoors. We ourselves can run nearly twenty-five miles an hour, for short spurts, and we have trained race horses to attain forty-five or fifty. It seems pretty fast; but when Nature undertakes to do her utmost she makes these figures look paltry. Pronghorn antelope can hit sixty. Blackbucks have been clocked at sixty-five. But it is in the cheetah, the lean, sleek hunting leopard of Asia, that Nature has really pulled out all the stops. A cheetah can flash along at seventy miles an hour. He is Nature's ultimate in speed on land, but in her aerial creatures, of course, she reaches out to still more amazing records. The fastest things on two wings in a straightaway are Indian swifts, timed over a two-mile course at the scarcely believable speed of two hundred miles an hour. In the stoop, or dive after quarry, Nature has carried speed to its utmost in the duck hawk. The dive is made at about one hundred eighty m.p.h. Strangely enough, one bird even holds something of a *land* record. When Nature denied the ostrich the power of flight, she did her utmost to compensate in leg power. The result is one of the most spectacular in Nature's whole parade of spectacles. An ostrich can outrun a racing greyhound.

It is not only in speed that Nature has developed athletic prodigies hard to believe. She has trained up incredible jumpers. The human world's record (1947) for the horizontal jump is twenty-six feet, eight and one-quarter inches. Kangaroos can make an easy leap of thirty feet. Gazelles can achieve a graceful arc of forty. Still, even these are not Nature's utmost. Her most spring-legged mammal is the little mouselike rodent called a jerboa. A jerboa's body is only four or five inches long, but Nature has elongated his hind legs and tempered his muscles to such a steel-spring strength that in one leap he can hurtle fifteen feet. A man, to make an equivalent jump in terms of his body length, would have to jump more than forty yards.

If the anteater's tongue is the tongue to end all tongues and the jerboa's jump the last word in spacehopping, Nature's utmost striving in the matter of *bigness*, of course, is whales. Although we all know this, it is hard actually to take in the facts about whales' enormousness. A blue whale may measure as much as 100 feet in length, and may reach a weight of more than 300,000 pounds. But whales' bigness extends to more than these mere dimensions. Whale babies, for instance, are not only the biggest babies on earth, but the biggest babies in terms of the relative size of their parents. A baby whale at birth is often one-third as long as its mother! Even an unborn blue whale, taken from the body of its mother, has been measured at twenty-five feet in length and 16,000 pounds in weight. *Everything* about whales is big, including the unbelievable depths of the dives they make. They are Nature's utmost effort, in the mammal world, to deal in whopping sizes. A few years ago a sperm whale got tangled in a communications cable on the bed of the ocean. It was necessary to haul up the cable, whale and all, to cut the monster free. When the whale ran afoul of the cable, the great beast had been cruising at a submarine depth of 3200 feet.[1]

When Nature does her utmost in bigness, she can be dazzlingly grandiose; but she can be just as astonishing in any of her other outbursts of extremity. Take horns, for instance. Nature has given a pair of horns to each of many species of animals; but, even in this matter, she has also burst loose with one wild "utmost" that still dumbfounds every naturalist who encounters it. The animal involved is a small antelope that lives in India and Burma. It has *four* horns. It represents Nature carrying the horn idea to a sort of stunning ultimate, as she has done with the tongue idea in anteaters and the eye idea in a bifocal fish. Or take bird flight. It is a wonderful

[1] See p. 69.

thing that sparrows and robins can skim through the air as they do. The sailing and soaring of hawks is a glory. But when Nature, in a burst of perfection, gives us the flight of the hummingbird, we are left dazzled and incredulous. The tiny, ruby-throated hummingbird, smaller than a man's finger, beats its delicate little wings more than 4000 times a minute; on its migration it zooms non-stop across the vast sweep of the Gulf of Mexico; and, in its feeding, it flies backwards for a short distance.

Or take, for a final prodigy, the practice of courtship. Courtship runs all through the animal kingdom, expressing itself in a thousand kinds of dances, caresses, little gifts from male to female. They are often strange. But then Nature does her utmost, and gives us not merely the strange but the incredible. Such is the courtship of the gardener bower-birds of New Guinea. They build, literally, a love bower. Sometimes both sexes work on it, sometimes only the male. First, out of twigs, there is built a two-foot-high house at the base of a tree. When it is finished, its top is covered over with a roof of moss. And then, in front of this honeymoon cottage, there is carefully constructed a soft green lawn of moss. The bower-birds, bowing and bobbing and curtsying to each other, embellish the lawn with the equivalent of flower beds. They bring bright flowers and brilliantly colored berries and place them decoratively around the grounds. No matter how long they inhabit their bower, they never let the garden lose its loveliness. As fast as the blooms and berries fade, they are removed and replaced with fresh, bright new ones. Of the several kinds of Australian bower-birds the master builder is the golden bower-bird. Dressed in brown and gold, with its neck collar and short crest a bright yellow, the male is also the most beautiful. Bowers covering an area of six by fourteen feet have been found, the structure rising to a height of four feet.

Nature is constantly producing, with the ease of infinite creativeness and prodigality, the most astonishing and improbable and unlikely things. But when Nature really does her utmost—well, *then*, as the Irish philosopher remarked, what she produces is the impossible.

SUGGESTIONS FOR STUDY:

1. Do you feel the restatement of the main idea at the end of the essay is helpful? Why?
2. Are the paragraphs rather regularly the main divisions of the essay?
3. Are the major elements in paragraphs 2 and 3 arranged haphazardly or in accordance with a plan?
4. Do other paragraphs use the same arrangement? What paragraphs vary the pattern?
5. Is comparison or contrast much used as a method of development? Is the comparison of the jerboa's leap to man's legitimate?
6. How else does Devoe develop his paragraphs to increase interest and conviction?
7. Does Devoe vary the topic sentences to avoid the monotony of *The first extreme is* . . . , *The second extreme is* . . . , etc.?
8. What word recurs most frequently as transition between paragraphs? Are references to preceding utmosts used to help knit the essay together?
9. What is the meaning of *fabulous mechanism, denizen, undulating, prodigality?*
10. Write a theme in which you support a main idea by a series of examples or illustrations; develop each paragraph fully.

India's dependence on the monsoon, which capriciously bring enough rain, too much, or too little, is described by the daughter of the former Indian ambassador to the United States.

THE WIND THAT MEANS LIFE TO INDIA
by Santha Rama Rau

SOMETIME at the end of every April winds spring up off the west coast of South America and these, so the meteorologists tentatively suggest, travel westward across more than half the world to produce one of the world's most spectacular climatic phenomena. In the early part of their annual journey they are not particularly dramatic winds. They move easily at about fifteen or twenty miles an hour as part of the trade winds of the southern hemisphere, blow across the Marquesas Islands, include Tahiti in their scope and carry with them, for the most part, clear days and warm nights.

By the middle of May the winds have reached the Samoan Islands and continue along the course determined for them by the turning earth. They move across the Ellice Islands, the Solomons and New Guinea, and the long island chain of Indonesia.

In June the winds reach the Indian Ocean, and it is only then that their whole character changes. They sweep entirely out of their course, slacken their speed, acquire a special name

Reprinted from The New York Times Magazine, June 8, 1952, by permission of the New York Times and the author.

and such enormous importance that without them the 500 million people who live in India, Pakistan, Ceylon, Burma, Indo-China and Siam would not be able to survive in their homelands. By the time the first rain clouds burst over the Malabar coast those winds have become the great southwest monsoon, India's most valued—and most capricious—blessing.

From the time of the spring equinox onward, as the sun's rays strike the earth more and more directly, the huge land mass of continental Asia begins to heat up. With growing intensity through the weeks that follow, the heat continues unrelieved. In late May and early June temperatures recorded in north India have reached as high as 126 degrees F. The capital city, Delhi, has an average daytime temperature for May of 104 degrees. Then the Government offices and the foreign embassies switch to summer hours—the working day begins at 7:30 A.M. and finishes at 1:30 P.M. A large part of every day becomes devoted simply to avoiding the heat. Chiks (the slatted, bamboo screens) are lowered all day over windows and verandas to keep the interiors of homes and offices cool and shaded from the sun and glare. Only after sunset are windows and houses opened up to the slightly cooler air of evening. Only in the late short twilight do people sit in their gardens or walk in the parks.

The sea's moderating influence does not spread very far inland and only the cities immediately on the coast benefit by reasonably temperate weather. But in the plains of the north and east of the great plateaus of the center of India the heat is a strong and a curiously personal enemy. The earth bakes into a hard cracked surface, rivers dry up entirely or shrink to thin opaque trickles, and all farming comes to a standstill. This is also the season of the Loo, a dreaded, searingly hot wind that blows in from the Rajasthan desert, raises the temperature by 15 or 20 degrees and sweeps the surface soil into dust storms. All kinds of illnesses and nervous ailments are attributed to it, heatstroke, hysteria and uncertain tempers, and, at the first hint of the rising Loo, doors and windows are shut and bolted against its dust, heat and evil influence.

At the end of May the prolonged and acute heat has formed an enormous low pressure area in the atmosphere over India, and something like a huge whirlwind begins to circulate around its edges. As the heat increases, the speed of the air circulation grows until at last it has acquired suction strong enough to reach below the equator and pull the southeastern trade winds into India. Here, as the monsoon, for three months they move east and north across the country pouring out the water accumulated over 10,000 miles of ocean. Eventually they are checked by the great mountain barriers of the Himalayas which serve to contain the monsoon and conserve the major force of the rains for India. This mountain wall makes it possible for parts of Assam to have a rainfall of 450 inches in one summer while beyond the Himalayas Tibet gets between five and ten inches a year.

As the sun enters its autumnal phase, the earth, already cooled by the rains, is further cooled by the sun's declining intensity, and gradually the monsoon retreats from India to rejoin its old route south of the equator. If anything were to interfere with the process—if, for instance, a string of large volcanic islands were to spring up between the African Coast and Cape Gormorin, the southern tip of India, to deflect the monsoon, or if the heat in Central Asia should, by the cooling of the earth, be reduced and the force to pull in the monsoon should vanish—then India would become a desert. Only a thin coastal strip and the banks of the Ganges might remain green and habitable.

It is not surprising, then, that the chief of the Vedic gods, the oldest of all India's deities and the father of the whole pantheon of gods, is Indra, the god of rain. A child born under his auspices is certain to be fortunate and prosperous, and the monsoon, his season, is traditionally connected with fertility, production and richness.

For weeks before the rains begin priests in the temples of the west coast compute from ancient scriptures and old astronomical charts the exact date the monsoon will arrive. With equal seriousness (and, according to the priests, hardly more reliable results) scientists and Government meteorologists collect data from their many coastal stations, study advance reports of weather conditions from island outposts in the Indian Ocean and attempt to predict when the rains will come. For days beforehand, prayers and chanting in the temples urge Indra not to withhold his gift. In some parts of India rain-dances and drumbeats are performed to call the rain. In Delhi, Government officials more prosaically get on with the job of seeing that plans for water storage, more and deeper wells and bigger irrigation schemes are completed in case this year, again, the monsoon should fail.

Some years ago, one of India's former Ministers of Finance, in presenting his budget to the Indian Parliament, opened his speech with the remark, "The Indian budget is a gamble in rain." Just as Indian agriculture depends entirely on the monsoon to provide its water to fill the country's rivers and reservoirs, and to make irrigation possible, so Indian industry relies to a great extent on the same sources for its power. The electric light and power supply in all the major cities depends on the water reserves which, in turn, are replenished only by the monsoon. Without question, the greatest single factor in maintaining the functioning economy of India is the rain of high summer.

Although the monsoon has never entirely failed to appear, there has never been a recorded year in which the rains have been satisfactory in every part of the country. The day the rains break there is an extraordinary relaxing of tension everywhere. Strangers in city streets smile at each other in relief that the heat has broken. Children rush out in yelling excitement to stand in the first downpour and adults touch the damp ground in gratitude. Every newspaper carries the news on the front page, and compares the arrival of this year's rain with previous monsoons. But after a night of singing and exhilaration and thanksgiving, the anxiety begins again.

So many things can go wrong. There can be too much rain all at once and this will cause floods. Lives will be lost, property damaged, and yet more of India's thin, infinitely precious top soil will get washed away. There may be too little rain and that will result in droughts and famine. There may be long breaks in the monsoon which can mean that the seeds which are sown immediately the rains begin don't germinate, or that, later, seedlings wither.

The rains may begin too early or too late, and continue too long or end too abruptly. Then crops will rot in the fields before they are ripe for harvesting, or they may dry up before they are fully grown. In fact, one of the most important of the monsoon festivals, Bombay's Coconut Day, comes at the end of the heavy rains. At that time the gods of the ocean are appeased and offerings of food and flowers and fruit are taken down to all the beaches so that the monsoon seas will abate and allow the fishing craft to leave the harbors again. In all the aspects of the arrival, distribution, timing and departure of the monsoon the Indian farmer most of all, the industrialist and the Indian Government must gamble on the rains.

SUGGESTIONS FOR STUDY:

1. Could you divide the essay into two parts labeled cause and effect? Where would you divide?
2. Does Miss Rau discuss causes and effects in that part of the essay you have labeled cause?
3. Do the geographical places named in the first three paragraphs assist you in tracing the course of the monsoon?
4. Does the third paragraph state the main idea of the essay—including the notion of cause and effect?
5. Does the word *capricious*, inserted in the last sentence of paragraph 3, apply to any section of the essay?
6. Does the statement in paragraph 7—". . . then India would become a desert"—repeat an idea previously stated? Is there a difference in Miss Rau's treatment of the two statements, and is there a value in the repetition?
7. How has Miss Rau arranged the specific detail of paragraph 9 to increase its effectiveness?
8. What is the meaning of *climatic phenomena, spring equinox, opaque trickles, prosaically?*
9. In a two-part theme describe fully a cause, then its effect.

"The man and the opportunity had met" when an Army doctor was called to attend an accidentally wounded ne'er-do-well. The result was an amazing episode in the long history of medicine.

THE WINDOW IN ST. MARTIN'S STOMACH
by Richard Match

ONE JUNE DAY in 1822 a party of tipsy fur trappers and *voyageurs* crowded into the store of John Jacob Astor's American Fur Company on Mackinac Island, Michigan. Somebody's gun went off accidentally, and a French-Canadian named Alexis St. Martin slumped to the floor with a huge wound in his side. The others thought he was dead.

This doubtless seemed no great loss. The wounded canoemen, though only about 18, was already known as a sly, shiftless and alcoholic character.

Bystanders ran to summon the surgeon at the army post nearby, Dr. William Beaumont. There was no other doctor within 300 miles. In this fantastic fashion came together the two men who were to compose American science's most curious research team.

Dr. Beaumont, 37, a handsome, erect figure in the high-collared blue uniform and flowing hair style of the period, knelt at St. Martin's side. In Sir William Osler's memorable phrase, "The man and the opportunity had met." As a result,

Reprinted from New Liberty, October 1951, by permission of New Liberty and The Reader's Digest.

Dr. Beaumont was to learn more about the human digestive apparatus than any doctor in the preceding 4,000 years. He was to achieve medical immortality by actually observing the inside of the human stomach at work—and making discoveries that became milestones in medical progress.

As Beaumont himself wrote later, his first quick examination revealed "an appalling and hopeless case." The full charge of duckshot had entered his patient's left side, gouging a ghastly hole as big as a man's hand. Beaumont did what he could to repair the damage, applied a dressing and ordered his patient moved to the station hospital, "not believing it possible for him to survive 20 minutes." For one thing, a portion of St. Martin's stomach was protruding through the hole in his side, and it was punctured.

To Beaumont's astonishment, the dark, wiry little fellow clung to life but for nearly a year the hold was precarious. By the following Spring healthy scar tissue had formed around the opening. But Beaumont's constant attempts to close it entirely were fruitless. The patient, not only conscious but cantankerous, refused to submit to an operation to suture its edges together. During all this time St. Martin felt no pain at all inside his stomach, not even nausea.

Instead of dropping back into his abdominal cavity, the rim of St. Martin's stomach puncture had adhered to the rim of his external wound, in much the same way that a trousers pocket is attached to the outside fabric of the suit. Doctors call such openings a gastric fistula.

Eventually an inner coat of St. Martin's stomach folded across the fistulous opening, forming a leakproof valve which could be easily depressed from the outside. There remained, permanently, a round hole large enough to admit the doctor's forefinger directly into the stomach.

Two years passed since the shooting. St. Martin now was not only up and around, but eating "crude food in abundant quantities." Dr. Beaumont took rueful note of the Frenchman's appetite, because he had been paying Alexis' grocery bills.

With a wife and children to support on his army pay of $40 a month, feeding this extra mouth must have been hard. Alexis, however, earned his keep as a household servant. When, on a rare occasion, he felt under par, the doctor promptly administered a cathartic, "as never medicine was before administered to man since the creation of the world—to wit, through the ribs"; it "operated briskly."

Beaumont continued dressing the fistula daily. In one of these sessions he made a momentous observation. "When Alexis lies on his right side," the doctor noticed, "I can look directly into the cavity of the stomach and almost see the process of digestion."

Suddenly Beaumont also saw a great light. He realized that St. Martin's fistula represented not so much a wound stubbornly unclosed as a window miraculously opened. A window into the stomach of a healthy, active human being! Never before in medical history had there been such an opportunity. Here was the means of solving the age-old riddle of how food is digested.

At that time there were a dozen competing theories as to how our digestive organs break food down to basic nutritive elements which can be utilized by the body. One school held that food in the stomach was merely ground to powder, mill-fashion; another that it was simply cooked by body heat; a third that it soaked in a watery fluid—"swallowed saliva"—till it fell apart.

That the human stomach did secrete a peculiar fluid of its own had been widely acknowledged, however, since the work of the Frenchman Reaumur and the great Italian Spallanzani in the preceding century. By swallowing a sponge tied to a string, Spallanzani had obtained some fluid from his own stomach. He claimed that it possessed the powers of a chemical solvent and named it the "gastric juice."

In 1824, an Englishman named Prout added that he had found hydrochloric acid in a freshly killed animal's gastric juice. But many "authorities" scoffed at the idea of living tissues producing a powerful acid capable of dissolving solids.

One morning in 1825 Beaumont sat down on St. Martin's bedside to look for himself into his "human test tube." Pushing the walls of St. Martin's fistula apart with his thermometer, Beaumont could see inside to a depth of five or six inches.

The walls were pale pink in color, soft and velvety looking, and filmed with a mucous fluid. Beaumont sprinkled a few bread crumbs through the opening in Alexis' side. Promptly the stomach lining's pink hue brightened, and hundreds of minute droplets began to rise through the mucous film and trickle down the walls.

Beaumont tasted this new fluid. It was perceptibly acid. Here at last was Spallanzani's "gastric juice," tasting distinctly of Prout's hydrochloric acid.

But was it really a potent chemical agent? Would it dissolve food?

Next morning Beaumont slid a rubber tube into the fistula and collected some gastric juice in a vial. He dropped a small chunk of boiled beef into the transparent fluid and heated it to the normal temperature of Alexis' stomach.

I quote from Dr. Beaumont's own record of this experiment, for it remains one of the most decisive ever performed in an American laboratory:

"In 40 minutes, digestion had distinctly commenced over the surface of the meat." In two hours, "the cellular texture seemed to be entirely destroyed, leaving the muscular fibers loose and unconnected, floating about in fine small shreds." Four hours later, "they were nearly all digested, a few fibers only remaining." In 10 hours, "every part of the meat was completely digested."

"So far from being 'inert as water,'" Beaumont declared, "gastric juice is the most general solvent in nature of alimentary matter. Even the hardest bone cannot withstand its action." He had tried the juice on a length of hog's rib. This was tough opposition, but after a month of soaking, the solid bone had been completely dissolved.

Physiologists cannot yet explain with certainty why, though constantly secreting this potent chemical, the normal human stomach does not digest its own walls—and why the stomachs of an unlucky minority may do just that. These unfortunates are the people who suffer from peptic ulcer.

Beaumont could see now that he had something big on his hands. To explore his discovery, access to libraries and laboratories was essential. He immediately requested a transfer eastward. When the transfer came, in a glow of optimism, Beaumont packed his wife, his children, and his obstreperous "patient digester" aboard a Niagara-bound Great Lakes steamer. His optimism, alas, was shortlived.

By bringing St. Martin so near Quebec, he had placed temptation in the easily tempted Frenchman's path. Before the Beaumonts reached Fort Niagara, Alexis vanished, presumably northward. Frantically but in vain the doctor alerted friends in Canada. They found no trace of Alexis. Hopes dashed, Beaumont glumly took up his routine army duties again.

It is possible to forgive St. Martin for running out on science. Body chemistry held no fascination for him. The only chemistry he cared about was that of alcoholic fermentation. And he could see ahead interminable tubes, strings, bags moving in and out of his stomach on the hour. Diets and fasts. The doctor's relentless thermometer probing his innards at all hours of the night.

Tirelessly Dr. Beaumont kept after the far-flung agents of the American Fur Company, urging them to watch for St. Martin, refunding search expenses. Four years went by before the truant was found living in a village near Montreal. Alexis had worked several winters as a canoeman in the Indian country, survived a cholera epidemic, married, and fathered two children.

He would come back now, yes, but only with his entire household. To this condition his benefactor reluctantly agreed, and shortly the St. Martins debarked *en masse* at Prairie du Chien, on the upper Mississippi, where Beaumont was now stationed.

In the four years following Alexis' return, Beaumont carried out an amazing variety of experiments in his fistulous Frenchman's stomach. He charted the fluctuations of gastric secretion under all possible conditions. He clocked the digestion times of endless staples and delicacies, from hash to venison steak, fat and lean, raw and cooked, chewed and whole.

Fortunately for science, Alexis was not the most cooperative of guinea pigs. Time and again in Beaumont's records we find notations like: "He became angry during this experiment," or "He was vexed at being detained from his breakfast."

After a while the doctor noticed a curious coincidence. Every time Alexis lost his temper during an experimental meal, digestion was measurably slower. Roast beef eaten in anger lingered in St. Martin's stomach twice as long as it did when Alexis was calm and contented.

Checking carefully, Beaumont arrived at one of his most important discoveries. "Fear and anger," he wrote, "check the secretion of the gastric juice." He had established for the first time the central role of emotion influences in digestion.

What happens to a bit of food after you swallow it? From Beaumont's observations we can construct a fairly accurate timetable. Six or seven seconds after it left your mouth, the food drops into your stomach cavity. The contact with, and stretching of, the stomach walls by the food promptly stimulate secretion from your 35 million gastric glands. Stretching also touches off a muscular churning motion of the stomach. In two minutes solids are broken up, and the admixture of gastric juice has begun to transform your entire meal into a single porridge-like semi-fluid mass called chyme.

Within 10 minutes, chymified food starts leaving the stomach. In three to four and a half hours, the entire meal has been disposed of and your stomach is empty and quiet again. The pancreatic and intestinal juices, and the bile secreted by the liver, finish the job of digestion.

"The sense of hunger," Beaumont declared, "resides in the stomach." But it may be allayed without food passing through the mouth. To prove his point, he delayed Alexis' dinner one evening. Then he pumped a large syringe-full of barley soup through the fistula. "It satisfied the appetite," he wrote, "and St. Martin said he had no desire to eat."

But thirst was a different matter for Alexis. He insisted that his taste for alcoholic beverages could not possibly be satisfied in any such newfangled scientific way, but only in the time-honored sociable fashion—over the tongue and down the hatch. And often, Beaumont's notes are studded with sentences like: "St. Martin has been drinking ardent spirits freely for eight or 10 days past."

In 1831 Mrs. St. Martin, never popular with the doctor, announced that she was going home to mother. Beaumont was almost glad to shed the burden of caring for the briskly multiplying St. Martins. He bought Alexis a large canoe, on the Frenchman's solemn promise to return. That Spring the fabulous invalid paddled his wife and children (four by now) down the Mississippi, up the Ohio, and through the Great Lakes and St. Lawrence to Montreal—some 2,000 miles.

Alexis, ever unpredictable, reappeared from Canada scrupulously on schedule. For two more years Beaumont worked ceaselessly to conclude his series of 238 experiments and publish his results. In 1833 he completed the book which Harvey Cushing, a century later, called "the most notable and original classic of American medicine," *Experiments And Observations On The Gastric Juice And The Physiology Of Digestion.*

Copies of the book found their way to the laboratories of Europe. Within three years a German scientist, Theodore Schwann, read the work and discovered pepsin, another digestive fluid. In Paris, the great Claude Bernard was imitating Beaumont's experiments in animals. The shotgun discharge that pierced St. Martin's stomach had opened a new era in physiology.

Enjoying scientific acclaim, Beaumont planned new experiments too. This time, however, there would be no nonsense from Alexis. He had signed the slippery *voyageur* to a written contract. In one of the strangest legal documents ever composed, Alexis, for $200 a year, agreed to "promote by all means in his power such experiments as the said William Beaumont shall direct or cause to be made on or in the stomach of him, the said Alexis, by means of the aperture or opening thereto." Alexis signed with his X.

Apparently this document gave the doctor a false sense of security. Before leaving for a new army assignment at St. Louis, he carelessly let Alexis make one more visit to Canada. It was a fatal mistake. He never saw Alexis again.

Dozens of Beaumont's observations could be profitably

memorized by every housewife who prepares three meals a day for her family. Several are worth listing for emphasis:

Fatty foods are difficult to digest. Meat fat must be converted into oil before digestion, and other fatty foods require extra digestive steps too.

Hot, humid weather depresses gastric secretion. A good argument, to the homemaker, for light, digestible Summer meals.

Alcohol in quantity does your stomach lining no good. One day Alexis got drunk and interrupted an experiment. Next morning Beaumont took a good look at the inner coat of the Frenchman's stomach. "Color darker red than natural, and arid," he recorded. "Mucous coat abraded in spots and rolled in shreds." At other such times, he mentions deep red pimples, tinges of blood in the gastric juice, shreds of tissue resembling blistered epidermis.

Most of us over-eat. A given amount of gastric juice is capable of combining with only limited quantities of food. "When more food is presented for its action than it will dissolve," wrote Beaumont, " 'indigestion' ensues. The excess food may remain undigested for 24 to 48 hours, as insoluble in the stomach as lead." "The system," Beaumont concluded, "requires much less than is generally supplied to it."

By this time Beaumont had built one of St. Louis' best civilian practices—an indulgence then permitted army doctors. But he never gave up trying to get his Frenchman back. For 20 years he bombarded Alexis with letters and emissaries. Then, one wintry evening, the aging Beaumont slipped and fell on a patient's front steps. He died shortly afterward.

Alexis St. Martin outlived his doctor by more than a quarter of a century. For a while he appeared in sideshows. Whatever strong drink did to his stomach lining, it apparently left his physique rugged. He sired 17 children in all, and at the time of his death in 1880 was chopping cordwood for a living.

He was then, by various estimates, between 76 and 83 years old. For 58 of those years he had lived comfortably with a hole in his vitals that ought to have killed him in 20 minutes.

SUGGESTIONS FOR STUDY:

1. In recreating this bit of history, is Match more concerned with the strangeness and humanness of the events and characters or in the importance of Beaumont's medical discoveries?
2. Why does Match begin with a shooting?
3. What do the frequent dates and references to time suggest about Match's arrangement of the parts of his article?
4. Does Match individualize St. Martin? Does he react humanly toward the ne'er-do-well? Does he make him seem ungrateful?
5. What scientific information does Match give the reader within his narrative framework?
6. What does the treatment of scientific terms like *gastric fistula, peptic ulcer, chyme* indicate about the intended audience?
7. Do you find any examples of colloquial language?
8. Do you find any examples of antithesis, paradox, irony?
9. Does the context give you a fairly good clue to the meaning of the italicized words: *protruding* through the hole, *suture* its edges, abdominal *cavity, fistulous* opening, *nutritive* elements, chemical *solvent, a mucous* fluid, *perceptibly* acid, juice in a *vial, inert* as water, *secreting* this *potent* chemical, *obstreperous* patient, *interminable* tubes, *relentless* thermometer, debarked *en masse,* charted the *fluctuations, staples* and delicacies, a curious *coincidence,* stimulate *secretion,* sense of hunger may be *allayed,* scientific *acclaim,* by means of the *aperture,* fat must be *converted,* letters and *emissaries*?
10. Write a theme on one of the following: an experiment, the human guinea pig, the human appeal buried in scientific writings or statistics, the importance of Osler's dictum: "The man and the opportunity had met."

The atomic age has made all of us aware of the dangers scientific discovery has posed for us. Here a scientist suggests that our troubles may lie with the scientists themselves, not merely in the bombs they create.

SCIENCE CAN BE SILLY
by Anthony Standen

WHEN a white-robed scientist, momentarily looking up from his microscope or his cyclotron, makes some pronouncement for the general public, he may not be understood, but at least he is certain to be believed. Statesmen, industrialists, ministers of religion, civic leaders, philosophers, all are questioned and criticized, but scientists—never. They are exalted beings, who, standing at the very topmost pinnacle of popular prestige, proudly practice their monopoly of the unchallenged formula: "It has been scientifically proved. . . ." The "IT" can be almost anything.

Our world has thus become divided into scientists, the infallible men of reason and research, and nonscientists, sometimes contemptuously called "laymen." The dividing line is drawn by the fact that science has achieved so much while the layman knows so little—not enough, certainly, to argue back. He might not even want to argue back, for the claims of science are extremely inviting. Its benefits—from television to penicillin—are legion, and a mere layman, his imagi-

Copyright 1950 by Anthony Standen. Published by E. P. Dutton, Inc.

nation stupefied by these wonders, is duly humble. Since it is only human nature to accept such flattery, the scientists easily come to share the laymen's opinion about themselves. The laymen, on the other hand, get their information about scientists from the scientists, and so the whole thing goes round and round like the Whip at Coney Island.

The individual scientist—it must be emphasized—is not inordinately conceited; on the contrary, he is often a most modest and diffident person. Yet, when he thinks of himself *as* a scientist, he almost always attributes to himself a delightful array of such qualities as accuracy, reasoning power, intellectual curiosity, tolerance and a kind of reverent humility before the facts of nature. So, as a group, these men of science have come to possess a fabulous collective ego, as inflated as a skillfully blown piece of bubble gum.

In our science-minded world, it is easy to begin to share the exhilaration of this collective ego at a fairly young age. The great masses of our youth have known "Biology I" in college, or at least "Introductory Science" in high school. They come out of the mill with one of three possible reactions: either 1) they hated it and have depressing memories of cutting up dogfish; 2) they found the subject interesting, but the teacher dull, and nourish for the rest of their lives a wistful yearning to know more; or 3) they gobble up everything and acquire a fierce faith that science can solve all the problems of the universe. People in the first two categories are genuine, understandable human beings. But the third class! So far are they from having learned any humility, they are known in every high school and among the freshmen and sophomores of every college as the most insufferable, cocksure know-it-alls. If they go on to be professional scientists their sharp corners are rubbed down but they undergo no fundamental change. As a group, they most decidedly are not set apart from the others by their tolerance, perceptiveness or patient humility, as their teachers would like to have us believe. Rather do they seem to think that they are entitled to pour scorn on other subjects from a very great height. They become technocrats. They seem to believe that no social or diplomatic problem is beyond their competence to discuss, if not to solve. They eat concentrated vitamins. They are, in the fullest sense of the word, uneducated.

That there are plenty of *good* reasons for knowing something about science goes without saying, whether you are farming or mending a Ford car. Atomic energy, of course, has given a great boost to science education, for persons of all ages from 5 to 100. Obviously we, or our elected representatives, should know as much as we possibly can about uranium 235 and the neutrons, for it is very little good having just a nodding acquaintance with a neutron.

Despite these excellent reasons for studying science in big doses, the scientists stick to their attitude that the *real* reason is something else, something higher and loftier altogether. They are like the Elizabethan poets, who would praise their mistress's eyes, nose, lips, neck, etc., and then say "but if you could see the virtue that dwells within her breast, you would find that even more delightful still." For it is not the base, utilitarian results of science that they advertise most: it is always the "scientific method" or the "scientific attitude" or a variety of other hidden mystical virtues. Useful facts are mere dross: it is this underlying "method" that purifies and refines the soul. And so a sanguine chemist, William J. Wissener, currently head of an industrial chemical research lab in Reading, Pa., tells us: "Science teaches us how to think straight, how to avoid deceit, and how to benefit mankind most by honoring the authority of Truth." Or take the words of another scientific educator, B. C. Gruenberg, most recently a special consultant with the National Health Council, who says: "Scientists have a special responsibility to help adults and adolescents to find new conceptions and ideas to replace the traditional religious beliefs about . . . the meaning and value of human life, which science has made untenable." (Explanatory note: Gruenberg means that the traditional beliefs have been made untenable, not human life.)

Now the disillusioning truth is that "the scientific method," however pretentious it sounds, quite often means only the patient use of horse sense. It is when scientists scorn horse sense and give "the scientific method" a rude yank to stretch it into a technique of philosophy that their antics become most comic. When they get into this expansive mood, they start murmuring reverently about "correlations," for this is one of their favorite words. They measure two things, and find that when one of them changes the other also changes: this is called a beautiful correlation, and it is pursued with a solemn, dead-pan intensity, as if a correlation were a thing in itself. Very often they argue that the one thing *caused* the other, when it might quite well have been the other way round. Thus they will offer an argument that, in principle, runs like this: a man gets drunk on Monday on rye and soda water; he gets drunk on Tuesday on Scotch and soda water, and on Wednesday on gin and soda water. What caused his drunkenness? Obviously, the common factor: the soda water.

Since scientists have such breathtaking confidence in their own ability—in their collective ability, that is to say—it is small wonder that they never pause long enough to teach what are the limitations of science. Yet there may be limits to what science can do. Consider this question: Can science disprove ghosts? The average science-ridden citizen assumes that, of course, it can. And yet, is that true? Suppose (just for the sake of amiable argument) that ghosts can occasionally appear when the psychological conditions are just right, and suppose—as might quite well be true—that one necessary condition for the appearance of a ghost is the *absence* of a scientist. Then "science" would go on investigating ghost after ghost, and would "disprove" every one of them while they kept on appearing whenever the scientists were not looking.

This is a simple case, perhaps not a very important one, illustrating the impossibility of proving anything negative by the scientific method. At least it is enough to suggest that if science has any more serious defects than the inability to perceive an occasional spook in the corner, it is of the utmost importance that all citizens should know what they are.

According to the cult of "the scientific method," scientists not only do wonderful things but also teach wonderful things. Teachers are, indeed, the front men of science, and it is therefore instructive to observe how funny they can be when they are trying to be most serious.

To woo students to their classes, some scientists offer this inducement: "Learn about our environment." This particular lure is emphasized by those who teach geology. The underlying idea is based on a saying that scientists like to trot out, "Man is the product of his heredity and his environment." What they mean is that *a* man is the product of his heredity and his environment, for no one knows what the heredity of "man" is. (The Missing Link is still missing.) The statement is open to dispute, because a strict Calvinist, for example, would say that the fate of man depends upon a predestination which overrides any amount of heredity and environment. But then a predestinarian Calvinist is not a scientist, so what he says doesn't count, and the scientists have said to one another so often, "Man is the product of his heredity and his environment," that they all believe it without question.

Professional educators play up the environment even more strongly than the regular scientists. The environment is regarded as a fixed, steady sort of *thing* that is there, and the recipient of the education must be adjusted to it. No education, obviously, should be designed to turn out social misfits, but it is *not* true that man *must* be adjusted to suit his environment. Man is remarkably capable of adjusting his environment to suit himself. In fact, science itself is probably man's greatest tool in effecting changes in his environment. If we meekly accepted the idea that man must be adjusted to his environment, where should we get our reformers from? Where our revolutionaries? And what would our scientists do for a living?

SUGGESTIONS FOR STUDY:

1. What is the main idea? Is it expressed completely in any one sentence?
2. Does Standen organize in two main divisions—the idol and debunking the idol? If so, where is the separation between divisions?
3. What attitude does Standen early suggest in words like "The 'IT' can be almost anything," "sometimes contemptuously called lay-

men," "like the Whip at Coney Island"? Cite other words or phrases used for the same purpose.
4. Do you find the imagined quotation from an Elizabethan poet in paragraph 6 effective? If not, do you know any Elizabethan poets?
5. Do you find the quotations from the scientists effective? Why?
6. Do you find the *reductio ad absurdum* about the intoxicating effect of soda water effective? Why?
7. What is the relationship of the last two paragraphs to the one immediately preceding?
8. Does the context help to explain the italicized words (or is a dictionary necessary): popular *prestige*, *infallible* men, *inordinately* conceited, *collective* ego, mere *dross*, a *sanguine* chemist, *disillusioning* truth, however *pretentious*, *amiable* argument, *predestinarian* Calvinist?
9. In a two-part theme first describe a popular misconception or idol, then let the light of your special knowledge play upon it. See also the selection from *Kon-Tiki*, p. 60.

A scientist is transformed.

ACADEMIC UPHEAVAL
by John T. Cox, Jr.

THE ATOM BOMB has brought about certain changes in one of the large, ivy-clad, Midwestern state universities. The university has always had a College of Liberal Arts and Sciences, but the most influential faculty members were in the College of Agriculture—the professors of Agronomy, Animal Husbandry, Beekeeping, etc., who were, as a class, men of large frame, large families, and unlimited con-

Reprinted by permission. Copyright 1946, The New Yorker Magazine, Inc.

fidence. They took command of faculty meetings, knowing that if there was a showdown they would be backed by the state legislators of the rural sectors. Their progress across the campus on a sunny day was impressive, almost gladiatorial.

Into this atmosphere, twelve years ago, came William Ames, B.S. (Harvard), Ph.D. (Oxon.), Professor of Physics. Ames was a slight man, with a progressive myopia which obliged him to wear thick-lensed spectacles. His wife, Clara, affected low-heeled, sensible shoes and was pretty in a dull way. Her remarks were never quoted. At faculty teas she was not asked to pour. She had no children, a circumstance which was emphasized by the bountiful fecundity of the other campus wives. In an effort to overcome this misfortune, she and the Professor read thick compendiums on genes, mutations of species, anthropology, and the breeding habits of aboriginal tribes.

As a student at Oxford, Ames had sat at the feet of the great Lord Rutherford and had learned the true and unrelenting nature of the laws that govern our unseen world. His classes in Advanced Physics, over the years, had few takers. His requests for apparatus for research were shouted down in faculty meetings by the Professor of Animal Husbandry and the Professor of Meat Cutting, who had their eyes on new cream separators and slicing machines, or by the Professor of Agronomy, who wanted a new tractor with four-wheel drive and radio. Professor Ames was a quiet man, a lamb among the rams, and resigned to his colorless career. Secretly, he admired the physique and the bullying manner of the Professor of Meat Cutting.

The summer of 1945 was idling by at the university, Germany had been defeated, the Army Specialized Training Program classes were drowsing in the heat of the plains. On August 6th, in one microsecond, the light of ten thousand suns broke over Hiroshima and an ugly mushroom cloud poked its head sixty thousand feet in the air. Nine days later the war was over. There was jubilation on the campus for a week, and then a hush set in as the papers began to relate in detail the work of the scientists, the long-haired scientists, the *physicists*, who held the secret of world military power in their formulas.

At the first faculty meeting of the school year, in October, the full professors were gathered in a large knot near the door, talking among themselves, waiting for the president to call them to their places. Simultaneously with the banging of his gavel, a hush fell over the group, and there was gentle shuffling and a parting of the mass as Professor Ames walked into the room and over to his accustomed place. He looked neither to the right nor to the left, and his small frame was as erect as a Prussian colonel general's at a color mount. As the meeting progressed, he asked for the floor, which he was given immediately and with sweeping deference. He stated that his classes in Advanced Physics were up to his expectations. With an enrollment of two hundred and fifty students, it was necessary to get an amount of new apparatus—a mass spectrometer, a small cyclotron, and some other electrical equipment. All in all, the Physics Department would need, roughly, a million two hundred thousand dollars. He turned around and, glaring at the assembly, asked if there were any objections from other departments. The Professor of Meat Cutting rose like a cobra listening to a flute and moved that the appropriation be made. It was seconded and passed. Professor Ames then turned on his heel, said, "Good day, gentlemen," and left the hall by the center aisle, erect, looking neither to the right nor to the left.

On May 13, 1946, the Professor's wife, Clara, gave birth to twin sons. Since then, Ames has been observed from time to time in local saloons, his foot on the brass rail, lecturing the barkeepers in loud tones.

SUGGESTIONS FOR STUDY:

1. Is the opening sentence a topic sentence?
2. Does this amusing parable concern a really significant change in public thinking since 1945?
3. How are the elements in the parable arranged?
4. What specific details strike you as most memorable?
5. Is this too exaggerated to be convincing?

6. To what previous part of the essay does the final paragraph relate? Is the final paragraph an effective ending? Why?
7. Does Cox use any interesting figures of speech or comparisons to enliven his narrative? For example?
8. What is the meaning of *Ph.D. (Oxon.), progressive myopia, bountiful fecundity, rose like a cobra listening to a flute?*
9. Write a theme on popular notions regarding or due to the atom bomb; or write a brief narrative, imagined or real, amusing or serious, which depends on a significant issue but does not deal directly with it.

One of the most far-reaching results of the atomic age will be the development of whole new clusters of jobs and careers. Here is an account of how a man developed one of the first careers in atomic energy.

CAREER AT Y-12
by Daniel Lang

THE WAR may be over and the period of reconversion under way, but one industry continues to do nothing but war work. It has never done anything else. This industry, the world's newest and possibly its last, is atomic energy. More than a hundred thousand Americans, working for the Manhattan District in various parts of the country, are engaged in it. Since large-scale atom-splitting is less than three years old, all these people can be regarded as pioneers in a business which has a future. Recently, when I was in Oak Ridge, Ten-

Reprinted by permission. Copyright 1946, The New Yorker Magazine, Inc.

nessee, the site of one of the major operations in this business, I spent an evening at the house of one of these pioneers, a man I'll name Edward Jackson, and heard about his career in what someone will inevitably call the atomic game. He also told me about the life he, his wife, and their infant son have been leading in the brand-new town of Oak Ridge. Jackson is an inspector at a huge plant run for the Army by the Tennessee Eastman Corporation. In this plant, known to Oak Ridgers as Y-12, an electromagnetic separation process is used in the complex, precise production of U-235. Jackson examines certain incoming equipment to see whether it conforms to blueprint specifications. If he thinks a piece is not up to standard, he lists the defects he has found, and the government rejects it. Frequently he disapproves equipment in which a single part is off by as little as one ten-thousandth of an inch, and occasionally the tolerance is even smaller. It is a responsible job. A favorable word from him on a defective piece of equipment could perhaps slow down the country's production of atomic bombs. That, of course, would make everybody miserable.

Jackson is a pudgy, black-haired man of thirty-five from near Pittsburgh. Before he came to Oak Ridge he had driven a truck for his father, who owns a fleet, and, after getting a ground instructor's license, had taught the students of a small Harrisburg technical school how to repair a plane's sheet-metal parts and read blueprints. His wife, Betty, and their baby were in the house the evening we talked, and I saw a good deal of them. It would have been hard not to. Like thousands of other Manhattan project workers, the Jacksons live in a prefabricated plywood house whose main feature is compactness. It is about the size of a caboose, I would say, but, because of a Venetian-blind arrangement in the middle of one room, the Jackson home is officially considered a three-room dwelling. Mrs. Jackson, a slender, pretty girl, is enthusiastic about it. We had scarcely been introduced before she showed me the numerous closets, contrivances that pulled out of the walls and from under window seats. "This house would be perfect to take along on a camping trip," she said. "It's what the Oak Ridge housing section calls an A-6 model," Jackson told me.

Jackson heard about the chances of getting a Manhattan District job in November, 1943, when he was teaching at the Harrisburg school. The school was about to close and the boss assembled his small faculty and, waving a bunch of application blanks, informed them that Tennessee Eastman was looking for men like them to work on an important project, about which he knew nothing. Most of the instructors didn't want to go South, but Jackson and another man stepped forward and took the forms. "I had another offer from some Miami outfit," Jackson said to me, "but a second iron in the fire couldn't hurt me. I couldn't afford to be out of work too long. Betty was in a family way." On Thanksgiving Day he got off a train in Knoxville to investigate Tennessee Eastman, at the company's invitation. He felt blue about being away from home on the holiday, and the sight of Knoxville's dreary railroad station didn't console him any. He was met by a company car and driven out to Oak Ridge, eighteen miles west, to be interviewed by a personnel man named Welch. "At the entrance gate," Jackson said, "guards searched us, checked the auto's pockets, and even lifted the hood, looking for weapons." Jackson didn't penetrate deep into Oak Ridge. All he could see, on his way to the personnel office, was vast stretches of red clay being churned up by bulldozers making roads, and a few wooden buildings. When he got out of the car and stepped into a gooey mass of thick, red clay, he felt even more depressed. Welch told Jackson that he could get on the payroll at once but that he couldn't know what the project was. He said that the work would help shorten the war and that Jackson stood a chance of learning a lot about some rather revolutionary machinery. "I asked him," Jackson said, "if this job could lead to postwar opportunities. Welch just smiled and said he thought so."

Jackson said he'd think it over. He went back to Knoxville and phoned his wife that he hated Oak Ridge. "Then don't take the job," she said. He hopped a train to Miami to see about his other iron in the fire. That job, it developed, was a State Department project for sending American mechanics to Brazil to teach Brazilians how to repair planes. He called Betty again, and she said she wouldn't dream of going to Brazil. "Are you *sure* that Tennessee place isn't O.K.?" she asked her husband. "I was phoning her from a booth that looked out on the Florida beach," Jackson told me. "It was a beautiful day. Blue sky and the temperature just right, and people were parading by in orange-colored beach clothes. I forgot all about that mud in Oak Ridge. When Betty asked me that question, I took one more look at the Florida beach and told her, 'Oh, Betty, it's beautiful.'"

Jackson spent his first three days as a Tennessee Eastman employee getting settled in the drafty dormitory to which he had been assigned and being processed. He was given a physical, was photographed and fingerprinted, and had to fill out innumerable forms. "Eighteen feet of paper!" Jackson said. "Every time I poked my nose around a corner, somebody stuck something at me to sign. Had to tell them my jobs for the last ten years, where I'd been, if I'd ever done time, and promise that if I invented anything on the job the rights belonged to Tennessee Eastman."

On the fourth day, Jackson was told to report, along with a couple of hundred other newly recruited men and women employees, to a training school, where they were herded into a large, bare room, full of benches, known as the "bull pen." Jackson was sitting there, waiting, when a man called out his name and asked him to come to the front of the room. The man, who turned out to be the superintendent of the school, told Jackson that because of his teaching experience, he ought to be a good man to address the gathering. He briefed Jackson on what to say, and Jackson stood up before his fellow-novices. "I told them to keep their mouths shut about Oak Ridge," he said, "or it might mean a ten-thousand-dollar fine or ten years in the cooler. I told them a lot of things like that. I started off rickety, but I warmed up as I went along, and by the time I finished I was pounding the table. I might have done even better if I'd known what I was talking about."

For the next couple of weeks, Jackson continued in

his state of authoritative bewilderment. "I'd lecture five, six times a day," he said. "I was a professor of security. All kinds of people were joining the project—architects, electricians, chemists, and young kids who were college graduates. Illiterates, too. I know that, because everyone had to sign an attendance sheet and there'd always be a few who'd ask me to write their names down for them. I always gave the same lecture, and they were as bored as I was. We were all getting investigated and waiting to be cleared. That could take quite a while. Sometimes I'd be in the middle of my spiel when an M.P. would walk into the room, tap someone on the shoulder, and I'd have one less pupil. The same thing could have happened to me, but there I was, sounding off on security." The recruits for the school had come from all over the country. There was a group of girls just out of Grinnell College; construction men who had been working on the Alcan Highway; middle-aged women who had read ads declaring, "When You're a Grandmother You'll Brag About Having Worked at Tennessee Eastman." There was also a large group of men who had worked in a magnesium plant out in Las Vegas, Nevada. The plant had shut down and a Tennessee Eastman man had flown out there to tell them about Oak Ridge.

After some weeks of specializing in security, Jackson's horizon was broadened. He was asked to tell his classes about the bus lines that were now operating on the reservation and to do a bit of morale work by assuring his listeners that any inconveniences they were suffering from, particularly in housing, were temporary and that a little patience and fortitude were necessary. "That was a hell of a thing for me to be lecturing about," Jackson told me. "Betty was writing me every day from Harrisburg bawling me out for not getting us a place to live. I'd kick to Welch and he'd recite my own lecture back at me." Two months after Jackson's arrival at Oak Ridge, his housing problem was solved. He was shown a huge map on which hundreds of squares, each one representing a plot of land, were drawn in pencil, and told to pick out his home. Jackson pointed to one of the squares, more or less at random. "An excellent choice! That means you're going to live in East Village," a housing official told him. Jackson, curious about what he had put his finger on, drove out to East Village just in time to see his home being unloaded in sections from a truck that had hauled it from Indiana. With the help of a crane, a crew was lifting pieces of it from the truck and gently setting them down on wooden foundation blocks. "You're getting a furnished demountable," one of the crew said.

Jackson took a train to Harrisburg and drove back to Oak Ridge with his wife in their car. He spent much of the trip warning her not to be troubled by her first impressions. It was pouring when they arrived, and the clay quagmires were at their softest. The car got stuck in the mud just as they pulled up in front of their house. "This is it," Jackson said, and, lifting his wife out of her seat, he carried her over the mud and into the A-6. In mid-March, two months later, their child was born, at the Oak Ridge hospital. "That makes him a hillbilly," Jackson says.

Shortly before Jackson got his house, he was at last cleared by Military Intelligence. He promptly informed the school superintendent that he wanted to work at Y-12 instead of hanging around a training school. "I told him," Jackson said, "that I was a first-class aircraft sheet-metal man and wanted to help make plane parts out at Y-12. That's what I thought they were making." The superintendent suggested patience and assigned Jackson to a new lecturing post—teaching people how to read blueprints. It wasn't until just before his child was born that Jackson got his break. A personnel man at the plant who had heard and liked his lectures asked him if he wanted to be maintenance-and-operations engineer at Y-12. Jackson enthusiastically said yes, and the next day he was sent out to the plant.

His first job had to do with the converting of a small building that had been used for chemical work into what was called a product-control unit. "I was warned that it was a very secret building," he said. "I was given a special badge without which no employee could enter it, no matter how many other buildings he could get into. The badge had a letter and a number on it. The letter O.K.'d me for the building, and the number showed how much could be discussed with me. The numbers ran from one to five, five being for the top dogs. My number was only one, but just the same I got a kick out of having the badge." Jackson's job was to help with the installation and maintenance of fluorescent lighting and air-conditioning and to oversee the repainting. He was also to act occasionally as a liaison man for his supervisor, Dr. Angus Cameron, which meant that he would be able to get around to other units of Y-12. In addition, he would have the opportunity to become acquainted with some of the machinery being used.

"It made all the difference, being at Y-12," Jackson said. "There was real activity. The grounds covered twelve thousand acres, and construction gangs were busy putting up new units." The building to which he was assigned had glass-brick walls. "No machinery in the place," he said, "but there were a lot of dials and meters." The temperature was kept constant and the air-conditioning purified the atmosphere. As Jackson continued to work for Dr. Cameron, he discovered the reason for all these precautions. It was the existence, in a small room in the building, of a delicate instrument used to determine the quality of something extremely important (U-235, but he didn't know that then). Thus, there could be no machinery in the building, because its vibrations might affect the instrument. Dust in the air could also have thrown it off. The entire building was painted white and the workers wore white uniforms; only chemical workers were supposed to wear white uniforms, to distinguish them, for reasons of security, from other classes of workers, each of which wore uniforms of a different color, and Dr. Cameron's product-control section, though not strictly chemical, was considered to be under the chemical people. However, the white uniforms served a purpose. "The place reminded us of a hospital, and that sort of kept you on your toes. You worried that if you got careless you'd mess up the whiteness and maybe something would be hurt."

Jackson thought a lot about the mystery of the delicate instrument in the small room. "That was one piece of equipment I never got to know well," he said. "Dr. Cameron kept people away from it." One day the air-conditioning inside the small room broke down, and Jackson fetched two repair men. The mechanics, who were dressed in blue uniforms, instantly caught Dr. Cameron's eye and he swooped down on them. They explained their mission, but Dr. Cameron wanted to know if they had to do their work inside the secret room. "Well, we can't fix it if you won't let us in," one of the maintenance men said. Dr. Cameron asked, "Can't you tell me what to do from outside?" They explained that would take a lot of his time. He finally let one man in the room for a few minutes a day until the air-conditioning was in shape again.

Everything about Y-12 was mysterious, Jackson said, but he found the place exhilarating rather than sinister. "So many screwy things went on," he said. "The workers in the building next to ours couldn't get into their place unless they had gas masks strapped to their sides. Sometimes a loud horn would go off, and that meant they were having a gas-alarm drill. They'd come hustling out with the masks pulled over their faces. There were chemical installations that smelled of ammonia and ether, and places where the employees got down on their knees every now and then to look for tiny bits of metal. In their hands they held Geiger counters, instruments that detect radioactive rays. Sometimes the counters would lead them to a tiny orange or black speck on someone's white uniform. The speck was very valuable. The uniforms of certain workers were always chemically treated before they were laundered or junked, to make sure that none of those precious bits would go down the drain.

"Then there was the huge main production plant," Jackson went on. "Anyone who could go on thinking about aircraft sheet metal after one look at the place was plain batty. There weren't any lathes or drills or presses. Just a mass of copper and stainless-steel pipes of the weirdest shapes you ever saw. It was an enormous building, with pipes all over the place. You'd see two of them running together for a stretch, but then they'd part company and go off to different ends of the building. And there were so many valves that the chains to operate them had to have different-colored tags on them so you could tell which valves they operated. The plant was very clean and quiet. All you could hear was the low sound

Career at Y-12   113

of generators. The lights were on the end of long, thin poles that came down from the ceiling through spaces between the pipes. You couldn't have the lights in the ceiling, because the pipes were so closely packed that they'd have blocked illumination. Off this area were the control rooms. That's where you found the cubicle operators, young girls who sat on high stools in steel boxes about ten feet high, fifteen feet deep, and five feet wide, with switchboards full of dials and meters. Those dials and meters told us whether or not the separation process was operating smoothly. The girls didn't really understand the readings they made, but they knew that the meter needles had to respond a certain way, that certain red and green and yellow and orange lights had to flash, and that they had to hear certain clicking sounds. If any of those things didn't happen, they phoned their supervisor, who was an electrical engineer, and he'd take over in the cubicle then. He'd check everything to find out where the trouble was, and he wouldn't leave until it was cleared up. Then the girl would climb back onto her stool and go on with her day's work. I didn't know then and I don't know today what all those dials and meters were indicating, but, whatever it was, it must have been the payoff."

Naturally, Jackson said, all the secrecy made the workers do a lot of guessing about what was being produced at Y-12. "We knew it couldn't be very big," he said, "and we were also pretty sure it wasn't mouse traps." One rumor Jackson heard was that the Army was developing a new and revolutionary type of gasoline. A paint that would make planes invisible was another candidate. One of Jackson's friends, certain that the secret product was rocket fuel, showed him a magazine article which said that something called uranium could lend itself to such a purpose. Another notion was that the plants were working on a death ray. "For a while," Jackson told me, "I heard that nylon stockings were being manufactured. I think that one got started because there are a couple of hosiery mills in the vicinity." Some workers believed that the place was the start of a postwar project, and thought it was a shame that so much manpower and material should be expended on it then. A batch of gag guesses were in circulation, too—that the plant was making Roosevelt campaign buttons, face powder for Wacs, dehydrated water for overseas troops, and "the confligulator." Jackson handed me a piece of tissue paper on which was typed, "Confligulator T-1 is the newest weapon ordnance has under consideration. Tactical uses are still secret, but it can be safely said the art of warfare will be revolutionized by it. Briefly and in nontechnical language, Confligulator T-1 is a combination of totalizer wheels arranged to be propelled through multiple predetermined circumferential superpositions and an intrinsically heterogeneous precomputed taxonomy of abutments controlled by nonconsecutive monodromic sequences of denominational seriatim concatenation. . . . Aw nuts—let's give the damn thing to the Japs!"

Some workers couldn't take all the secrecy. "They wanted to know why they were showing up day in and day out at Y-12," Jackson said, "and they weren't supposed to know, so they quit." The problem never bothered him. To begin with, he was too busy. Then, too, he'd always had a passion for machines. "Every time I'd learn something new about Y-12 equipment, I felt good," he said. " 'My God,' I'd tell myself, 'nobody in history has ever worked on this equipment before, and here I am fooling around with it.' And then you got into a daily routine, seeing friends at night, picking up the groceries, and such stuff, and the secret product got to be like the question of salvation—you just didn't think about it. Once in a while I'd think maybe it was a boondoggle, but then it became a case of whether or not you had faith. I just couldn't believe the government was pouring all that dough into nothing."

After five months of working for Dr. Cameron, all the installations in this particular unit had been completed, and Jackson was given a choice of two new jobs. Dr. Cameron wanted Jackson to stay with the product-control unit, and he also was offered a chance to spend a couple of months at the Westinghouse factory in East Pittsburgh inspecting devices the company was making for Y-12. "I decided on the Westinghouse deal," Jackson said, somewhat hesitantly, "because I'd get to know more about the machinery." Mrs. Jackson, who had put her baby to sleep some time before and was now listening to us, laughed. "It was my fault," she said. "I got tired of the wooden walks they have here in Oak Ridge. I wanted to see solid sidewalks again. I felt homesick, too, and we've got people—Eddie's family—up near Westinghouse." "It doesn't much matter whose fault it was," Jackson said. "It worked out fine." He explained that when they returned to Pennsylvania they realized, to their surprise, that they had become attached to Oak Ridge. Mrs. Jackson even found that she missed the wooden walks and her A-6.

At the Westinghouse plant, Jackson discovered that he was a celebrity to the workers. They asked him to tell them all about the Manhattan District, and they were impressed at the knowing way he inspected what they were making for the project. They said that after the war they wanted to visit the District's installations and find out how the parts they had been making were used. Jackson would smile cryptically and they would be even more impressed. "They sure made me feel as though I were on the inside," he said. "They'd give the parts they were making such names as bazooka, Mae West, bread pan, and sailboat. But I knew the code names and if they were made right for us and how they looked when they were assembled at Y-12." As for Mrs. Jackson, she found her old friends too commiserating. They kept feeling sorry for her because her house was so small and she didn't have a cellar. Finally, she told them off—said that her house saved steps and that the reason she didn't have a cellar was that it never got cold enough down there for people to need a furnace.

After the two months at Westinghouse were up, the Jacksons went back to Oak Ridge. That was in February, 1945. "When we got back," Jackson said, "we looked up all our friends. It was nice to listen again to the Tennesseeans talking in their funny way about that 'storm' of theirs. If one of them is talking, they say he's talking up a storm, or if he's working, he's working up a storm—always that storm. We went on our Sunday auto trips again, with the baby sleeping in a hammock in the back of the car, to the Great Smokies and to see the T.V.A. dams. Sometimes we'd drive down to Chattanooga to see Lookout Mountain. There was still plenty of mud in Oak Ridge, but I was glad to be back." On his return, Jackson was informed that he had been promoted to inspector of equipment, his present job. He liked the job better than his old one with Dr. Cameron because he had even more to do with equipment. The construction work had let up somewhat by then, he said, but the activity in Y-12 was as great as ever. "Everyone was used to his job now," Jackson said. "Employees were trained, assigned, transferred, fired, promoted, and went on two-week vacations." During the months just before Hiroshima was bombed, Y-12 was functioning as smoothly as if it had been going fifty years.

Jackson's own vacation began on August 4th, and that day he, his wife, and the baby started on a leisurely trip to visit Mrs. Jackson's relatives in a small Pennsylvania town near Altoona. Toward noon of August 6th, they were driving along, some thirty miles from his mother-in-law's house, when his wife casually turned on the radio. The big news was just being announced. "I got goose pimples," Jackson said. "I pushed the accelerator down to the floor and I didn't know I was doing sixty-five until Betty asked me where the fire was. She kept dialling all the stations. Every announcer was saying the same thing. After the sixth station, Betty said to me, 'So you were really doing something down there after all.' 'Some nylon stockings I made!' I told her."

When they reached their destination, they found Mrs Jackson's mother, who had also heard the news, very nervous. "She didn't think that Oak Ridge should have been mentioned on the air," Jackson said. "She said Japanese spies would attack the place and kill Betty, the baby, and me." After his mother-in-law had been reassured, the reunion with family and friends became jolly. A young brother-in-law, home on furlough from Europe, shook Jackson's hand and said, "You saved me from going to Japan." Other relatives and neighbors congratulated Jackson not only for having worked on the bomb but also for having kept quiet all that time. Jackson insisted that he hadn't known what he was making, but everyone thought he was a great kidder. Late that night, after everyone else had gone to bed, he got out an atlas in the living room and looked up Hiroshima. "It's thirty-four degrees latitude, one hundred and thirty-two degrees longitude, and three hundred and forty-three thousand Japs lived there," he told me.

The Jacksons started back to Oak Ridge next day. Jackson wanted to know what had happened in the town when the reason for its existence had at last been disclosed. Some people, particularly those in less responsible positions, had, it seemed, claimed that they had always known that U-235 was being made at Oak Ridge; the run on newspapers had been so big that copies had sold at a dollar apiece; inside the plant, workers had gathered in groups to discuss the news, but their now knowledgeable foremen had persuaded them back to their posts by saying, "Come on, let's break it up—uranium's running all over the floor." The next day the absentee rate was as low as usual. On the whole there had been no particularly spirited outbursts. When Nagasaki was bombed, Jackson and his friends were discouraged. "We began to wonder how many atomic bombs were going to have to be dropped," he said. But then, a few days later, the war ended. "Well, we *had* helped shorten the war, after all," Jackson said.

"Well," Jackson said, "that's the way it's been up to now. You haven't seen much excitement since you've been in Oak Ridge, have you? You're not going to, either. People have settled down here to live and work. It's a funny thing. In the old days they used to have a poster around here that said, 'YOU CAN LICK JAPAN!' Now they've got one that says, 'YOU HOLD THE KEY TO WORLD PEACE.' And we're working the same way with the new poster as we did with the old one. We show up at Y-12 on time, come home, keep a date, wonder if we're going to get a raise, or maybe hear a tip about a bigger house to move into. It's a business now, and I'm in it. I've forgotten all about going back to planes. I used to think they were the coming thing and how I'd open up a plane garage. But this thing I'm in now is basic. I'm in on the ground floor, and so far I've been doing all right."

SUGGESTIONS FOR STUDY:

1. Is Lang's purpose primarily narrative or expository?
2. What kind of phrase does Lang use frequently in opening a new paragraph to indicate the basic arrangement of his essay?

Current Prose

3. Do most paragraphs have topic sentences? Do the paragraphs have a definite unity whether a topic sentence is present or not?
4. Do the quotations from Jackson vary the presentation of facts about Oak Ridge? Effectively?
5. Cite some words in Jackson's speech that are appropriate to casual conversation but not to formal writing.
6. Is Mrs. Jackson's breaking into the interview, or her reaction to wooden walks, effective?
7. Is the detailed description of Confligulator T-1 convincing? Are all the words appropriate? Is *tolerance* in paragraph 1 a technical term?
8. Has the *nylon-stocking* reaction to the bombing of Hiroshima been prepared for?
9. What is the meaning of *fortitude, furnished demountable, dehydrated water?*
10. Write an expository narrative about a job or occupation—e.g., my summer in a lawyer's office, a day during the haying season, the routine of an army cook.

A noted anthropologist, a pioneer in the comparative study of cultures, discusses war as it appears in a variety of cultural patterns.

ON WAR
by Ruth Benedict

WARFARE is a social theme that may or may not be used in any culture. Where war is made much of, it may be with contrasting objectives, with contrasting organization in relation to the state, and with contrasting sanctions. War

From *Patterns of Culture*, by Ruth Benedict. Reprinted by permission of Houghton Mifflin Company, publishers.

may be, as it was among the Aztecs, a way of getting captives for the religious sacrifices. Since the Spaniards fought to kill, according to Aztec standards they broke the rules of the game. The Aztecs fell back in dismay and Cortez walked as victor into the capital.

There are even quainter notions, from our standpoint, associated with warfare in different parts of the world. For our purposes it is sufficient to notice those regions where organized resort to mutual slaughter never occurs between social groups. Only our familiarity with war makes it intelligible that a state of warfare should alternate with a state of peace in one tribe's dealings with another. The idea is quite common over the world, of course. But on the one hand it is impossible for certain peoples to conceive the possibility of a state of peace, which in their notion would be equivalent to admitting enemy tribes to the category of human beings, which by definition they are not even though the excluded tribe may be of their own race and culture.

On the other hand, it may be just as impossible for a people to conceive of the possibility of a state of war. Rasmussen tells of the blankness with which the Eskimo met his exposition of our custom. Eskimos very well understand the act of killing a man. If he is in your way, you cast up your estimate of your own strength, and if you are ready to take it upon yourself, you kill him. If you are strong, there is no social retribution. But the idea of an Eskimo village going out against another Eskimo village in battle array or a tribe against tribe, or even of another village being fair game in ambush warfare, is alien to them. All killing comes under one head, and is not separated, as ours is, into categories, the one meritorious, the other a capital offence.

I myself tried to talk of warfare to the Mission Indians of California, but it was impossible. Their misunderstanding of warfare was abysmal. They did not have the basis in their own culture upon which the idea could exist, and their attempts to reason it out reduced the great wars to which we are able to dedicate ourselves with moral fervour to the level of alley brawls. They did not happen to have a cultural pattern that distinguished between them.

War is, we have been forced to admit even in the face of its huge place in our own civilization, an asocial trait. In the chaos following the World War all the wartime arguments that expounded its fostering of courage, of altruism, of spiritual values, gave out a false and offensive ring. War in our own civilization is as good an illustration as one can take of the destructive lengths to which the development of a culturally selected trait may go. If we justify war, it is because all peoples always justify the traits of which they find themselves possessed, not because war will bear an objective examination of its merits.

SUGGESTIONS FOR STUDY:

1. What is the main idea and where is it expressed?
2. What evidence does Miss Benedict use to support the generalization that war may or may not be used in any culture?
3. What evidence does she use to support the generalization that war will not bear an objective examination of its merits?
4. What is the meaning of contrasting *objectives,* an *objective* examination, *sanctions,* social *retribution, meritorious* killing, *abysmal* misunderstanding, *asocial* trait, *altruism,* a *culturally selected* trait, *category* of human beings?
5. What tone do the above words give to the selection?
6. Write a theme showing why some idea or attitude generally accepted in your community is provincial rather than universal.

Everyone who hasn't been to war, and especially anyone who may be called on to go, wonders how afraid he will be when the time comes. Many people, of course, serve with distinction through entire wars and never hear a shot fired in anger. Others hear too many. In this essay, a Korean veteran tells what it was like to reach the breaking point.

JOURNEY INTO FEAR
by *William D. Blair, Jr.*

A VERY FEW hours after arrival at the port of Pusan in Korea we were on a train, jerking toward the west and the enemy. There had been word of guerrillas firing on our convoys, and on every flatcar of the train men were holding weapons ready to fire. Sometime during this five-hour journey war came to us all. Wonder at the strangeness of the place brought with it loneliness and a yearning for home—and then came fear.

It may have come first to some as they looked at the skyline and thought about what it would be like to be shot at, to have someone aiming a rifle at them, actually trying to kill them. Probably it came to others at a station, when they saw a South Korean infantryman whose only weapon was a single grenade, hanging by a string from his belt. Maybe some felt it first when we passed a hospital train, returning from the unknown with its load of silent, bandaged figures, or when

Reprinted by courtesy V. F. W. Magazine, July, 1951, official publication of the Veterans of Foreign Wars, and by courtesy of the publishers of The Reader's Digest.

they noticed the two rigid bodies floating slowly down the river which ran close to the tracks.

This first feeling was only a dull fear, hardly more than uneasiness. We were uncertain what lay ahead, we were realizing reluctantly that whatever control we had over our destinies was slipping from us.

Arrival in the combat area did nothing to reassure us. A group of lightly wounded soldiers was playing cards on the road near our debarkation point, and one of the newly arrived Marines, mustering his self-confidence, jeered:

"Is that the way you people fight a war?"

"This isn't the movies, Marines." The cardplayers were tired but superior. "You'll be goddam lucky to do as well as the 27th!" That was the unit the newcomers were to relieve.

"You the 27th?"

"We're what's left of it."

There were many things you weren't afraid of, not knowing; you have to see them first. Death isn't very frightening till you've seen some of its horrible methods. The words "disfigurement," "disablement," don't mean much until you've seen a head without features, and have heard it moan: "Can my wife still love me, with a face like I'll have?"

There had been hard fighting at Chindong-ni for over a week. A company of the 27th had been cut off from the rest of the regiment a small distance away and was still surrounded, desperately short of ammunition, water, and rations. Several Marine units were dispatched to effect a rescue. As they set out along a dusty track and under a malicious sun which made every rod a mile, there was no conversation. Dungarees quickly grew dark with sweat under the heavy loads, and you settled into the automatic, slouching pace which for a time makes thinking unnecessary and postpones fatigue. Instead of excitement there was lethargy, almost unconsciousness as you plodded along past the ruins of Chindong-ni, its mud hovels crumbled and smouldering. Past dead cattle, their legs jutting stiffly in air. Past a dry stream bed. Past an ammunition bearer, who had fainted from heat exhaustion. Past bamboo clumps. And into fear, as two hidden machine guns opened fire from the flank.

We stared, ignorantly amazed; then squad by squad we understood and leaped for cover, feeling the sudden singe of terror as we saw the bullets splash dust in the road.

Pusan had been the title page, the train ride the preface. This was Chapter One of the text. This was a deeper fear than before; it wiped out the past and the future—every frame of reference except the utter and immediate necessity for safety. We were animals till we found it—wild with fear and moving by instinct alone. In ditches and behind rocks we finally saw that this wasn't, after all, unbearable—not while we lay in relatively safe cover and the danger was only a couple of not very expert machine gunners. Fear subsided, though it didn't altogether disappear, and we were prepared to stay in our ditches indefinitely. And then the officers, swearing, exhorting, brandishing their carbines, stood exposed on the road and ordered us up and on.

It is one thing to lie in a snug trench while you listen to the bullets ricocheting from the stones over your head or smacking the turf just beyond; you are calmly afraid, almost pleasurably afraid, as you might be for the hero of a romance. It is another thing to stand where you can easily and unromantically receive a small, hard missile in the hollow of your temple—which itches expectantly at the thought; or in your stomach—which is now bottomless and sick; or in other parts of your so susceptible body. The fear is not nice. It's a frenzied pounding in the breast, a feeling of nakedness, a frantic attempt to blot out everything but the sight of the ground directly ahead and the sound of the voice of command; and to go on, and on, and on until it's done. In days, or weeks, a fear like that becomes determination, which is not the opposite of being afraid. Or it festers into panic, hysteria, and collapse. It makes man of boy, or child of man.

It's a wonderful thing to discover that you're not as afraid as you thought you'd be. It gives green youths an immeasurable lift in their first days of fire. After these initiations they look at each other and smile, because they've shown themselves, maybe for the first time, that they aren't cowards. Unfortunately, the discovery loses its potency in repetition. Mind and body are worn thin; the last drop of willpower is wrung out, and you need something more. Providentially, it comes—emotion takes over. The result is a truly marvelous exhilaration, born of the endless fear, and it sweeps the endangered along heedless, even fiercely jubilant, to whatever end of the road. For the survivor, the memory of the interval often lingers. It's like a remembered orgy, which exerts a fascination and arouses a craving. The victim feels a need to indulge it again. It becomes horrible, for men still inflamed by the ecstasy will go back from safety to the battle when for them there is no call.

I think it must be this driving intoxication which inspires heroes, the men who hug grenades to their chests to save their fellows, or dash singly against impregnable enemy positions. It must be the thing that makes warriors—for there are some who enjoy war. These are contemporary Achilleses, Launcelots, Rolands, of whom one wants to say that they were born after their time. There was a bearded young lieutenant, possibly still living, in command of a platoon at the bank of the Nam River. Communist raiders were slipping by night into the no-man's-land village on the far bank, setting up mortars and machine guns to harass our outposts. They did little damage, but the insolence piqued the lieutenant's pride. He lay in wait for the raider band alone in a maze of rubble. The trick worked. He killed nearly 20 North Koreans before they could turn and run, and came grinning back to his lines. He was as happy at his work as any man I've known.

But the danger-lust is more remarkable in non-warrior types, doing their job as best they can and finding no pleasure in it. These, the fever can transform into something wholly foreign to their natures. One company of soldiers stayed five days on a tiny, T-shaped ridge, surrounded by ten times their number. They ran out of food and low on water, and watched supplies aimed at them drop tantalizingly from American planes into the hands of the enemy. In the night the enemy around would slink into their midst, and in the morning bodies of some soldiers would be found crumpled with knife wounds in their hearts. After what must have been an eternity, a friendly force cut its way to the rescue, and the agonized soldiers could fall back. But they seemed to take no joy in their salvation. "They were so doggone mad they didn't care if they *ever* came back!" marveled a member of the relief.

The gruesome sights of the battlefield, in their effect on the soldier, are also subject to the law of diminishing returns. You expect to be shocked and sickened—but that must be an artificial feeling because you don't react fastidiously for long. Burning or crushed or dismembered bodies are only dirt, as the preacher likes to point out, and the sight of them, when the novelty is gone, is little more obnoxious. It's true that at first you are nauseated, and terrified by the thought of the ghastly deaths some of these flesh-heaps have obviously suffered. But you learn to waste little sympathy on the irreparable.

There is one true horror, and it has no remedy. I watched two surgeons in a mobile field hospital toil for hours over an almost faceless man. The formless flesh tumbled and came away between the probing instruments. After a long time one of the surgeons sighed and murmured, "I'm sorry, fella." The surgeons tried to make something clean and firm out of a ghastly pulp. Then they bandaged what was left of the head, leaving only an opening for the one functioning eye, and sent him away. "He will die," they said. And horror was the vista of that man's future—not death, but the intervening time in the hospitals, with the opening in the bandage like a window in a tenement, from which the wretched can overlook the vile.

Green, scared troops approach their first test by fire, and begin to feel how dependent they are on each other. They begin to reappraise each other, and pray fervently that every man will turn out true. One man's laxity or weakness can kill all the rest. Afterward the survivors feel a hot pride in their collective achievement and a glow of gratitude and trust for each other. In very little time a bond is forged in a company which is stronger than most family ties, for the price of its dissolution is often death. Take a soldier out of a unit like that and he will be acutely unhappy and afraid; he can't be sure in his new place that the men on his right and left will still be there when the assault waves start to arrive. Many soldiers, comfortably convalescing from wounds in rear-area hospitals, have moved heaven and earth to be sent back to their company, from the first day they could rise out of bed. They would rather go back and fight beside their friends than take their full measure of rest and risk being sent to a different unit.

The fraternity of such soldiers is infectious, and it spreads over a whole combat area. Every man who does his job under fire becomes the brother of every other who is in the same fix. After a while you love just about every man you see—each one is suffering for you. It is a common remark among soldiers that the further back you go from the fighting, the less sympathetic are the people. The less hardship the man knows, the less he is driven into the arms of his neighbor, and the more he is just what he was in his peaceful home—self-centered, unfeeling. Under stress, a man is noble; left to himself, he is mean. I don't know which is truly the man.

Aboard a hospital ship, where men are crowded into a cabin with eight or nine others, mutual sympathy and respect create friendships quickly. The young Marine lieutenant had been speaking of his dread of combat, shame for his postbattle tears, and his greatest terror—when he heard above him in the night the ominous sound of a dozen grenades being primed in unison, to be dropped on his platoon.

"But nature is wonderful," he went on. "She doesn't let you remember all the sounds we heard, or all the awful feeling we had or things we saw. It's just a blur. Just that one sound—the time they banged their grenades, all together, right over us—that stays with me. I'll always remember it. But mostly you forget."

So it is. The details, the shades of feeling, the little horrors and pains and fright—these are forgotten. But enough remains to evoke the terrible anguish, the stunning terror again, and always again.

Sometimes I wonder what goes into being afraid for your life. Perhaps it is all the other fears which you recognize when you have time to think about your emotions, violently mixed in one moment. Fear that family and friends will suffer, that a wife will be a widow, that children will be fatherless. Fear that all the little pleasures and joys you find in your life will be felt no more. Fear that you will be judged by your errors; that you will never demonstrate your beliefs. Fear that you will never have lived.

In the dense fog near Seoul, a young soldier scrambled back and forth over the hill. His platoon had left him. The order to pull back somehow never had reached him, and finally from the uncanny silence came the conviction that he was alone on the barren height. He tried, frantically, to follow his comrades, but the mist was like a blindfold. After every desperate 20-yard rush he stopped, uncertain, staring at the little space he could see around him. And then, as panic mounted, he heard the scratches of feet against stone, the metallic snick of metal on metal and metal on rock. He had been a soldier long enough, and he knew the sounds. It wasn't his platoon. The impulse to scream was almost too strong to control, but he bit it down. Miraculously, right there in front of him, loomed a huge boulder, reaching angularly away from him out of the ground. He leaped around it and crouched in the tiny cave it afforded. Suddenly two pairs of soft-shoed feet stepped onto the flat rock top above his head, and two voices murmured—not in English. His heart was like a pneumatic drill, crashing and blasting its way through his frame; his eyes blurred with stinging tears. Time became meaningless. The human being can stand no more than so much and slowly he relaxed. It didn't matter, now, once you knew; and it was so peaceful. Life had seldom given him a sweeter moment than this acceptance of its limit. Then he got up, careless and yet confident that his step in the dark would sound like any other, and walked down the hill and through the fields and back to the arms of his brothers.

That, in the end, is what war is: Fear. Fear for your life, primarily, till one is so afraid that he can be afraid no more.

SUGGESTIONS FOR STUDY:

1. Is the essay loosely or closely organized?
2. What sections or paragraphs illustrate compact organization?
3. Is the detail specific enough to be effective? For example?

4. Is the diction forceful and appropriate? For example? Is the nonstandard speech in the dialog convincing?
5. Do the narrative examples add force and conviction?
6. Do you find Blair's approach to a difficult and personal problem honest or falsely heroic and sentimental? Why?
7. What word is repeated frequently throughout the essay and especially in the third last paragraph? Is the repetition effective?
8. What is the author doing to the abstraction *fear* in such details as *the itching temple, the bottomless stomach, the pounding breast?*
9. What is meant by *guerrillas, lethargy, the law of diminishing returns?*
10. Write a theme in which you describe or analyze an emotion.

Woman's work is never done.

WAR AND THE LADY CORRESPONDENT
by Walter Bernstein

AS A LOVER of the theatre, I have been alarmed lately by its tendency to romanticize female war correspondents. I ran into one of the sisterhood during the war, and I still carry the scars.

I met this particular lady in Naples one bleak, celibate winter, at a time when any variety of American woman was a rare sight. The only female correspondent I had met until then was a hard-bitten tomato from a Midwestern paper, who wore pants as though she had never worn anything else. She

Reprinted by permission. Copyright 1947, The New Yorker Magazine, Inc.

was so much more masculine than most of the male correspondents that no one regarded her as a real woman, except possibly the desperate infantrymen back from the front. The female who showed up in Naples was nothing like that. She wore a blond feather bob, pancake makeup, and fawn-colored gabardine slacks; she shimmered in a mist of Chanel; and the afternoon she blew into the pressroom, everyone knew that here was a Woman. She hesitated on the threshold for a moment, giving everyone the eye; then she saw a photographer she knew (a *Life* photographer, of course), flew up to him, and began spraying him with breathless French. I knew the *Life* man was from Staten Island, where French is not the native tongue, so I asked a man from the Chicago *Sun* if the lady was from France.

"No," the *Sun* man said. "She's from Minneapolis."

That was the first time I saw her. As an enlisted correspondent, I naturally did not get near enough to touch the cuffs of her slacks, but I saw her from time to time around the pressroom, often speaking English, and occasionally I could hear her gay laughter rising above the partition that separated the enlisted men's mess from that of the civilian correspondents, who had vitamin pills on their table. Once, she even went up to Cassino in a jeep with two of the more intrepid correspondents and a shell landed in the same valley, but she took it well, rarely talking about it afterward unless asked.

Then, one day, I had to go to Bari, which is an Italian city on the Adriatic. Bari is about an hour's trip by plane from Naples and I had the promise of a ride in a B-25. The airport was about ten miles out of Naples and the plane was scheduled to leave at noon, so I got up early that morning and stood out in the road and caught a ride in a British weapons carrier. The day was damp and drizzly and I thought perhaps the planes would be grounded, but the guard at the gate said they were flying. No one was in my plane when I got to it, but an Army car stood beside it and I went up to that. I opened the door, and there, in the back seat, was an Air Forces public-relations captain and next to him was the lady correspondent, her creases just as sharp as ever, looking as fresh and as radiant as if the sun were shining and she were on her way to the Minneapolis Country Club. I asked the captain when the plane would leave, and he said as soon as the pilot arrived. It was raining harder, so I asked if I could sit in the car until then. The captain didn't seem overjoyed, but he said I could, and I climbed into the front. He and the lady were talking intimately in the back, not quite baby talk, and holding hands, but I didn't pay much attention. It was warm and pleasant in the car, the rain plunking softly on the roof, and I settled down and began whistling quietly to myself. All of a sudden, I felt a clutch on my shoulder.

"That song!" the lady correspondent said tensely.

"What song?" I said, trying to collect myself. She'd scared the hell out of me.

"That song!" she said.

"What song?" I said.

"The one you were whistling," she said impatiently.

I tried to think what I had been whistling, and finally remembered it was one of the songs the International Brigade sang in Spain during the Franco rebellion. "What about that song?" I said.

"Where did you learn it?"

"In New York," I said, "where I learn all my songs."

She leaned back, her eyes on something very far away. "I haven't heard that song since Spain," she whispered.

"Were you in Spain recently?" the captain asked.

She didn't bother to answer. She just said simply, "We had a people's army in Spain."

"You did?" said the captain.

"I'm on my way now to Yugoslavia," she said to me. "I hear they have a people's army there." I figured she collected people's armies. "I want to see if it's a *real* people's army," she said sternly. I said I hoped she got there. "I was in Spain," she reminded me.

"Well, well," the captain said.

Just then, the pilot showed up, saving the captain from any further conversational strain. With him were the co-pilot and the flight engineer, both of whom climbed into the nose of the plane. The captain called to the pilot, who came over to the car. We all got out to meet him. The pilot had a Purple Heart and two D.F.C.s and the Air Medal with clusters, but he was out of his league here. When the captain introduced him, Madame X just smiled and gave him the grip, and I could see his knees buckle. He finally managed to ask her if she wanted to ride up front.

"*Enchantée*," she said, flawlessly. She climbed into the nose, disdaining the pilot's eager aid. He started to follow her, then saw me.

"Are you coming, too?" he said. I nodded and smiled feebly. "Well, get in the back," he said. He climbed in after the lady. I wriggled up into the tail section of the plane, which is separate from the pilot's compartment, and the captain closed the hatch after me. I could see him through the waist windows, as the engines kicked up, waving his handkerchief at the lady.

I settled down for the ride. That is, I *tried* to settle down. The first hint that woman's work is never done came when we took off as if the pilot were showing her how he and Jimmy Doolittle took off from the deck of that carrier. The plane didn't go fifty feet before it stood on its tail and shot straight up into the air. From then on, it was every man for himself. I tried to stay in one place, but there wasn't a chance. The pilot buzzed everything he saw and a lot of things he didn't see. He did twists; he did turns; when he ran out of the standard tricks, he invented new ones. God knows what was going on in the front of that plane. First, he would bank hard and I would be slammed against the waist guns. Then he would climb and I would rattle on down to the rear blister. I felt like a ball in a bowling alley. I don't know how long the ride took, but he landed the way he took off, probably saying to her, "Look, no hands!" He came in at top speed and jammed on the brakes and I went from one end of the plane to the other without touching a thing. After that, I just lay where I fell, breathing heavily. I could hear the pilot talking to the lady as they climbed down. I waited for a while, then knocked politely on the hatch. The voices were receding in the distance. I knocked again. I pounded. I had never heard of anyone's starving to death in a B-25, but there was no reason why it couldn't be done. I pounded some more, and then I began to yell. Someone fumbled at the hatch and pulled it open, and I climbed down, aching all over. The pilot and the lady correspondent stood there, looking annoyed.

"Be careful of that airplane, soldier," the pilot said sharply. "It's not one of your damned tanks." He examined the plane carefully to see if I had scratched it. Then, apparently satisfied, he walked away, arm in arm with the lady. I followed as best I could, watching as they got into a waiting staff car and set off for Bari. The lady smiled at me as the car roared past, but maybe the window glass robbed the smile of some of its vital elements, the way it does with ultra-violet rays, because I didn't feel a thing. I limped after them down to the main road and finally got a hitch into town.

I never saw the lady correspondent again, but I heard about her the next day. The night she arrived, she had visited the Yugoslav mission, escorted by one of the top American Intelligence men in Bari, and had asked to be taken into Yugoslavia. I asked some Partisans I knew if they were taking her. One of them, a colonel, looked startled.

"We have troubles enough of our own," he said. "She would disrupt our entire Army." He shook his head, remembering the lady, and said in disbelief, "Tell me, are all American women like that?" I said I wasn't sure any more; I had been away too long. He muttered something in Yugoslav and walked away.

I asked another Yugoslav what the colonel had said.

"He says he feels sorry for the American men," the other Yugoslav said.

SUGGESTIONS FOR STUDY:

1. What is Bernstein's purpose? What is his attitude toward his subject? Where are both revealed?
2. Do the various incidents characterize the lady? Is the Yugoslav colonel's remark an apt one?
3. Why is the unfeminine correspondent brought into paragraph 2?
4. Is any reader unlikely to know that French is not the native

language of Staten Island? Why does the author mention the fact?
5. Do the quotations enliven the narrative? Do they comment on the lady? On the other characters?
6. Does the airplane ride strike you as funny? What makes it funny, or not?
7. What is the significance of the references to Spain, people's army, General Doolittle and the carrier?
8. Is Bernstein fair to the lady? Give examples.
9. What is the meaning of *intrepid, enchantée, rear blister?*
10. Write a theme about your pet peeve; or write a theme about an incident or several incidents, the chief purpose of which is to characterize a person.

* * *

Intelligent people generally, not merely language specialists, find the subject of language fascinating. The following selections should prove the point, dealing as they do with six of the infinite variations of the subject, like . . .

1. SLANG AND TRADE JARGON——

NEW AMERICAN LANGUAGE
by *John Crosby*

MY FRIEND, Jim Mainwaring, and I were kicking it around the other day, just seeing how far we could go.

"Television," said Jim, "is pricing itself out of the market."

Copyright 1952, The New York Herald Tribune, Inc.

That's as good as any to start with—an ad-agency truism that has seen good service and yet is as up to date as Variety, where it was kicked around plenty thoroughly last week.

"You mean, money-wise, the whole picture has changed?" I inquired.

"You're tuned in on my antenna," said Jim, who knows every agency cliche in the book. "Only it's not money-wise this season. It's dollar-wise."

"Dollar-wise, then, the whole picture has changed."

"Dollar-wise and agency-wise and copy-wise and talent-wise," said Jim, warming to his task, "television is pricing itself out of the market."

"How do you know?" I asked him. "The precincts aren't all in. You're sitting around Ad Alley thinking that outside New York it's all Jersey. You gotta check the trade and get out in the field. Or else you're talking to yourself. You're not tuned in on my antenna."

"You mean, it doesn't jell with you?" asked Jim.

"I mean I won't buy it."

"Well then," said Jim, who is an expert at the Machiavellian maneuver. "Well then, let's spin the compass and see where we're at."

Right away, I saw what he was up to. And he was.

"The ball's in your court now," said Jim firmly.

I toyed with it a while, not knowing whether to run with it or kick.

"Let's start from the top," I said cautiously. "If television is pricing itself out of the market, then the big play goes back to radio."

"It figures."

"It figures?" This is high praise from Jim. "You mean I'm tuned in on your antenna?"

"Well," said Jim cautiously, "not quite. Let's take this ball of wax and motherhen it. Let's woodshed it. Let's iron the bugs out of it."

The ball was back in his court now.

"Okay," I said, "let's do all of those things. Let's think on our feet, shall we? Let's put wheels on it."

"Well," said Jim, venting a new expression that doesn't

quite know its way around yet. "I'm allowed one crazy idea a month and this is it. If you'll just let me run off at the mouth a bit."

"Go ahead, big boy, fill me in."

"Well, I was talking to a guy on a plane from Cincinnati —I realize this is just a one-man survey—and he updated me on a couple of gimmicks he's got on the hopper."

"New wrinkles on his pitch, eh?"

"Yeah, but he hasn't quite cleared it with the top brass. So I hope you're soundproof."

"I'm deaf and dumb. Update me, big boy."

Jim lowered his voice to a whisper. "He says dollar-wise the Big Act has got to go co-op. That's straight from the upper echelons. Of course, plans haven't been finalized yet."

"You mean they haven't covered all the bases?"

"No, but he's trying to get the client to firm up. It's just possible he may put the wrap-up on it next week. You think it figures?"

"Well, I can only call 'em as I see 'em and I'd like to have the research department dig out the facts and take a good look at the numbers before I make a firm commitment but— just thinking on my feet here—I'd say it comes off, though not perhaps from every angle or when the over-all picture is considered."

"Good boy," said Jim with admiration. "That's one of the most beautiful qualified statements I ever heard. You really hit me where I live."

SUGGESTIONS FOR STUDY:

1. What is Crosby's purpose?
2. Do Crosby and Mainwaring get anywhere in this conversation?
3. What occupations besides television contribute terms to this new American language?
4. Is the selection easy to read? Why?

136 *Current Prose*

∎∎∎∎∎∎∎∎∎∎∎

2. LEARNED WORDS——

THE ACID TEST
by Roscoe Fleming

A PLUMBER once wrote the United States Bureau of Reclamation that he had found hydrochloric acid good for cleaning out pipes.

Someone in the bureau wrote back: "The efficacy of hydrochloric acid is indisputable, but the corrosive residue is incompatible with metallic permanence."

The plumber replied that he was glad the bureau agreed with him. The bureau came back:

"We cannot assume responsibility for the production of toxic and noxious residue with hydrochloric acid, and suggest you adopt an alternative procedure."

The plumber wrote back that he was still glad to know the bureau thought his plan O.K.

In desperation the government man finally broke down and wrote:

"DON'T use hydrochloric acid. It eats the inside out of the pipes."

Incidents like this helped to initiate a movement for simplifying the language used by governmental officials.

Chief Engineer Leslie N. McClellan of the Reclamation Bureau led this campaign. He began by putting into more un-

∎∎∎∎∎∎∎∎∎∎∎∎∎∎∎∎∎∎
Reprinted from The Christian Science Monitor, November 23, 1951.

derstandable language the English used by bureau employees and officials, which he found to be ponderous, stilted, and overtechnical.

"Suggestion sheets" containing examples of awkward-letter-writing and advice about simplifying it have been sent around bureau offices here since 1950.

This simple program saves time and money for the government and increases the respect its correspondents feel for it.

Authors of the "sheets" say letters can usually be trimmed by one-third to 60 per cent, and do their job better.

Answering technical letters has become a big chore in itself, since hundreds are received monthly from all parts of the world. The chief engineer's office is now recognized as one of the world centers of engineering information and research. The writers ask this question:

"What would you think if a man you had invited to lunch called back and said:

" 'Reference is made to your recent phone call, the contents of which have been duly noted. Please be advised that the recipient of your kind invitation is otherwise occupied for lunch on the day mentioned. It is suggested, however, that you invite the speaker to lunch again at some future time.' "

The writers also say that some letters to the government likewise err on the side of "gobbledygook" and confusion. Their advice can be summed up: "Be simple. Be clear. Be candid. Go on to the end and stop. Think through what you want to say before you start writing."

SUGGESTIONS FOR STUDY:

1. What difference in word length do you find between the first two government letters and the third?
2. Is there a further difference between "the production of toxic and noxious residue with hydrochloric acid" and "It eats the inside out of the pipes"?
3. Does this difference suggest that *toxic, noxious, residue* may be used appropriately in other contexts and for a different reader?

3. NATIONAL DIALECTS——

AMERICAN ENGLISH
by Ivor Brown

THERE is no such thing as the American Language any more than there is such a thing as the English Language. There are half a dozen species of each and some of them are more or less identical. I have, for example, just been reading through some editorials in *The New York Times* and *The London Times*. As far as style and vocabulary are concerned you could slip the writing of one into the columns of the other without anybody noticing any difference in their excellence.

There is, indeed, in the case of these two countries, a unified, editorial-writer's language, which has its own formalities on both sides of the ocean. For example, both in Times Square and in Printing House Square the builders of opinion are apt to observe that "It is incumbent on us all" or "To vote is an obligation and privilege of citizenship." Yet nobody supposes that when they are setting out in the afternoon to write their evening pieces of grave counsel for the morrow they say, on parting from the ever-loving wife, "It is an obligation and privilege to ask the Simpsons back to dinner and it is incumbent on you to see that the dinner is a good one."

I am not decrying the formalities. It is a particular pleasure to a conservative Englishman to discover how much of

Reprinted from The New York Times Book Review, May 4, 1952.

his language's old leisured stateliness has been preserved in America. The "gotten" of U.S.A. is still preferred by an Englishman of literary taste to the snappy English "got," and all lovers of the eighteenth century and its classical elevation of style must like to hear of an elevator operated and not of a lift worked; there is more distinction in the aloofness of an apartment than in the levelness of the curt, undignified flat.

Shakespeare and Milton, if their shades revisited a Hollywood film, might recognize many words which were the English of their time and some of which have been lost. Christopher Morley has reminded me that Shakespeare wrote of a "deck" of cards and not of a pack. Milton's use of "homely" is preserved in America, having changed its meaning in England, and he would have called a sidewalk just that, whereas this simple and precisely explanatory term has been lost by the English, who use the vague "pavement" instead. So it is pleasant for one who has had pleasant hours among the minds of the seventeenth century to meet their vocabulary still alive in another continent.

Where the languages might naturally fall apart is in their slang; but are they so far sundered? The Englishman who cannot grasp and enjoy the vivacity and pungency and metaphorical richness of the various American slangs is either a prig or a fool. In his introduction to a collection of Damon Runyon stories, which shares place of honor with the Sherlock Holmes collection at my bedside, E. C. Bentley has very properly denounced the feeble English habit of asking for glossaries of American slang. Good American speech of the people declares its meaning by its force and picturesqueness of imagery and he who cannot understand it must, in my view as well as Bentley's and in Runyon's idiom, be such a guy as is more than somewhat dumb.

There may be some words spoken at Lindy's that are strange to our eyes and ears, but Runyon is ready to explain them. Fink, for example. Joe the Blow Fly is a fink, a fink being "such a guy as is extra nothing"—and also "a character who is lower than a mud-cat's vest pocket." Yet even in my Runyon I find, among the conversations of such as Hot-Horse Herbie and Regret the Horseplayer the use of dast for darest; and that at once sets the bells of the seventeenth century ringing in the ears, just as such a grave, admonitory name as Regret reminds one of the old moralists. Here Runyon and Bunyan commingle.

Few in England would now call a hammer a "mawl," yet this old word for the mallet used in the game of Pall Mall (and so giving London one of its most august street names) turns up when Rusty Charley enters Nathan Detroit's crap-game. The players "are packed so close you cannot get a needle between two guys with a mawl."

The formal and the fresh, the classic cadence and the invention of the last minute—America retains them so fondly and creates so fruitfully. At one time the American language is still strolling with the silken ladies of Pomander Walk; at another it is the utterance of guys and dolls. Guys? Yes, they are older than Guy Fawkes and one stalks majestic in Scottish Dunbar's famous praise of London. Of London's Lord Mayor that fifteenth-century balladist wrote that "No Lord of Parys, Venyce, or Floraunce" was the equal in dignity of this civic "exampler, lode-star, and guye." Great guy indeed!

Guys and dolls, not to mention molls, are familiar in American fiction and "musicals." Yet here is the guye in the London of Henry VII, while Doll or Doll-Common was Ben Jonson's name for a woman of the town and Molls or Moll-Commons were of the same low company in that high period of comedy. Incidentally, Ben Jonson used "beat it" for go. Continually the lingo of new Broadway is linked with that of old Bankside. How can any word-lover resist such a language?

SUGGESTIONS FOR STUDY:

1. Does the author recognize a formal and an informal tone in language on both sides of the Atlantic?
2. Are you inclined to think of American English as less snappy, more classically elevated than British English? Are Brown's examples to the point?
3. Can you add to the list of archaisms preserved in America?
4. What does the author mean by "Here Runyon and Bunyan commingle"?

4. LOCAL DIALECTS——

MAINE SPEECH
by E. B. White

I FIND that, whether I will or no, my speech is gradually changing, to conform to the language of the country. The tongue spoken here in Maine is as different from the tongue spoken in New York as Dutch is from German. Part of this difference is in the meaning of words, part in the pronunciation, part in the grammar. But the difference is very great. Sometimes when a child is talking it is all one can do to translate until one has mastered the language. Our boy came home from school the first day and said the school was peachy but he couldn't understand what anybody was saying. This lasted only a couple of days.

For the word "all" you use the phrase "the whole of." You ask, "Is that the whole of it?" And whole is pronounced hull. Is that the hull of it? It sounds as though you might mean a ship.

For lift, the word is heft. You heft a thing to see how much it weighs. When you are holding a wedge for somebody to tap with a hammer, you say: "Tunk it a little." I've never heard the word tap used. It is always tunk.

Baster (pronounced bayster) is a popular word with boys. All the kids use it. He's an old baster, they say, when they pull an eel out of an eel trap. It probably derives from

From *One Man's Meat* by E. B. White. Copyright, 1940, by E. B. White. Reprinted by permission of Harper & Brothers.

bastard, but it sounds quite proper and innocent when you hear it, and rather descriptive. I regard lots of things now (and some people) as old basters.

A person who is sensitive to cold is spleeny. We have never put a heater in our car, for fear we might get spleeny. When a pasture is sparse and isn't providing enough feed for the stock, you say the pasture is pretty snug. And a man who walks and talks slowly or lazily is called mod'rate. He's a powerful mod'rate man, you say.

When you're prying something with a pole and put a rock under the pole as a fulcrum, the rock is called a bait. Few people use the word "difference." When they want to say it makes no difference, they say it doesn't make any odds.

If you have enough wood for winter but not enough to carry you beyond that, you need wood "to spring out on." And when a ewe shows an udder, she "bags out." Ewe is pronounced yo.

This ewe and yo business had me licked at first. It seemed an affectation to say yo when I was talking about a female sheep. But that was when I was still thinking of them as yews. After a while I thought of them as yos, and then it seemed perfectly all right. In fact, yo is a better-sounding word, all in all, than yew. For a while I tried to pronounce it half way between yew and yo. This proved fatal. A man has to make up his mind and then go boldly ahead. A ewe can't stand an umlaut any more than she can a terrier.

Hunting or shooting is called gunning. Tamarack is always hackmatack. Tackle is pronounced taykle. You rig a block and taykle.

If one of your sheep is tamer than the others, and the others follow her, you say she will "toll" the others in. The chopped clams which you spread upon the waters to keep the mackerel schooling around your boat, are called toll bait. Or chum bait. A windy day is a "rough" day, whether you are on land or sea. Mild weather is "soft." And there is a distinction between weather overhead and weather underfoot. Lots of times, in spring when the ground is muddy, you will have a "nice day overhead."

Manure is always dressing, never manure. I think, although I'm not sure, that manure is considered a nasty word, not fit for polite company. The word dung is used some but not as much as dressing. But a manure fork is always a dung fork.

Wood that hasn't properly seasoned is dozy. The lunch hour is one's nooning. A small cove full of mud and eelgrass is a gunkhole. When a pullet slips off and lays in the blackberry bushes she "steals away a nest." If you get through the winter without dying or starving you "wintered well."

Persons who are not native to this locality are "from away." We are from away ourselves, and always shall be, even if we live here the rest of our lives. You've got to be born here—otherwise you're from away.

People get born, but lambs and calves get dropped. This is literally true of course. The lamb actually does get dropped. (It doesn't hurt it any—or at any rate it never complains.) When a sow has little ones, she "pigs." Mine pigged on a Sunday morning, the ol' baster.

The road is often called "the tar." And road is pronounced rud. The other day I heard someone call President Roosevelt a "war mongrel." Statute is called statue. Lawyers are busy studying the statues. Library is liberry. Chimney is chimley.

Fish weir is pronounced fish ware. Right now they're not getting anything in the wares.

Hoist is pronounced hist. I heard a tall story the other day about a man who was histed up on the end of a derrick boom while his companions accused him of making free with another man's wife. "Come on, confess!" they shouted. "Isn't it true you went with her all last year?" For a while he swung at the end of the boom and denied the charges. But he got tired finally. "You did, didn't you?" they persisted. "Well, once, boys," he replied. "Now hist me down."

The most difficult sound is the "a." I've been in Maine, off and on, all my life, but I still have to pause sometimes when somebody asks me something with an "a" in it. The other day a friend met me in front of the store, and asked, "How's the famine comin' along?" I had to think fast before I got the word "farming" out of his famine.

The word dear is pronounced dee-ah. Yet the word deer is pronounced deer. All children are called dee-ah, by men and women alike.

The final "y" of a word becomes "ay." Our boy used to call our dog Freddie. Now he calls him Fredday. Sometimes he calls him Fredday dee-ah; other times he calls him Fredday you ol' baster.

Country talk is alive and accurate, and contains more pictures and images than city talk. It usually has an unmistakable sincerity which gives it distinction. I think there is less talking merely for the sound which it makes. At any rate, I seldom tire listening to even the most commonplace stuff, directly and sincerely spoken; and I still recall with dread the feeling that occasionally used to come over me at parties in town when the air was crowded with loud intellectual formations—the feeling that there wasn't a remark in the room that couldn't be brought down with a common pin.

....

BUT ME NO SHOULDER BUTTS
by H. I. B.

FROM REPORTS in our favorite newspaper about an English family, plus dog, that recently came to the United States, it would seem that the family is having more trouble than the dog in understanding English as Americans understand it.

But it should be pointed out that one doesn't have to cross the ocean to have one's English misunderstood. One can be thoroughly misunderstood within the boundaries of one's own state.

....

Reprinted from The Christian Science Monitor, June 28, 1952.

But Me No Shoulder Butts

Take the case of that succulent bit of smoked, boneless pork which is so delicious when boiled gently with green beans or cabbage. In our family, it was always known as smoked neck, and any butcher in the City of Brotherly Love knew what you wanted when you asked for it.

But, alas, we moved to a little town in the coal regions. The long hard winter brought the butcher out in a sleigh; thrice weekly the merry tinkle of a cowbell announced his approach. He served us well, we got on famously together, but he had never heard of a smoked neck.

As winter thawed toward spring, we were getting increasingly hungry for a good dish of smoked neck with beans, and one day went up into the heart of town to see what could be done about it.

Ah! a strange butcher; but the meat looked familiar. We asked about it. He shook his head. We didn't understand. There in the case was a beautiful smoked neck, about 2½ pounds, just the right size and not too fatty. Wasn't it for sale? He still shook his head.

Now we had been taught as a child never to point at anything. But these were extenuating circumstances and we were desperate. We pointed. The butcher laughed indulgently, "Oh, you mean a nugget." We agreed, weakly.

That smoked neck-nugget was one of the most delicious we've ever tasted. But then we were transferred to the capital of the state, and we soon found that if we expected to enjoy the same tender, tasty bit of pork in that city, we would have to ask for a boneless butt. Now, when is a "neck" a "butt"? Never, according to the dictionary. We had yet to learn, however.

One day last summer we were cooking a smoked neck-nugget-boneless butt and our neighbor remarked, "Something smells awfully good, what are you cooking?"

Remembering that she came from upstate, we answered confidently, "A nugget."

A look of perplexity stole over her usually placid face as she took a long sniff. She was invited in for a longer sniff and a peep into the white enameled cooking pot. "Oh, a pork daisy," she laughed. "Whatever made you call it a nugget?"

146 *Current Prose*

We explained. If we didn't agree on its name, we did agree on its goodness. She then offered to lend us a page of recipes cut from a magazine describing different ways to prepare to serve this particular cut of meat. The article was entitled, "They Call Them Little Hams."

As we said, we are genuinely concerned. With English writers' wives in danger of encountering smoked neck-nugget-boneless butt-pork daisy-little ham-shoulder butts in a butcher's gleaming case, this sort of thing could even strain international relations.

SUGGESTION FOR STUDY:

Can you cite other geographical variations of terms for objects and actions such as these two essays illustrate? A little investigation among friends from other parts of the country should reveal many, both in their speech and in yours.

....

5. SPELLING——

FONY AND FANTOM
by William Chapman White

THIS LOVELY month of June, when the flox is in the garden and the foebe in the tree, is marred for eleven-year-olds by one thing, the final exams in spelling. The minute they are over the pupils should hurry down to Mr. E. V. Kraus in New Brunswick, N. J., and wish him good luck. If he has his way June, some day, will be pleasanter for all those

....

Copyright 1952, The New York Herald Tribune, Inc.

who face the fenomena of English spelling. Mr. Kraus is the guiding spirit behind The Reformed Spelling Society, Inc.

He is a retired merchant, now eighty-two. In early life he had an experience that few of us have had. Coming here from Czechoslovakia in 1887, he ran headlong into the English language and had to learn it as a grown-up. Somehow he mastered the intricacies of "dough, through, bough, cough," "loose, truce, juice, deuce," "physical, fiscal" and the many other idiocies of English spelling. Mr. Kraus began at once to do something about them. Back in the 'nineties he talked spelling reform to any one who would listen and even interested Teddy Roosevelt, who tried for a while to do something about it. Eventually Mr. Kraus got his society going and set up a program.

Many people besides Teddy Roosevelt and Bernard Shaw have tried to make sense in English spelling. One change after another has been suggested but all of them ran into hostility from some purists and inertia from almost every one else. Many of the programs for reformed spelling have been too complex to introduce in one piece and have usually set supporters to arguing what to reform instead of how to bring about any reform. Melville Dewey, of the Dewey classification system used in libraries, carried simplified spelling to such a complicated point that even his followers stopped following.

Mr. Kraus has a different idea. He wants to reform English spelling a step at a time. When people are accustomed to the first change, the next step will be less difficult to introduce. For the first step, Mr. Kraus emfatically urges every one to toss the old Greek hangover of "ph" for "f" out of the language. It might look odd for a time to see "fysician, flegm, Fillip, Afrodite, fone, filosofy, and fotograf" but they would look no odder than the result of being fonetically logical and changing all "f"s to "ph." As in, "Phiphty-phive Phrench phlags phluttered phreely phrom phiphty-phive phriendly phoreign phrigates Phriday Phebruary Phirst."

When Mr. Kraus felt that people were used to seeing "ph" gone from spelling he would introduce his second step. This would rid English of the "ugh" and "ough" spellings for an assortment of sounds—and a blessing that would be for any one who has to try to teach English spelling to foreigners. The third step would be to throw out the "ch" in "choir, chimera," and similar words and use "k." When these changes and others were firmly established Mr. Kraus would turn to streamlining vowels.

Maybe people will follow where Mr. Kraus leads. Over the years some spelling in common usage has been simplified. "Plough" is now "plow," "draft" stands for "draught." "Thru and thruout" are sometimes acceptable, "altho" is sometimes allowed and even "thoro" for "thorough" may escape the blue pencil.

Among the members of Mr. Kraus' society are some educators, lawyers, clergymen, and even two ex-mayors. In addition he has a large number of instinctive converts among eleven-year-old boys. Quite naturally, many of them write "fonograf, fony, and fantom," not because of any program of The Reformed Spelling Society, Inc., but because that's the way they sound and that's obviously the logical way to spell them. The only trouble with the logic is that, in the final exam, the teacher marks that spelling wrong.

Maybe Mr. Kraus should start a society to reform teachers.

SUGGESTIONS FOR STUDY:

1. Do you agree that English spelling is characterized by many idiocies?
2. Do you approve of or object to the changes Mr. Kraus suggests?
3. Is the reform of teachers a good idea?

HAYWIRE
by John Allan May

ONE of the great advantages of occupying an editorial chair is that you have the most prolific inventors of new words and fancies working for you every day of the week.

In this particular case I am not referring to the correspondents of *The Christian Science Monitor*. I mean specifically the teleprinting machines that are housed in that abode of mystery, the Wire Room, where messages come in from correspondents and agencies the world over. Sometimes, reading messages that have come from the Wire Room, an editor dimly begins to understand the derivation of the word "haywire." These are the times when a machine gets whimsical.

The most common type of haywire goes like this: "Mr. Godfrey Crummidge declared, 'The whole affair can best be described as G739&%¾z!.'" In these cases, however, the machine is not really trying, and a good wire operator can defeat its machinations by quickly translating the jumble back into daytime English. He will send a message through, "For G739-&%¾z! in line five read unfortunate," and the bubble of wonder bursts and vanishes.

I was delighted, however, the other day when one of our machines scored a resounding victory. A message from London clattered its way frantically into the office, and in the middle of it was the following remarkable sentence: "This is the first evidence of the required new sense of ujlibility."

Ujlibility! There is a fine new word for you. I was enthralled as I read further. The operators had interrupted the

Reprinted from The Christian Science Monitor, June 20, 1952.

cable to hold a conversation by teleprinter, and there it was in type. It went like this:

What is ujlibility in first line paragraph four?

Have no idea. . . . They will probably send a correction. If not we will get one from them in time for first edition. They have tieline troble.

They had indeed. Plenty troble, I should say. And nobody sent a correction. (The reader will notice the splendid economy with which the teleprinter clinched its success with the introduction of the final word "troble.")

In this case, after due consideration, I decided to use stability instead of ujlibility. It seemed to fit almost as well. But an even more difficult word came through shortly afterward. It was "oylsslucoations." With this one it was necessary to concede utter defeat.

At other times the teleprinters hit on misprints that seem delightfully appropriate, like a reference I have beside me to "Joint labor management beards." One can just see the picture. It might be the 12,659th meeting of a steel committee. Or maybe the result of a presidential decision to seize the barbering industry.

Another example that pleased me was the statement, "Students demanded a vhoice in the proceedings." These were Irish students. And a sturdy Scottish ring was given to a message that read, "Mconfidence is returning." While the tang of Welsh mists swirled in the description of a certain British socialist group as "Aneurin Bevan and his fogovbers."

But occasionally one receives a complete story that is straight out of the world of Lewis Carroll. I shall always treasure this haywire:

"Winsoon Churchill addressing 3000 housewivzy at Silver jububilee meeting of women's advisory commiotee of canservative party made an impassioned plea for more time. His plea followed local elections wherein socialists secured resounding vcitory at pogls. 'Eeven if we had wisdom of Solomon and power thaos never been wizled by moroals,' Churchill said, 'you cannot chaneg in a few months evigs that have been gorzing for years.'"

Of course you can't.

SUGGESTIONS FOR STUDY:

1. Do you find the sketch amusing?
2. Can you name another professional group who sometimes find dull chores enlivened by egregious misspellings?

....

6. MEANING——

RETROACTIVE WEATHER
by John Crosby

GOT ANOTHER little note on popular education. That tireless investigator of other people's business, Allen Funt, took his "Candid Camera" and his concealed microphone out the other day to find out how many people knew what the word *retroactive* meant. He walked up to an elevator starter and declared belligerently: "Listen, I think you ought to know that the last elevator on the right side is retroactive."

"Gee," said the starter, "haven't heard any complaints from the elevator man."

"It's dangerous."

"Gee, we'll have to look into it. You think it's very dangerous?"

"It certainly is dangerous. You can get into all kinds of trouble with that."

Mr. Funt then wandered out, smiling his sadistic smile,
....
Copyright 1950, The New York Herald Tribune, Inc.

and accosted a young lady at a soda fountain. "Boy," he exclaimed, "isn't this weather retroactive, though." She agreed heartily that it was.

"Most retroactive day we've had," said Funt.

"Yes," said the girl. "Terrible."

"You know what retroactive weather is, don't you?" asked Funt.

"Very hot without stopping," said the girl firmly.

The next victim was a gentleman window shopping. "Hey, buddy," said Funt grimly. "If I were you I wouldn't go into that store."

"Why not?"

"Those people in there, they're very retroactive . . . I mean if a store is retroactive, the least you can do is pass 'em by."

"Well," said the man uncertainly, "as long as you insist."

"I don't insist. It's just my advice. Would you—do you—ever go into stores that are retroactive?"

"Well, I've taken chances before."

SUGGESTIONS FOR STUDY:

1. What does *retroactive* mean?
2. Is this episode convincing? Do you believe it really happened?

"WHEN YOUR MOTHER IS HUNG"
by Catherine Drinker Bowen

AND ON the steps of Montgomery Place a small boy sat under an iron trellis and watched the world go by. One afternoon the butcher's boy stopped to talk. This was complimentary; the butcher's boy was big, and occupied with great businesses. Preparing at last to move on to regions of his own the butcher's boy made his salute. "Good-bye!" he said genially. "See you when your mother is hung."

Wendell Holmes sat frozen, glued to the steps. Why had they not told him? *When* would she be hanged? At sunrise? He had heard they did it at sunrise. Going inside, Wendell sought his mother, looked at her mutely. . . . At supper nobody talked of hanging. Wendell went up to bed; his mother came and kissed him goodnight, heard his prayers. When she was gone he lay trembling. Downstairs on his mother's desk lay the new album she had given him for stamps. She had promised to help label the rarest ones. They were going to do it the first thing in the morning.

See you when your mother is hung . . . when your mother is hung. . . .

Wendell fell asleep. In the morning when he woke, the sun was shining; downstairs he heard his mother's voice.

Why, the butcher boy lied! The butcher boy was joking! Sitting on the side of his bed, hearing from below the blessed, familiar sounds of morning, Wendell's breath came deep with relief.

From *Yankee on Olympus*, by Catherine Drinker Bowen, by permission of Little, Brown, & Company and the Atlantic Monthly Press.

154   Current Prose

Springing to his feet, he threw on his clothes and clattered joyfully down the stairs to breakfast.

SUGGESTIONS FOR STUDY:

1. What is the basis of the six-year-old Wendell Holmes' misunderstanding?
2. Have you read Ring Lardner's "Haircut" or any other story that depends for its point on a literal interpretation of words not so intended?
3. Write a theme on some aspect of language, using any of the essays in this group (*New American Language* through *When Your Mother is Hung*) as a model or point of departure. Specify which essay you use.

∎∎∎

Is letter writing a chore? Mr. Shipp believes it should be a pleasure, and he has some novel ideas on how to go about it.

HOW TO WRITE A LETTER
by Cameron Shipp

A MAN I know recently scrawled on the back of his bank statement: "We are eating three times a day. How are you?" and mailed it to me.

My family and I were amused by this novel bit of correspondence. Not many of us, of course, have the nerve or the wit to send our bank statement to a friend in place of the letter we have been putting off for weeks, but if this man had

∎∎∎∎∎∎∎∎∎∎∎∎∎∎∎∎∎
Reprinted from The Christian Science Monitor, May 27, 1952, by permission of the Christian Science Monitor and The Reader's Digest.

polished phrases for hours he could not have written a more interesting letter. We spent an evening trying to figure out his income and how he spent his money—which was precisely what he had intended.

Why is it so difficult for us to write a few short words on a small piece of paper? Why is it that a man who can be as interesting as a tax rebate when you meet him in the locker room of your golf club becomes as inarticulate as a fish the moment he takes pen in hand? And why does the brightest, friendliest woman you know, always the life of the party, swear she'd prefer to plow fields or slave in salt mines rather than write a letter? Why do you hate to write letters?

It's important to write them. There is no surer, more satisfactory way of making or of holding friendships than by the easy, inexpensive fun of putting a few sentences on paper. Yet few of us regard letter writing as anything except drudgery.

I think I know why. We have been taught that letter writing is a formal sort of thing, like drawing up one's will. We have been taught that letters must be written on proper, expensive paper, with stately salutations and false-modest endings. We have been made to feel that the document—even to old friends or relatives—has to be a society gesture, else the person who receives it will conclude that we don't know the rules of polite social intercourse.

All this is ridiculous, especially in a country which prides itself on informality. But they are true reasons. And there are two other main reasons, I believe, why we shudder at the thought of writing a letter. They are:

I can't think of anything to say, and

Who stole my pen?

These are as nonsensical as the first set of inhibitions, and all of them have been disposed of long ago by straight-thinking persons. Consider the instance of Richard Armour. Armour heads a department at Scripps College; he is also one of our most prolific writers of light verse; a colonel in the reserves who drills one night every week; a lecturer in cities far from home. Busy man, obviously. Yet he is a faithful, constant correspondent who turns out an average of a dozen written messages a day to friends and business acquaintances.

I said "written messages," because Armour seldom writes letters. He has discovered the twopenny post card. He knows he seldom has anything to say that can't be put in less than the 100 words of typing a post card will hold, and he generally stays within 20 words. No salutation or closing. Just something like this:

"Good to see you last week. Kathleen and I leaving for San Francisco tomorrow. Agent likes my new book. Call you Monday when we return. Dick."

Nothing unusual about it. No attempt at wit. No literary pretensions. Just 25 words typed on a post card, but how effective! He recalled a pleasant meeting, gave me two pieces of news, made an appointment. Most important, he kept in touch, let me know he had me in mind. This cost Armour two cents in money and perhaps one minute of time. If he can get away with this sort of thing, why not you?

Matter of fact, you can go him one better. Air-mail post cards cost only four cents. One hundred words delivered anywhere in the United States the next day for less than a nickel is the best bargain I know. If you want to, you can personalize the cards by having your name and address printed in one chaste line across the top, as Armour does.

The most famous letter writer in America today is the novelist and humorist Homer Croy. It was he who sent me his bank statement. He usually writes on odd bits of stationery picked up in odd corners of the world. His letters seldom run more than a dozen words.

Homer realizes one of the fundamental weaknesses of human character—the desire to look over someone else's shoulder or to peek into someone else's business. He types or scrawls his lines on the backs of letters that people have written to him. A recent example: "Cam—I saw Dale yesterday and we mentioned your name. Favorably, too. H. C."

That was all. He had seen an old friend, and they had talked about me. This casual, unnewsworthy hail came across the continent and bound me to Homer Croy with hoops of steel. He did it with 12 words.

I turned the letter over. There was a note from a magazine editor accepting a story Croy had written. Mentioned the price, too. I was in on something I had no business knowing. Croy had let me look over his shoulder. Anybody can do the same. My Aunt Margaret in North Carolina once did.

She sent me a receipted bill for her new hat, which had cost $28.75. On the reverse side Aunt Margaret wrote an eloquent letter:

"Whee!" she said.

How much more exciting that one word than eight or nine pages about Aunt Margaret's recalcitrant tulips or her reasons for not having written sooner!

Croy has other tricks in his bag besides letting someone else write a letter for him. He is a newspaper clipper. My name seldom appears in newspapers, but if it does and Croy sees it he clips and mails it to me, often pasting it on a post card. But he is more likely to send along something about my home state, North Carolina; about fruit trees, in which I once had a disastrously expensive interest, or anything at all. It takes a little time and it's surely one of the happiest ways to get around writing a letter.

Business letters are a special department, and a big one. I am told that experts are making great strides in cleaning up the correspondence of many corporations, eliminating the hackneyed "Yours of the 15th instant received and contents noted" kind of thing. There is even a movement afoot to delete the absurd "dear" in front of people's names.

Why, indeed, call a man "dear" when you are about to complain that his company has been negligent with your order of an electric refrigerator? The absurd, insincere "dear" will be with us a while, but it is a hopeful sign that at least a few sharp persons are eliminating it. The trend in all business correspondence today is toward informality. We have come a long way forward since Grandfather was everybody's respectful, "ob't s'vt."

Once I got a job through a one-word letter. I had called several times on the late W. C. Dowd, Jr., publisher of the *Charlotte News*, but he had no opening. Three months later, from another city, I wrote him a letter. It said:

"Dear Mr. Dowd:

"Yes?"
"Sincerely,
"Cameron Shipp."

Mr. Dowd hired me, apparently believing that brevity might be a good thing in a reporter.

There's not very much more that anybody can say.

To sum it all up, here are a few simple rules about letter writing:

1. Be brief.

2. Offer a piece of news, or enclose something, such as a clipping, that will be of interest to your friend.

3. Don't try to show off your literary abilities. The real literary people never write literarily.

4. Forget the book of etiquette. Be informal, spontaneous, even unconventional. Be funny if you can, but don't try too hard.

5. Write at least a few lines every day. Start now. There's always a pencil in the house. (There's no law requiring you to use pen and ink.)

6. Use post cards liberally. The four-cent air-mail card is the greatest advance in cheap communication since the smoke signal.

Now, get going! There's no excuse, what with post cards for people in a hurry, tom-toms for Africans, pens that write under water for mermaids, a dictionary full of short words for writing to short people, and a lot of tall words to use if she is taller than you. Writing letters can be fun!

SUGGESTIONS FOR STUDY:

1. What is the purpose of the first paragraph?
2. Is the organization of the essay compact or loose? Explain.
3. Does this organization fit the tone of the essay, as indicated by some of the diction?
4. Do the rather frequent sentence fragments fit this tone?
5. What distinctive method does Shipp use in paragraphs 3 and 4?
6. Does the introduction of personal references and Aunt Margaret increase the appeal of the essay?
7. Does the essay suggest the importance of a writer's need to adapt his writing to his reader?

8. What is the meaning of *inhibitions, recalcitrant tulips, hackneyed?*
9. Write a personal letter, giving it some of the appeal indicated in the examples in this essay.

∙∙∙

The pleasures of research depend on an inquiring mind. Here a writer possessed with the necessary curiosity recounts how it confined him to the first 21 pages of the front matter of a 3300 page unabridged dictionary.

AN ENTIRELY NEW BOOK
by E. J. Kahn, Jr.

THE 1945 PRINTING of the second edition of Webster's New International Dictionary (G. & C. Merriam Co., Springfield, Massachusetts) is a volume much prized by booklovers. It has such an extraordinary appeal that a few months ago, when a bibliophilic scoundrel broke into the display window of a local bookstore, the only book he chose to take, of the dozens within his grasp, was a New International Dictionary, which must have been the most difficult of the lot to haul away. My mother, who had been trying to buy the book for me, shortly thereafter did, by honorable means, get hold of a copy. It is a handsome work, printed on India paper, bound in rich brown leather stamped in gilt, and bearing on its title page the announcement "An entirely new book utilizing all the experience and resources of more than one hundred years of genuine Webster dictionaries." You can

∙∙∙∙∙∙∙∙∙∙∙∙∙∙∙∙∙∙

Reprinted by permission. Copyright 1946, The New Yorker Magazine, Inc.

imagine with what happiness I welcomed it into my library.

I had expected to do considerable browsing through the dictionary's pages, but I have read practically none of its 3,210 Arabic-numbered pages, and in the preceding cxii Roman-numbered ones, I have not yet browsed beyond page xxi. I got stuck there. At the bottom of that page, I came across this editorial note: "The following persons, committees, and business firms are a few among the many who have co-operated by furnishing information of great value. For their co-operation the Publishers herewith express their grateful acknowledgment." Then came this list:

Baldwin Locomotive Works
  Philadelphia, Penn.
Bethlehem Shipbuilding Corp.
  New York, N.Y.
Brook Brothers
  Madison Ave., New York, N.Y.
Porter B. Chase, Adjutant General
  State House, Boston, Mass.
Columbia Phonograph Co.
  Bridgeport, Conn. (Factory) &
  New York, N.Y. (Office)
Committee on Publication of The First Church of Christ, Scientist
  (Clifford P. Smith)
  Boston, Mass.
Mr. William P. Cutter
  Asst. Librarian, Baker Library, Harvard University
  Graduate School of Business Administration
  Cambridge, Mass.
Fairbanks, Morse & Co.
  Three Rivers, Mich.
Habicht, Braun & Co.
  New York, N.Y.
Hart, Schaffner & Marx
  New York, N.Y.
J. Lichtman & Co.
  Newark, N. J.
Miehle Printing Press & Mfg. Co.
  Chicago, Ill.
National Paper Box Mfrs. Assoc.
  Philadelphia, Penn.

An Entirely New Book

National Spiritual Assembly of the Bahá'ís
  New York, N.Y.
Westinghouse Electric & Mfg. Co.
  East Pittsburgh, Penn.

What a peculiar bunch, I thought, to be singled out for special credit from among the thousands of sources the publishers of the dictionary must have had occasion to consult. I reread the names, slowly: "Brook Brothers, Madison Ave., New York, N.Y." Hmm. I have a charge account at the famous old men's-clothing store called Brooks Brothers, on Madison Avenue, in New York, but I had never before heard of Brook Brothers. I checked the Manhattan Telephone Directory—no Brook Brothers there, on Madison or any other avenue. Well, perhaps it was a typographical error. But, conceding the unexpected presence of a typographical error in the dictionary, how explain that Brooks and Hart, Schaffner & Marx were both in there? Two men's-clothes firms out of a total of fifteen credits seemed an abnormally high proportion. I looked up a couple of definitions in the body of the volume, to see if men's wear had been overplayed. "Tweed," I found, had been given no more space than "tweak," and "gabardine" ran a poor second to "gabble." To be sure, there was a small illustration of the Ascot tie, which Brooks Brothers have done much to keep alive in the world of fashion, but even that perhaps telltale drawing was overshadowed by a larger one, directly above it, of the ascon, a variety of sponge.

By this time, my curiosity had got much the better of me. I wrote to the G. & C. Merriam Co., explained how proud I was to own the dictionary, and asked if they would mind telling me what information it was that the selected fifteen had supplied to earn them such prominent mention in so distinguished and scholarly a reference work. I received a prompt reply from a lady who identified herself as Secretary to the General Editor. She said:

> The files containing correspondence with the various firms and others about which you inquire have been stored away and it would take considerable time to ferret out the information

you wish. However, the writer may say that she remembers about some of the material furnished by those listed on page xxi. For example: Baldwin Locomotive Works furnished us information about trains; Bethlehem Shipbuilding Corporation about ships; Brook Brothers and Hart, Schaffner & Marx about certain types of men's clothing; Columbia Phonograph Company about their product; Fairbanks, Morse & Co. about scales; and National Spiritual Assembly of the Bahá'ís gave us information about their organization.

Some of this I think I could have guessed myself, but I was surprised by one thing: the Merriam people persisted in referring to "Brook Brothers." Perhaps my assumption that it was a typographical error was wrong. I wrote to the Secretary to the General Editor, thanking her for her kindness and asking if I was right in surmising that she meant "Brooks Brothers" when she said "Brook Brothers." She answered that I was. "As a matter of fact," she wrote, "we noted this error some time ago and notified the printers to correct it in the plates. As we know you realize, it often takes a long time, due to manufacturing processes, before such a change appears in printed books."

Well, that matter had been cleared up. I was still puzzled, however, about the "information of great value" furnished by the fifteen persons, committees, and business firms. Finally, I wrote letters to the big fifteen, using, except in the case of Brooks Brothers, the names and addresses exactly as they appeared on page xxi. I explained that my curiosity had been aroused and that the Merriam Company hadn't been able to satisfy it, and I asked what special contribution they had made to the dictionary. I had eleven replies.

The first answer came, appropriately enough, from the advertising manager of Brooks Brothers, who telephoned me. He said he was afraid that he couldn't tell me about his firm's share in the work, but he was naturally grateful for the dictionary's kind mention. "I can't even guess what it's all about," he said. "If it had happened in the last thirty years, it would have passed across my desk, but I don't remember any dealings with the dictionary people. Maybe they took some catalogue or historical booklet we got up and used it as authority for some of their definitions without letting us know. In our ads, you know, we spell 'woollens' and 'travellers' with two 'l's—a British survival, I think. Perhaps they used us as the authority for that. I didn't even know our name was in the dictionary." I told him as gently as I could that their name was not in the dictionary, that there was merely an approximation of it. "How could that have happened?" he murmured. *"Everybody* knows about Brooks Brothers." Then I asked him to hold the phone while I checked the Webster listings of "woollen" and "traveller." In each case, the single "l" was given preferential listing. I asked him if he knew of any literary connection between Brooks and Hart, Schaffner & Marx. There was a slight pause. "Well, there was that business about the camel's-hair overcoat," he finally said, in a grudging tone. I pressed him for details, and it slowly came out that, in the spring of 1937, *Time* had run a story crediting Hart, Schaffner & Marx with a number of "firsts" in the clothing game—with having established the first "all-wool policy," for instance, in 1900, and with having brought forth the first camel's-hair coat, in 1912. A few weeks later, a fellow from Dumont, New Jersey, was represented in *Time's* "Letters" column by an indignant communication in which he sharply pointed out that Brooks Brothers had had an all-wool policy since about 1815 and had featured a camel's-hair ulster in its 1908 catalogue. I thanked the advertising manager for his news, hung up, and turned back to my dictionary. There was no definition of "all-wool." Alongside a handsome drawing of a Bactrian camel there was a definition of "camel's hair," but there was nothing about who had brought out the first coat made of it.

A moment later, my midmorning mail arrived. On top of the pile was a letter from a Hart, Schaffner & Marx man in Chicago:

> It's evident that something must have passed between G. & C. Merriam Company, Springfield, Massachusetts, and ourselves . . . but despite a diligent search on our part, we are unable to discover from what point in our organization the information they had from us originated. . . . The conclusion we have reached is that whatever correspondence we had with G. & C. Merriam Company took place far enough back that for

space economy reasons our copies of it have been destroyed. However, it occurs to us that one of our items we most likely would have made available in a case of this sort is a booklet we prepared a few seasons ago entitled "Behind the Seams" and on the possibility that it was data from this booklet which prompted the courtesy of our being given special credit we are mailing you a copy of it.

I could hardly wait till "Behind the Seams" arrived, which it did a few days later. It is a handsome, loose-leaf, tab-indexed, opulently colored volume of two hundred and eight pages, a second edition (just like my dictionary) "brought up to date and modernized to fit 1942 conditions." The first edition of "Behind the Seams," published in 1938, had, according to the second edition, been so compelling that extra copies had been requested by "salesmen, buyers, store executives, college professors, heads of big corporations in other industries, university libraries, etc." There was no mention of the G. & C. Merriam Co., but I figured that the dictionary publishers could be included under that "etc.," or that they might have obtained a copy of the book from any one of the ninety or so college professors in the list of the dictionary's Special Editors. I noted with interest that "Behind the Seams" credited Hart, Schaffner & Marx with having been the first clothing manufacturers to adopt an all-wool policy, but it gave 1907 as the date—seven years later than *Time's* date and ninety-two years later than the date the friend of Brooks Brothers claimed for Brooks. The booklet was illustrated with a hunk of raw wool and with swatches of Shetland, twist, sharkskin, flannel, serge, cheviot, crash, basket weave, hopsack weave, covert, and "gaberdine." I was about to start looking some of these up in the dictionary when I remembered that I already knew that the Webster people favored "gabardine" as a spelling. I decided that if G. & C. Merriam and Hart, S. & M. couldn't even get together on a simple word like that there was no point in my probing further into the extent of their relationship.[1]

[1] Anyone who insists on probing further will quickly discover that whereas H.,S.&M. maintain that buttons were first worn by a thirteenth-century English lord, G.&C.M. say that they originated in the thirteenth or fourteenth century, in southern Europe.

An Entirely New Book 165

While I was still exploring "Behind the Seams," a courier arrived with a letter from the sales-promotion manager of Fairbanks, Morse & Co. He wrote:

> As regards our furnishing the Webster's New International Dictionary, published by G. & C. Merriam Company of Springfield, Massachusetts, on data concerning our product, we are of the opinion that we did so, a couple of years ago, but we cannot find anything in our file concerning the matter. . . . To give you a more complete picture of our company, its history, and its part in World War II, I am sending you under separate cover with our compliments a copy of our new company book entitled "Pioneers in Industry."

"Pioneers in Industry" proved to be even more splendid than "Behind the Seams." It is a massive work of a hundred and sixty glossy pages, as large as the pages of my dictionary. "Pioneers" told the full history of Fairbanks, Morse, which manufactures not only scales but many other kinds of machines, including Diesel engines. Among the illustrations were photographs of two parts of such engines—a "blower impeller" and a "nozzle tip"—for neither of which was I able to find a definition in my dictionary. "Pioneers" also contained a quotation from a book about life in America in the eighteen-forties, when people were

> buying cosmoramas and *periphanoscopes* for their children . . . playing battledore and dumb crambo . . . wearing *gros de Naples* and velvet collars . . . drinking sangarees and *timber doodles*, spitting tobacco juice into 1,000,000 spittoons. . . .

I have taken the liberty of italicizing the phrases of this passage that are not mentioned in my dictionary.[2] Clearly, Fairbanks, Morse and G. & C. Merriam are not solidly en rapport.

I had a fairly lively correspondence with Mr. Cecil Lichtman, assistant treasurer of J. Lichtman & Co., of Newark, who turned out to be tanners and leather manufacturers. Mr. Lichtman explained that "we have been unable to locate immediately a 1945 edition of the Webster Dictionary" (a dis-

---

[2] It would perhaps be unfair not to point out that, although "gros de Naples" is missing, the dictionary does list "gros de Londres."

turbing comment on culture in Newark) and asked me to send him the names of the fourteen persons, committees, and business firms honored by Merriam along with his own outfit, in the hope that these might give him a clue. After I had done so, he reported that he still had no idea what the Lichtman contribution was. "It occurred to us," he nevertheless went on, "that they may possibly refer to some assistance that this company gave in the preparation of a book on tanning and leather procedure, and leather terminology. The reference made by Merrian [sic] may or may not refer to this book." He did not offer to send me a copy of it, and I was too proud to ask him for one.

My appeal to the Columbia Phonograph Co. was answered by the executive vice-president of the Columbia Recording Corporation. "No one in the company has any idea as to what the reference in the Webster's Dictionary signifies," he wrote. "I can find no one who has any recollection of any discussion at all with the publishers." I wrote back and asked him how come the Columbia Recording Corporation happened to be answering mail addressed to the Columbia Phonograph Co., the outfit Merriam and I were concerned with. The executive vice-president replied that "the American Record Corporation (Columbia Recording Corporation is the same corporation, simply by change of name) acquired Columbia Phonograph Company, Inc., on July 1, 1934. Columbia Recording Corporation actually absorbed the assets of Columbia Phonograph Company, Inc., on December 28th, 1940, and thereafter dissolved the corporation." No matter which date you take, all this happened a considerable while before my dictionary went to press.

The secretary of the National Paper Box Mfrs. Assoc. reported that he could find no record of any correspondence with the Merriam Company. "It may be, however," he wrote, "that their reference was directed to a series of surveys covering twenty-one industries made for this Association by Moore and Company during 1944 and 1945." Before I quite knew what had happened, these surveys of twenty-one industries, plus four others thrown in for good measure, had landed on my desk, wrapped in a copy of the *Wall Street Journal* and encased in a paper box. Some night next winter, I am going to sit down with a glass of ale and those twenty-five surveys and have a hell of a time.

By now, the mail was pouring in. Clifford P. Smith, it developed, was no longer manager of Committees on Publication of The First Church of Christ, Scientist. (The dictionary calls it "Committee," but the Church, I judged from its letterhead, prefers the plural.) The present manager, a Mr. Kilpatrick, informed me that "Judge Smith, who formerly filled this position, has passed on." Mr. Kilpatrick knew, though, what it was that the Committees had done for the dictionary. Some time before, they had furnished the Merriam Company with "Christian Science definitions of many words that are used in Christian Science with special meanings . . . [and] the phraseology of these definitions, including special capitalization and meaning, as distinguished from that customarily employed." I thanked Mr. Kilpatrick for his help and asked him for a list of some of these words. He sent them along: "atonement," "baptism," "Christ," "Christian Science," "death," "devil," "error," "eucharist," "flesh," "God," "intelligence," "Jesus," "man," "matter," "mind," "miracle," "mortal mind," "principle," "prophet," "resurrection," "salvation," "scientist," "soul," "spirit," and "substance." All these are given Christian Science definitions in my dictionary, and I began to feel better about the book, even though it had misled me about Judge Smith. Here, at least, was a clear-cut case of real coöperation. Then I happened to recall that on page xix the dictionary had, in its "Special Editors" list, given credit to the same Judge Smith for the same definitions. No wonder the book is so heavy.

My next letter gave me additional pause. It was from a Mr. Clark, the assistant librarian of the Baker Library at Harvard, who said that Mr. Cutter, listed by the dictionary as the assistant librarian, had left that post in 1932 and had died in 1935. "Therefore, your query as to his contribution to the Webster Dictionary must remain unanswered," Mr. Clark wrote. Mr. Cutter, he added, had devised a system for the classification of business literature—the only one of its kind—and had been looked upon as a specialist in the field of business terminology. "No doubt, it was through this connection that he made his contribution to the Dictionary," the incumbent said. By this time, my mind was so cluttered with doubts that I was glad to be able to dismiss one of them. No doubt, I repeated to myself reassuringly. Then, with nervous fingers, I proceeded to open a letter from the assistant sales manager of the Miehle Printing Press & Mfg. Co. He said:

> You seem to have brought from the tomb a skeleton which cannot be identified.
> Search and inquiry has been made at this office to ascertain the exact material furnished to publishers of Webster's New International Dictionary. This material was furnished quite a long time ago and without any particular record being made in this office.
> As I recall, it had to do with printing equipment ancient and modern, and the meaning of the terms used in the printing industry, together with illustrations of old and modern presses.

There are more than twelve thousand illustrations in my dictionary, according to the publishers' count, but only two of them, by my count, are of printing presses.

All things considered, I was not one bit surprised when my letter to the Bethlehem Shipbuilding Corp., of New York, N.Y., was answered by the manager of publications of the Bethlehem Steel Company, Inc., of Bethlehem, Pa. He wrote, of his corporation's relations with the dictionary:

> We have frequent requests of this type, and it is not always easy to recall particulars later on. When we contribute major articles and illustrations, as is the case with many handbooks and cyclopedias, it is a different matter.

He added that the dictionary was

> likely referring to some earlier edition for which we may have checked some of the material in our field. . . . Our guess is, that like a large number of firms, outstanding in their field, we have been selected to check and advise on certain pertinent data, and that we have had the good fortune to be one of the few that have been singled out for special mention.

But that was only a guess. It remained for the secretary of the National Spiritual Assembly of the Bahá'ís of the United States and Canada, of Wilmette, Illinois—replying to the letter the dictionary had told me to address to the National Spiritual Assembly of the Bahá'ís in New York—to send me some facts. The secretary wrote:

> I have gone over our records and can give you the following information.
>
> During the month of March, 1928, we had correspondence with the G. & C. Merriam Company in which we pointed out that Webster's New International Dictionary gave an erroneous impression of the Baha'i faith in its definition of Babism and Baha'i.
>
> We sent literature giving them sources of correct information, for which we received their courteous thanks. The fact that this correspondence took place some eighteen years ago is obviously the reason why the Merriam Company is not able at present to give you these simple details.

It appeared, then, that the "information of great value" furnished by the Bahá'ís for my dictionary had been merely a letter of protest about a mistake in an earlier edition, sent in 1928.[3] And what was all this from Bethlehem Steel about "some earlier edition"? I went over to the Public Library, found a 1934 printing of my dictionary, and turned to page xxi. There was the same editorial note of gratitude, the same list of fifteen, the same missing final "s" on Brooks Brothers. I began to wonder what sort of entirely new book my mother had palmed off on me. I also began to appreciate the confusion of the people who had received my letters of inquiry, and I began to understand why four of those letters had not been answered. I sat down and wrote a cross note to the Secretary to the General Editor. I did not ask her all the questions that

[3] Despite this ancient plea of the Bahá'ís for accuracy, neither they nor the Merriam Company seem to be able to make up their minds about the acute-accented vowels. The Bahá'ís' secretary ignored these accents in the body of his letter, though they appeared several times in his letterhead. The dictionary ignores the accents on page xxi, and then, on page 204, in defining "Bahai," omits not only the accents but also the apostrophe which it used on page xxi.

170 *Current Prose*

were running through my head. Why, for instance, was the late Mr. Cutter still listed as holding a job he had left two years before the 1934 printing came out? Why did the Merriam Company arbitrarily assume that fifteen persons, committees, and business firms would go through an especially trying decade unnicked by the scythe of time? Was it possible that *I* would be listed in some future edition of the dictionary, years after my death, for having called attention to the error in the spelling of Brooks Brothers?[4] As I say, I did not ask the Secretary to the General Editor all these questions. I merely reported on some of my findings and said that I was even more puzzled. "How do you account for all this?" I asked her sternly.

The Secretary to the General Editor did not reply.[5] Instead, I received a letter from a Merriam man who did not give his title but whom I was able to identify, by consulting the dictionary, as one of the four editors who had been engaged in "adjusting and harmonizing the complex material" of the volume and also as the Special Editor in change of Fancy Diving. He said:

> In further reply to your inquiries about certain names mentioned in the front matter of our Webster's New International Dictionary, Second Edition, we are aware that these listings are the same in the 1945 printing as they were in the first printing of the book in 1934. Reference to the copyright of this dictionary will show you that no new copyright has been taken out since 1934 on the part of the book about which you are inquiring. Copyrights later than 1934 are specifically designated as applying to the "New Words Section." This no doubt answers your question.

Huh?[6]

[4] "We noted this error some time ago and notified the printers to correct it in the plates," the Secretary to the General Editor had, you remember, written me, adding that it is often a long time before such changes appear in printed books. It sure is.
[5] I hope nothing has happened to her.
[6] "An exclamation expressing contempt, interrogation, a grunt, etc."
—*Webster's New International Dictionary.*

SUGGESTIONS FOR STUDY:

1. Is Kahn's apparent purpose his real purpose? State both.
2. Do transitional phrases indicate that the parts of the essay are arranged chronologically? For example? Do these parts move toward a climax? How?
3. Do the paragraphs serve as definite units in the essay?
4. Does the sentence in paragraph 2, "I got stuck there," contrast with the other sentences in the paragraph? Effectively?
5. Does Kahn use similar sentences elsewhere? For example?
6. What is the basis of humor in the Brooks Brothers episode?
7. What is the basis of the humor in the sentence, "I began to wonder what sort of entirely new book my mother had palmed off on me"?
8. Is there a difference in tone between footnotes 1 and 5? Does this difference reflect a progressive change in tone throughout the essay?
9. What is the meaning of *bibliophilic, ascon, Bactrian, hopsack weave, periphanoscopes, cyclopedia, acute-accented, huh*?
10. Write a theme, satiric or serious, on a pretentious advertisement or public pronouncement.

The most famous blues writer of them all tells how he wrote the most famous of all the blues.

BIRTH OF THE ST. LOUIS BLUES
by *W. C. Handy*

WELL, the *Jogo Blues* got a play. Michael Markels of New York was one Broadway band leader who featured it successfully. A St. Louis millionaire, Russell Gardiner, "The

From *Father of the Blues*, by W. C. Handy, copyright 1941 by W. C. Handy and used with permission of The Macmillan Company.

Banner Buggy Man," liked it so well he sent me a twenty-dollar note every time we played it—which was every night when he was present. But *Jogo Blues* never became a hit and never fulfilled the hope I had entertained for a success.

The trouble may have been partly because *Jogo* was an instrumental number. Then another disadvantage was that only Negro musicians understood the title and the music. On the other hand, while my men liked it a great deal, many bands couldn't play it well because it was considered over the head of the ordinary pianist and too difficult for the average orchestra. I had made an orchestral arrangement too difficult for the average player, and profits in musical compositions come from widely repeated sales, not from an occasional yellowback from a single rich enthusiast. In short, I was still looking for that second hit.

It occurred to me that I could perhaps make more headway in this direction without the questionable help of my four lively and robust youngsters at home, all bent on using my legs for teeterboards. The noisy rumpus warmed the heart but it put a crimp in my work. I could feel the blues coming on, and I didn't want to be distracted, so I packed my grip and made my getaway.

I rented a room in the Beale Street section and went to work. Outside, the lights flickered. Chitterling joints were as crowded as the more fashionable resorts like the Iroquois. Piano thumpers tickled the ivories in the saloons to attract customers, furnishing a theme for the prayers at Beale Street Baptist Church and Avery Chapel (Methodist). Scores of powerfully built roustabouts from river boats sauntered along the pavement, elbowing fashionable browns in beautiful gowns. Pimps in boxback coats and undented Stetsons came out to get a breath of early evening air and to welcome the young night. The pool-hall crowd grew livelier than they had been during the day. All that contributed to the color and spell of Beale Street mingled outside, but I neither saw nor heard it that night. I had a song to write.

My first decision was that my new song would be another blues, true to the soil and in the tradition of *Memphis Blues*. Ragtime, I had decided, was passing out. But this number would go beyond its predecessor and break new ground. I would begin with a down-home ditty fit to go with twanging banjos and yellow shoes. Songs of this sort could become tremendous hits sometimes. On the levee at St. Louis I had heard *Looking for the Bully* sung by the roustabouts, which later was adopted and nationally popularized by May Irwin. I had watched the joy-spreaders rarin' to go when it was played by the bands on the *Gray Eagle,* or the *Spread Eagle.* I wanted such a success, but I was determined that my song would have an important difference. The emotions that it expressed were going to be real. Moreover, it was going to be cut to the native blues pattern.

A flood of memories filled my mind. First, there was the picture I had of myself, broke, unshaven, wanting even a decent meal, and standing before the lighted saloon in St. Louis without a shirt under my frayed coat. There was also from that same period a curious and dramatic little fragment that till now had seemed to have little or no importance. While occupied with my own miseries during that sojourn, I had seen a woman whose pain seemed even greater. She had tried to take the edge off her grief by heavy drinking, but it hadn't worked. Stumbling along the poorly lighted street, she muttered as she walked, "Ma man's got a heart like a rock cast in de sea."

The expression interested me, and I stopped another woman to inquire what she meant. She replied, "Lawd, man, it's hard and gone so far from her she can't reach it." Her language was the same down-home medium that conveyed the laughable woe of lamp-blacked lovers in hundreds of frothy songs, but her plight was much too real to provoke much laughter. My song was taking shape. I had now settled upon the mood.

Another recollection pressed in upon me. It was the memory of that odd gent who called figures for the Kentucky breakdown—the one who everlastingly pitched his tones in the key of G and moaned the calls like a presiding elder preaching at a revival meeting. Ah, there was my key—I'd do the song in G.

Well, that was the beginning. I was definitely on my

way. But when I got started, I found that many other considerations also went into the composition. Ragtime had usually sacrificed melody for an exhilarating syncopation. My aim would be to combine ragtime syncopation with a real melody in the spiritual tradition. There was something from the tango that I wanted too. The dancers at Dixie Park had convinced me that there was something racial in their response to this rhythm, and I had used it in a disguised form in the *Memphis Blues*. Indeed, the very word "tango," as I now know, was derived from the African "tangana," and signified this same tom-tom beat. This would figure in my introduction, as well as in the middle strain.

In the lyric I decided to use Negro phraseology and dialect. I felt then, as I feel now, that this often implies more than well-chosen English can briefly express. My plot centered round the wail of a lovesick woman for her lost man, but in the telling of it I resorted to the humorous spirit of the bygone coon songs. I used the folk blues' three-line stanza that created the twelve-measure strain.

The primitive Southern Negro as he sang was sure to bear down on the third and seventh tones of the scales, slurring between major and minor. Whether in the cotton fields of the Delta or on the levee up St. Louis way, it was always the same. Till then, however, I had never heard this slur used by a more sophisticated Negro, or by any white man. I had tried to convey this effect in *Memphis Blues* by introducing flat thirds and sevenths (now called "blue notes") into my song, although its prevailing key was the major; and I carried this device into my new melody as well. I also struck upon the idea of using the dominant seventh as the opening chord of the verse. This was a distinct departure, but as it turned out, it touched the spot.

In the folk blues the singer fills up occasional gaps with words like "Oh, lawdy" or "Oh, baby" and the like. This meant that in writing a melody to be sung in the blues manner one would have to provide gaps or waits. In my composition I decided to embellish the piano and orchestra score at these points. This kind of business is called a "break"; entire books of different "breaks" for a single song can be found on the music counters today, and the breaks become a fertile source of the orchestral improvisation which became the essence of jazz. In the chorus I used plagal chords to give spiritual effects in the harmony. Altogether, I aimed to use all that is characteristic of the Negro from Africa to Alabama. By the time I had done all this heavy thinking and remembering, I figured it was time to get something down on paper, so I wrote, "I hate to see de evenin' sun go down." And if you ever had to sleep on the cobbles down by the river in St. Louis, you'll understand that complaint.

St. Louis had come into the composition in more ways than one before the sun peeped through my window. So when the song was completed, I dedicated the new piece to Mr. Russell Gardiner, the St. Louis man who had liked *Jogo Blues*, and I proudly christened it the *St. Louis Blues*. The same day on Pee Wee's cigar stand I orchestrated the number and jotted down scores for the men of my band.

The song was off my chest, and secretly I was pleased with it, but I could scarcely wait for the public verdict. Blurry-eyed from loss of sleep, I went with the band to the evening's engagement on the Alaskan Roof.

The one-step, maxixe and other dances had been done to the tempo of *Memphis Blues*, which the Vernon Castles slowed up to introduce their original dance, the fox-trot. When *St. Louis Blues* was written the tango was the vogue. I tricked the dancers by arranging a tango introduction, breaking abruptly then into a low-down blues. My eyes swept the floor anxiously, then suddenly I saw the lightning strike. The dancers seemed electrified. Something within them came suddenly to life. An instinct that wanted so much to live, to fling its arms and to spread joy, took them by the heels. By this I was convinced that my new song was accepted.

When the evening was over, the band piled into cabs and followed me home to celebrate the birth of the new blues. But Maggie, arms akimbo and rolling pin poised, was waiting for Jiggs at the door. I had been away from home twenty-four hours, burning up worlds of energy to produce a song, but maybe I should have stated where I was going and what I intended to do. Failing to make that clear, I presume the fault was mine. But it's an awkward thing to announce in advance your intention of composing a song hit between midnight and dawn. The talk more naturally follows the act, and that is what ultimately happened in my case.

The men of the band got a big kick out of my domestic drama. But after all, heads are made to be lumped in this funny-paper world—aren't they?

SUGGESTIONS FOR STUDY:

1. Is Handy's purpose expository or narrative?
2. For how many paragraphs does "A flood of memories filled my mind" serve as topic sentence? Why?
3. Does the reader need some knowledge of music to understand the essay completely? Is the essay enjoyable without this knowledge?
4. Is phraseology like "put a crimp in my work" and "made my getaway" appropriate to the tone of the essay?
5. Is the specific detail with which the essay is filled a real merit? How?
6. How many times is the verb *to be* used in paragraph 4? How many times the passive voice? How many times the active voice of action verbs?
7. What is meant by *yellowback, chitterling, roustabouts, flat thirds and sevenths, cobblers, maxixe, funny-paper world*?
8. Is the essay successful in making precise the intangibles that go into the creation of music or song? Why?
9. Write a theme in which you make as precise as you can the intangibles in a composition—in music, art, writing.

Definitions, as the student writer who attempts one will find, are notoriously difficult to write. This one clarifies a much-used term.

SWING MUSIC
by James A. Poling

SWING is a form of music indigenous to America. Its history is vague but it is conventionally believed that swing music originated in the deep South around the first decade of this century. Certainly the first recognized great swing musician was Buddy Balden, a black New Orleans cornetist, and, musically speaking, the grandfather of Louis Armstrong, recognized to-day as one of the greatest swing artists of all time.

Swing music made its first important bid for popular approval in 1916, with the appearance at Reisenweber's restaurant in New York of The Original Dixieland Jazz Band. Ted Lewis and Paul Whiteman helped spread its popularity and they in turn were followed by Red Nichols and countless other bands until the popularity of swing became international. Swing music's popularity was climaxed in 1938 with the appearance at Carnegie Hall of Benny Goodman (the greatest clarinetist of his time) and his band in an all-swing concert.

Swing differs from other music in that in other musical

From *The Music Lovers' Encyclopedia*, compiled by Rupert Hughes, completely revised and newly edited by Deems Taylor and Russell Kerr. Used by permission of Doubleday & Company, Inc.

forms the orchestra re-creates the composer's musical ideas just as the composer conceived them. The performer is in a secondary rôle. In swing the performer appears in a more creative rôle. Through improvisation (*the soul and heartblood of swing*) the performer transforms the composer's fundamental melodic idea into his own conception of the theme. In other words, the swing musician does not simply convey to the listener what was original with the composer; he himself *creates* the musical substance his auditors hear. Hugh Panassie in his book *Hot Jazz* says, "To ignore the talent of the orchestra in jazz (swing) is like ignoring the talent of the composer in classical music."

Swing is characterized by a musical idiom and attitude, rather than by a tempo. It is generally polyphonic music composed of melodies that support one another, as contrasted to homophonic music in which the melody is supported by chords. *Ad lib* variations on a simple theme; counterpoint, particularly of the fourth or syncopated variety; involved harmonies; and syncopation, in which the accent is shifted to the unstressed part of a beat or measure—these are fundamental to swing.

Whether or not swing is a transient musical form is a subject of considerable debate. The answer generally given by swing addicts is the now classic statement of Louis Armstrong, greatest cornetist of them all, "Folks, take it from me—we couldn't live without a little *swing* now and then, mostly then."

SUGGESTIONS FOR STUDY:

1. Does this definition of swing music differentiate it from other forms of music?
2. Is there more than one differentia? What?
3. Is a knowledge of musical vocabulary necessary to a full understanding of the definition?
4. What are the several divisions of the essay?
5. Are the quotations effective?
6. Is the triple use of *greatest* effective?
7. How does this essay compare in tone, purpose, and interest with the previous one?

8. Do swing, jazz, ragtime differ? Was *St. Louis Blues* any of them?
9. What is the meaning of *indigenous, improvisation, auditors, ad lib, transient, addict?* Are these restricted to musical diction?
10. Write a theme in which you define a kind of music, a prejudice, success, college spirit, sportsmanship, a religious belief, or other intangible. Use as much specific, concrete detail as possible.

The trend toward seriousness and realism in modern musical comedies, and the deeper question of the function of art as escape, are considered in a lively argument between a radio man and one of the leading writers of the serious musical comedy.

DOWN WITH SENSE
by Fred Lounsberry

SOME MONTHS ago I was browsing through some old sheet music and came upon Irving Berlin's "My Walking Stick." Reading it through, I found the lines: "I'd go insane without my cane." And it struck me that there, in six words, was the thing we are in danger of losing in our musical theatre. The old essence of gaiety, goofiness and abandon which allows a performer to be applauded for elaborating such trivia is falling into disrepute and is, I fear, in the very shadow of extinction.

The reason is, of course, the melancholy sense of responsibility that has been acquired by the leading practitioners of the musical-drama art. In the beginning, we have "Okla-

Reprinted by permission from The New York Times, June 22, 1952.

homa!" to blame. But it is not all the old horse's fault. The people who actually made "Oklahoma!" the well-spring of our troubles were the critics who were so overwhelmed by perfect entertainment that they went on a transcendental binge and called it "a pure slice of Americana," "folk art," and all the other things that city people seem to find tolerable about life in the country.

That "Oklahoma!" may have been these things, I will not deny. But if it was, it was an irrelevant coincidence. The popularity of "Oklahoma!" can be traced mainly, believe it or not, to a fine book, fine songs, fine performances, and the always necessary luck of having been produced when it was just what the world wanted. It was excellent entertainment and still is. But the appraisers called it something more, and Rodgers and Hammerstein, suddenly seized with a mission, set out to do something worth while in the musical theatre.

"Carousel" followed and was awfully good. "Allegro," leaving entertainment back in the mist and justifying itself almost exclusively on its social-artistic weight, was terrible. Regaining their equilibrium, Rodgers and Hammerstein restored the factor of entertainment to their work and delivered "South Pacific," which has done fantastically well. And lately we have had "The King and I," delightful to attend, but musically and lyrically again showing the frightening inclination to leave entertainment behind and advance with art.

Now I am not fool enough to launch a severe criticism against Rodgers and Hammerstein. They are, Heaven knows, excellent creative men. Their shows and songs are good, the songs especially so in view of the current popular music as a whole.

What I might criticize is that special aspect of their output, the leaning toward seriousness and sense, and the leaning away from carefree fun. I criticize this because I dread to see it carried to its obvious extreme, and I feel it is necessary to make the criticism because our journalists who happen to be working as theatre critics seem to feel that this seriousness is not only the coming thing but the only thing.

Thus, there is apt to be not only an extension of the trend in the work of Rodgers and Hammerstein but also an imitation of it in the work of less skilled craftsmen. As a matter of fact, this has already begun. "The Little Foxes," a morbid play, was made into the musical drama, "Regina," which, they say, was morbid in more ways than the atmospheric. A musical is planned with Eugene O'Neill's "Desire Under the Elms" as its basis. I am crazy about O'Neill, but the thought of seeing his grim tragedy set to music depresses me. There are other examples on Broadway, but let's take a brief look at the motion picture.

Go to see an old Marx Brothers film, and you will be instantly impressed with how serious our modern musical comedies of the screen have become. Today, everything has to make sense, be logical, and be explained. There is little or no tomfoolery left. You seldom see, in a current comedy, a scene inserted simply because it is funny. The concern today is with story line and that means sense and seriousness and responsibility. If no one were going to the movies these days, I would say, "No wonder no one's going to the movies these days!"

This dilemma is the outgrowth of the fanaticism to which we are, to a large degree, addicted in this country. It is all or nothing. We have had some successful musicals which overlapped into the drama field and, as a result, these are the thing, and anything else is fluff. An interesting demonstration of this is a comparison of the press received by two shows which opened within a few months of each other, "Kiss me, Kate" and "South Pacific."

No one is going to tell me that "South Pacific" is musically or lyrically up to "Kiss Me, Kate." Nor is anyone going to convince me that Ezio Pinza and Mary Martin were any more compelling than Alfred Drake and Patricia Morison. Both shows, as we all know, did handsomely.

But read the Broadway and Hollywood columnists, or listen to the comedians, and what do you find being referred to as the one and only apex of musical theatre art? "South Pacific." This despite the fact that "Kiss Me, Kate" cleaned up on endless tours in the United States, cleaned up in London where it got a better reception than "South Pacific," and also cleaned up in Stockholm, where its opening was hailed as the greatest event in the history of the Swedish theatre, which, you'll recall, had considerable dealings with one of the most exciting dramatists of all time, August Strindberg.

I am not griping about "Kiss Me, Kate's" luck; after all, it has made out fine. But I am trying to point out that it has been mysteriously sloughed off in certain influential quarters. Why? Because it is fluff, not drama. It has no significance. It happens to be brilliantly entertaining, but apparently that is a stigma. I hope we have many more shows with an equally emphatic stigma.

It is well and good to experiment with everything. The experiments of Rodgers and Hammerstein are laudable. But let us not make the mistake of depriving the theatre of its right to entertain, without further obligation.

To have the theatre reflect life is, we can be thankful, an accepted objective. But there is no ground for demanding that it do so all the time. Escape is recognized as a valid part of life. Escape is why sensible people go to ball games and concerts and parties. Escape is what Noel Coward wrote "Blithe Spirit" for, when London was in its worst days of World War II.

So, let us, while reserving seats five months ahead for the latest hit by Rodgers and Hammerstein, also plan to give ourselves an uncomplicated treat by attending a foolish show about an implausible character who would go insane without his cane, or his latest equivalent.

The next time somebody praises a musical show to me because it has realism or meaning or depth, I will take Irving Berlin's walking stick and flail the conscientious non-objector over the head with it.

SUGGESTIONS FOR STUDY:

1. What is the main idea and where is it expressed?
2. What evidence does Lounsberry cite?
3. Is the paragraph that begins with the Marx Brothers convincing? Why?
4. Does the comparison between "South Pacific" and "Kiss Me, Kate" bear directly on the main idea?
5. What is the meaning of *trivia*, a *transcendental* binge, an *irrele-*

vant coincidence, equilibrium, dilemma, fanaticism, musically or lyrically, apex of art, a stigma?
6. Lounsberry's original title was "My Walking Stick." Is this a better title than the present one? Do you think the present title had anything to do with the tone of Rodgers' reply? Why?

IN DEFENSE OF SENSE
by Richard Rodgers

WHEN I was a small boy, a little band of us used to roam through the outskirts of the Long Island village in which we lived, searching for a vacant house. Our pleasures were simple and direct in those days. All we wanted to do was break some windows. There was something delightful about the smack of the stone as it hit the smooth surface and something almost funny in the tinkle of the glass as it fell to the floor inside.

It's safe to assume that when small boys grow up most of them turn to more constructive pursuits. Occasionally, however, we find a man, mature in years, who still finds something pleasurable in the tinkle of the glass he has broken. The stone he throws may even be verbal instead of mineral. Such a case is one Mr. Fred Lounsberry.

There's a big difference, however. This house is not vacant. It's a musical comedy house and it's inhabited by people who do their best to dispense entertainment for gain. Any attempt to discomfort them by the unwarranted destruction of their property is likely to bring forth howls of rage. Have a howl: Mr. Lounsberry resorts to an ancient and specious technique—that of making a misstatement and attempting to make it appear true by means of other misstatements or

Reprinted by permission from The New York Times, June 29, 1952.

half-truths. His first misstatement is the basis for his entire article. He declares that in the present-day musical comedy theatre "the old essence of gaiety, goofiness and abandon . . . is falling into disrepute and is in the very shadow of extinction."

I wonder where anything goofier than Phil Silvers in "Top Banana" can be found. I would be willing to pay a very stiff price for a pair of tickets to see it. I cannot conceive of any more gaiety (and charm and wit) than there is in the current "New Faces" and for abandon, give me "Guys and Dolls."

Mr. Lounsberry holds Rodgers and Hammerstein largely responsible for this deplorable condition in our musical theatre, but, at the moment, the three carefree and irresponsible musicals named above outnumber the two that might be labeled "serious," although, perhaps, they don't out-gross them. He traces the downfall of musical comedy back to "Oklahoma!" and accuses the critics of being "so overwhelmed by perfect entertainment that they went on a transcendental binge and called it 'folk art,' etc." Then comes his best piece of logic. "The popularity of 'Oklahoma!' can be traced mainly, believe it or not, to a fine book, fine songs, fine performances and the always-necessary luck of having been produced when it was just what the world wanted. It was excellent entertainment and still is."

So far, I don't understand what the man is criticizing, but I can't help thinking of something that happened when we gave a birthday party for one of my daughters who was then 5 years old. There was the inevitable magician and the inevitable dog that fetched the proper-colored handkerchief and could bark up to five or six at command. One of my daughter's guests, a little boy about her age, suddenly said in a thoroughly disgusted tone, "Aw, he's trained." I find it surprising that Mr. Lounsberry is smart enough to realize that "Oklahoma!" was produced at exactly the proper time, but doesn't give us credit for having known it ourselves and accuses us of being lucky.

He presents us with a very interesting sentence regarding "The King and I." He calls it "delightful to attend, but musically and lyrically again showing the frightening inclination to leave entertainment behind and advance with art." I'd like to know how anything that shows a frightening inclination to leave entertainment behind can possibly be delightful to attend. The critics certainly don't need me to defend them, but I resent this man's implication that our men who write of the theatre are stupid enough to be pushed around by any bogus art attempt. Certainly, the seriousness with which Mr. Lounsberry believes the critics are being seduced didn't do us much good in the case of "Allegro." They gave it a trouncing.

In case Mr. Lounsberry wonders why I have not thrown the rather phenomenal success of "Pal Joey" in his teeth, I have been saving it because I have a special point to make. First of all, our friend will have to admit that this is a very unserious evening in the theatre and that its only overtones are those of laughter. Then we might examine the fact that when the piece was first produced in 1941, although it was done superbly at that time, it had a comparatively small public. I submit that its success today, with an equally superb production, is due to the fact that the musical theatre has made sufficient strides in its concept of entertainment to be able to treat a subject matter that offended certain portions of the public and the press eleven years ago.

This advance in thinking was due, I believe, to such shows as "Carousel" and "South Pacific." The horizon was broadened considerably by musical plays of this type and today the theatregoer buys his musical comedy ticket with no preconceptions.

I will happily grant Mr. Lounsberry his premise that "Kiss Me, Kate" was, in general, more lighthearted and less serious than "South Pacific" and I do not wish to quarrel with his artistic criteria when he says "no one is going to tell me that 'South Pacific' is musically or lyrically up to 'Kiss Me, Kate.'" Conceivably we could find someone who might tell him just that but perhaps what he means is that he wouldn't be willing to listen. What is annoying is that once again he challenges the critics with having fallen for something without validity in preferring "South Pacific" and hints that the public knew better.

I must point out here that "Kiss Me, Kate" played 1,077 performances in New York and that "South Pacific" at the close of business last Saturday night (June 21) played its 1,318th performance and last week grossed $44,066.50. All this in the large Majestic Theatre, whereas "Kiss Me, Kate" eventually had to go to the Shubert Theatre, a comparatively small house. "Kiss Me, Kate" played thirty-three weeks in Chicago and that company is now permanently closed. "South Pacific" played sixty-seven weeks in Chicago and is still touring. Three weeks ago it played to $72,015.

Mr. Lounsberry is not the first one to raise the question of the so-called serious musical but I am convinced that all this excitement is over nothing. When Mr. Lounsberry refers to "Oklahoma!" as "the old horse," I must admit that he is 50 per cent qualified to judge, but I believe there is no more chance of eliminating comedy in the musical theatre than there is of eliminating love in the song-writing profession.

The theatre as a whole has come on hard times. It isn't the picnic it used to be by any means and at this moment the only truly healthy segment of the living theatre is its musical wing. The healthiest and most successful portion of this wing is to be found in the comparatively serious efforts. These are doing by far the biggest business so, perhaps, if Mr. Lounsberry loves the theatre so much and wishes it to stay open so that he can have his nights of carefree goofiness, he might do well to support what he calls the serious musical and stop thinking of it as a menace.

SUGGESTIONS FOR STUDY:

1. Does the introductory analogy set the tone of Rodgers' reply? Does Rodgers use analogy again?
2. Is the evidence in paragraph 4 sufficient to answer Lounsberry's thesis?
3. Do you find Rodgers justified in wondering what Lounsberry is criticizing in the statement about "Oklahoma!"?

4. Does Rodgers suggest that Lounsberry's statement about "The King and I" is nonsense? Is he justified?
5. Is Rodgers justified in his inference that Lounsberry considers the critics stupid or easily imposed on?
6. Who do you think has the best of the argument? Why?
7. Does Rodgers' tone soften in the last four paragraphs?
8. Has the concern with financial success in the last paragraphs been suggested in an early paragraph?
9. What is the meaning of a *verbal* stone, *unwarranted* destruction, *specious* technique, *deplorable* condition, *irresponsible* musicals, *bogus* art, *phenomenal* success, *preconceptions*, *validity*, artistic *criteria?*
10. Write a theme on your favorite art form; or write on an issue about which you are sufficiently informed to offer specific evidence for your thesis, and about which you can expect opposition.

The thoughts of youth are long, long thoughts . . .

WE WERE SIXTEEN
by Thomas Sancton

ONE SUMMER when I was sixteen a party of us, paddling upstream to buy some candy at a crossroads store, came upon three young girls who were bathing in a sandy cove. There were four of us in the long pirogue, all of an age. For a long moment we were speechless. At last we said hello, and they answered in warm gay voices. We drifted the boat into the cove and began to speak to them. Two of the girls were sisters. The three of them had come to visit a relative who kept a fine summer lodge in the woods across the bayou

---
Copyright Feb. 1944, Harper & Brothers.

from the camp. One of the sisters was fifteen and the others were seventeen. They were aglow with fresh and slender beauty, and their bathing suits were bright flags of color. Their impact upon us was overwhelming. We grew silly, tongue-tied, said foolish things we did not mean to say, shoved one another about in the boat, and finally overturned it. The loreleis laughed musical little laughs. They seemed unbearably beautiful. We had no idea what to do about it.

The girls had been at the lodge for a week. They missed their beaux in New Orleans, they missed the dating and the dancing and the music. It was a gay town in the summertime. The older girls looked upon us as children; but still—they must have reflected—we were not such children at that. The younger sister, a slender child with thick brown hair and heavily crimsoned lips, sat on the bank and regarded us with a happy open face.

At last we took courage and asked if we could call on them that night.

"Oh, yes!" they cried eagerly. Life at that moment was dazzling.

Making this rendezvous was an impulsive thing to do, for it was midweek and we should have to steal away after taps and walk down a path without flashlights through a snake-infested lowland and—because the boats were counted and chained at nightfall—swim across the bayou, holding our clothes above our heads.

We crept from our cabins at ten o'clock that night and met in the pine woods. One of us intoned a counting-out rhyme; the loser had to walk first down the path through the snake hole. He cut a long gum sapling and rattled it down the path ahead of us. We walked bunched tightly together, tense with fear, giggling at our own unbelievable audacity, trembling in our eagerness. At the bayou's edge we slipped out of our shorts and shirts and sneakers and, holding them above our heads with one hand, we felt our way round the knees and along the sunken roots of a cypress tree, and pushed off into the bayou and began to swim.

The moon had not yet risen. We had only the silhouettes of trees to guide us. We swam closely together, cautioning one another to silence, bursting into convulsive squeals as water lilies brushed against our bodies or when a fish broke the surface near us. We swam upstream from the camp, past two bends, and waded from the water in the cove where we had met the girls. Now we were laughing with relief and excitement, and popping one another on the backsides. We scraped the glistening water from our bodies, dressed, and combed our wet hair and hurried off down the wagon path into the woods. Long ago the cove had been a landing stage for small schooners which came to load pine firewood for New Orleans.

The girls were waiting for us, dressed in bright print cotton dresses and wearing hair ribbons. The soft light gave age and mystery to their youthful shoulders, to their slender bodies; and, like nameless night-blooming vines in the woods about us, they bore a splendid fragrance all their own, a fragrance of youth and cleanliness and fresh cosmetics. They were playing a phonograph on the wide porch of the lodge. This was the summer of Maurice Chevalier's great success in American movies. The little sister sang his song, rolling her eyes, turning out her soft pink lip:

>   If ze night-ting gail
>   Cood zing lak you . . .

And she sang another:

>   . . . you make me feel so grand
>   I want to hand the world to you.
>   You seem to understand
>   Each foolish little dream I'm dreaming,
>   scheme I'm scheming . . .

I was so in love with her I could hardly catch my breath. I was in love with the other sister too, and with their friend. All of the boys were in love with all of the girls; the girls—so they said—had crushes on each of us. Our hearts were afire.

We walked hand in hand down the wagon trail to the cove and built a bonfire. We stretched out on blankets, laughing, singing. We sang the songs that people always sing by rivers and campfires, "There's a Long, Long Trail A-wind-ing," "The Sweetheart of Sigma Chi," all the rest. We kissed the girls and they held fast to us. Before this night we had been only boys, holding hands with girls in movies, not quite sure why we pursued them and acted silly. Now, lying beneath the open sky, for the first time we understood the poignance and the beauty of the human heritage.

Every night for two weeks we came to see them. And when they told us good-by the last kiss was as much a discovery as the first, and we knew that love was a thing that could never grow old. After they had gone we would steal from our cabins to sit on the back porch of the camp hospital, on a hill, where we could see the bayou and the cove and the woods where we had found them; and we sat there talking late into the night, like daemon lovers in the ballads of old. I never passed the cove again, even years later when I would paddle down the bayou fishing, without remembering our meetings with a suddenly racing heart. First love is unforgettable.

I had no lessons to do in those summer months of camp life. There was plenty of time to think. I was living a communal life with other boys. Among us were embryonic bullies, scoundrels, cheats, promoters, Babbitts, Christers, and stuffed shirts; and there were also the boys of good heart, the unselfish, the humorous, the courageous, boys who were the salt of the earth, but who, often in their later lives, would be misled and preyed upon and set against one another by the sharp ones. One and all we lived together, ate together, slept together. Our personalities clashed, fermented, or formed amalgams. Sitting together at night in the lamplit cabins, with darkness and towering woods closing in upon us, we had our first grave talks about religion, about death, about sex. The future stretching before us was wide and fathomless. And all about us, in the grass, in the underbrush, in towering summer skies, we beheld the face of nature and the earth's wide harmonies as they had never been revealed in our city lives. At night we could stretch out upon the field, observe the stars, and grasp for the first time the fact that some were vastly deeper in space than others. In our star-study courses we heard phrases like "light years." It began to seep into the consciousness of many of us that a hundred years or the life of an individual had little meaning in the total universe; and from this point some of us began our first gropings after moral philosophy, gropings for a belief that could give the total universe a meaning in our own lives.

There was a bugler in our camp who was the first consummate expert, in any field, that I had known. He had no other talent but his music. He was a good-natured, chubby, curly-headed Italian boy, rather lazy, and when he was not back in the woods practicing his cornet he walked round with a dreamy look, as though our own handicrafts could not possibly be of interest to him.

Paolo had a silver trumpet and he preferred it to the bugle. He wanted to be a great musician. He would take his horn and music back into a pine clearing a quarter of a mile from the camp and all day long we could hear him practicing the runs. He blew the trumpet with a clear, sweet tone. We had supreme confidence as we stood at attention on the parade grounds and the flag came down the creaking flagpole pulley in the late afternoon sunlight, and Paolo stood alone, with everyone watching, and bugled. We were proud of him when visitors came. He had that ability of experts to create a sense of possessiveness in others.

It was at bedtime that Paolo gathered up into his clear, thin music all the ineffable hungering of our awakening lives. At ten o'clock he climbed a high ladder to a life-guard platform we had nailed into the branches of a tall cypress tree beside the bayou. Paolo lived for this moment and, with the whole camp silent and listening below him in the darkness, he blew taps with a soft and ghostly beauty all his own. Somehow the music spoke for us, uttered the thing we knew but had no words for, set up a wailing in the pine trees of the brevity and splendor of human life. Lying in our bunks in the darkness of the cabin, some of us fell into sleep; but some lay in silence thinking longer, alive to the night, and I was of these.

One night some ten years later I entered a smoke-filled

tavern in another city where Paolo was playing in a band. By this time he had made a small reputation as a boy with a hot trumpet. I watched his now older face as he tore through the hot routines. He was tired. The silver horn made noise but, though I knew little about it, I could see that he was not a great jazz musician.

I did not go to see him any more. I wanted to remember Paolo before he had lost something, before any of us had lost it, a kind of innocence. I wanted to remember him in the land of our first discoveries, when he had climbed into a cypress tree to blow his horn, and there was a kind of Gothic night-drench in our lives.

SUGGESTIONS FOR STUDY:

1. In expressing his ideas and emotions, does Sancton rely primarily on general labels and abstract terms or on the concrete and factual? Cite details to justify your answer.
2. What is the voice of the verbs in "Our personalities clashed, fermented, or formed amalgams"?
3. Are action verbs and the active voice characteristic of the essay? Do they help in giving a sense of immediate action?
4. Does Sancton vary his sentence length? Examine the paragraph beginning, "Making this rendezvous . . ." and the last paragraph in each section.
5. Does the contrast between the younger and older Paolo serve to clarify Sancton's meaning?
6. Is the first section a unit? Is the second?
7. Does the first gain effectiveness from being an element in the second?
8. Does the concrete detail with which Sancton sustains his tone help you to grasp the meaning of *pirogue, loreleis, rendezvous, consummate, amalgams, fathomless, heritage, poignance, ineffable,* a kind of *Gothic night-drench?* What does each word mean?
9. Write a theme about an experience of your own in which you came to new questions "about religion, about death, about sex," to new perceptions of "the brevity and splendor of human life."

The slowly expanding world of a sensitive girl is recaptured in this selection from the autobiography of a well-known writer.

from MY STORY
by Mary Roberts Rinehart

VERY SLOWLY my world enlarged.
I went to school. It was my first real contact with other children, and I did not like it. One day the baker's daughter, out of a clear sky, slapped me on the face, and I stood stunned. Why had she slapped me? I still have no idea. Only a few years ago I saw her, a big buxom woman, on the street, and the old puzzle arose in my mind. Why did you slap me?
It had never occurred to me to slap her in return.
Other things were happening, too. One day my father, always interested in anything mechanical, took me in to an empty storeroom to see something new and novel. On an unpainted wooden table sat a curious mechanism, with a yellow wax cylinder. A demonstrator wound up this strange affair, the yellow cylinder revolved, and—talked.
But it made little or no impression on me. Already at home I had a talking doll. It was a lady doll, and when it was wound it moved forward on small wheels and said something vaguely supposed to be "mama." This very first phonograph, then, was not strange to me. It bore about the same relation to the present ones as the early crystal set radios did to those at present in use.

From *MY STORY*, Copyright 1931, 1948 by Mary Roberts Rinehart, and reprinted by permission of Rinehart & Company, Inc., Publishers.

Looking back, I can see now how my father's interest in the mechanical was always to the fore. Long before the first moving picture was made I was familiar with the principle. He brought home one day a kinetoscope; a long tape with pictures was placed inside it, you revolved the barrel while keeping an eye at the eye-piece, and the figures in the pictures moved, took on life.

Things were prospering with us. There came a time of great excitement when a new and shiny Hardman upright piano was moved in, and I took my first music lesson. Natural gas came, and there was the luxury and cleanliness of it. It burned in big open grates day and night, at a cost of something like a dollar a month for every grate. The grates were filled with broken fire bricks, and twice a year or more these bricks were dipped in whitewash. Then indeed the fires were lovely; the grates painted black, the bricks white, and the blue and yellow flames playing over them.

My mother was a housekeeper. Nothing was ever so immaculate as her house, so white as the oilcloth on the kitchen table, so red as the legs of those tables, so smooth as her beds. On Saturday mornings the brick pavement was scrubbed and reddened. A pail of red wash was prepared, and with this and a broom the "girl" painted the bricks. On Fridays every room in the house was turned out, the heavy carpets swept, the heavy furniture moved about.

And she liked change. One never knew, after Fridays, where the bed would be, or the bureau. There was one time, too, when we were shut out of the parlor for days, and then ushered in, my father, my little sister and myself, to see the transformation.

It was indeed transformed. My grandmother had given up the gray house now, and we had the rosewood furniture and the mirror. But my mother had loathed the rosewood, with its black horsehair. So now we stood and rubbed our eyes. She had made slip covers of rose and white linen for the chairs and the sofa, a long silk scarf, nattily caught up at each end, draped the mantel; and the same on the piano. And crowning glory of all, there stood on that mantel two figures in terra cotta. One was the Greek Slave, the other was Eve, holding up a very round apple.

We were stunned with that vision of beauty and gaiety, nor did the fact that there were strips of white crash tacked to the new carpet and leading to divers chairs and the sofa, detract from it. To this moment I can see that gay little room, my gay and smiling mother, my amused father.

But Eve and the Greek Slave did not remain long in their pristine nudeness. Representations were made, and so my mother was obliged to clothe them. After that each of them wore a "drape" of soft satin, thrown negligently over the shoulder and so arranged as to do the most good.

Looking back, those two chaste figures in their satin camouflage represent to me not only the strange narrowness of the 80's, but also my mother's innate sense of the beautiful and the right. She hated having to clothe them. Yet in her own way she was as narrow as the rest of the world she knew. A remote connection of the family was assaulted by the family coachman, a youngish man, and an illegitimate child was the result. It was years before I learned that story, but I remember well enough that relations with that family were broken off, and that I never saw this unfortunate girl again, until we were both women. The secret had been well kept, and I am glad to say that her husband married her, knowing the story. But her name, if mentioned at all, was spoken in whispers. She was "never to darken our doors."

Sin was sin. Unbaptized children were damned. Hell was real, a place of eternal burning in eternal fires. In the 90's the same fierce righteousness maintained. In my early teens a girl of fifteen bore an illegitimate child. I had only a nodding acquaintance with her, but after that I was not allowed to look in her direction. And over all this sat a God, the Jehovah of wrath and punishment, who had a long white beard like that of the minister who had married my parents and baptized me, and who never forgot and never forgave, unless one was converted and loved Him.

He was a hard God to love, and the attempt to repent my sinless life and to love Him with a single heart almost produced a neurosis in my early girlhood. As for the result, I can look over the descendants of that large family, and I believe that only two of them have turned to religion for comfort. One is one of the aunts, a woman now in her seventies and finding in her church—although she would deny this—more of a satisfaction of her social instinct than of real faith in God. The other is myself, and although I conform to the tenets of my church and its outward forms, I am fully aware that my religion of today has no relation to those early experiences, save that I have retained the conviction of sin; that I have built for myself a mystic faith of my own, in which God is a real and controlling factor in my life, and prayer an essential matter, but which conforms to no doctrine and subscribes to no dogma. For in the end each of us builds his own conception of religion, forms his own idea of what is God.

In this confusing world, in which sin was sin, but with my father accepting no God whatever to whom to answer for sin, this child who was myself lived her small and unimportant life. No great people came, to provide me with pen pictures today; the Mayor sometimes stopped and sat on the steps. He was "Your Honor" to the neighborhood. He was a little man with a twisted back. Now and then a fine and distinguished looking old man came down the street and stopped. He had been a colonel in the Civil War and retained his title, and he was a distant relative. Sometimes he borrowed a little money, but in spite of this he had a beautiful place in the country, with a carriage and an open surrey.

When I was twelve I was madly in love with his son, who was tall, blond and twenty-five. I would visit at the country place, and spend hours before a mirror brushing my two long black braids and in despair examining my face for blemishes. Then I would hang on the gate casually and wait for him. Sometimes he saw me there; as often as not he never noticed me. But that was later.

This child, then, lived in a slowly expanding world. The street had extended. It now included the public school; one carried a slate and used one's right hand, and bad boys were slapped with a ruler on their palms. It included church, a store or two, and my father's office. It included a remote spot called the alley, where one went for colored help, and with a planing mill on a corner which hummed and sang in weird and eerie tones. The board would go under the saw, the tone would slowly rise as the plank moved on, and then lower and finally stop. I would stand fascinated and watch. It was the only machinery I had ever seen. But soon I was to see other machinery. A laundry moved in, next door to the row of little houses, and was greatly resented by the neighbors.

Finally a fascinating bit of machinery was installed, a novelty consisting of two hot rollers. A girl sat inside the window and fed it collars, and these collars came out smooth and shiny, and as hard as sheet metal.

One day I heard terrible screams from that window, and I ran there. All the houses opened, and people ran out. The girl was sitting there screaming, and one of her hands was caught between the hot rollers. It took a long time to release her, and before they did it I was found and taken home. But she lost her hand, and for years I saw her around the laundry doing odd jobs, with a small gray shawl pinned over her shoulders to hide her deformity.

It left me with a horror of machinery. Some years ago my youngest son entered a huge press in Tennessee; he was going into the publishing business and was to learn the technical side of book-making. I lay awake at night, filled with terrors, for not only had I seen this girl, but later on in the hospital one night I was to admit a boy whose hand had been caught in a press, and who, by lifting the towel which covered it, showed me something crushed beyond recognition.

I was only seventeen then, and one remembers.

SUGGESTIONS FOR STUDY:

1. Is Mrs. Rinehart specific and factual?
2. Does the first sentence announce the main idea?
3. Is the sentence in the fifth paragraph from the end, "The street had extended," to be taken literally? Does it fit the notion of the opening sentence?
4. In the second paragraph, what is the point in changing "Why had she slapped me?" to "Why did you slap me?" Does this change fit the last sentence in the selection?

5. Does Mrs. Rinehart account logically for her reaction to the phonograph and moving picture? Her present horror of machinery?
6. Is the transition from "My mother was a housekeeper" to "He was a hard God to love" natural?
7. Do the details given here agree with anything else you may have read about life in America in the 1880's and 90's?
8. What part of this essay is most like the previous essay?
9. What is the meaning of *crystal set radios, kinetoscope, terra cotta, dogma?*
10. Write a theme on your early memories or on early influences that caused a present attitude.

* * *

A great comedian recalls the dog that started him on his career.

I LOVE NELLY
by Jimmy Savo

ONE of the greatest loves of my life has been the love of dogs. I don't mean especially the elegant and beautifully cared-for pets whose owners pamper them, though they often are good friends too. I love the ruined dogs.

I cannot resist the look in the eyes of a homeless, dirty, hungry dog when I meet him in the street, that please-take-me-home look. I take him home. I have been taking dogs home all my life, ever since I was six and saw that look for the first time in the eyes of a dog named Nelly.

What my life would have been if I had never met that kind, homeless creature I can't guess. All I know is that I owe

------

Copyright 1952 by United Newspapers Magazine Corporation. Reprinted by permission of the author.

a great deal to her. She made for me the first dollar I ever earned in the theater. In fact, I'm not sure that I ever would have become an actor if it hadn't been for her.

Nelly had had a good home for a while. Then she hurt her leg in an automobile accident and her owners didn't want her any longer. She got the look that homeless dogs get. I recognize it the minute I see it.

I think probably most people owe a lot to dogs, though sometimes they don't know it. When you are a child and a dog loves you it gives you a happy feeling and confidence that means everything. A dog's warmth and affection bring you that security we all need so much and that many children never have, as the psychiatrists tell us.

I often wonder what many of us would be today if we hadn't had a dog to give us courage and pride and belief in ourselves. It may seem foolish to say this, but Nelly was a mother to me. My real mother died when I was a baby. Nelly, in her kind way, brought me up. She was older than I and wiser. And she was bigger, too. I felt safe with her along. I told her all my troubles and my troubles were hers.

When I took her in, Nelly was a problem. My family was poor. What would Nelly eat? Before long it became apparent that she and I were both losing weight. Nelly was under the table and got my ration of bread. This made us both skinny.

I really had to do something. So every night Nelly and I went out on the streets selling papers. She was bigger than I but both of us were bold. I got courage from her. What a little boy would be frightened to do alone he can do confidently when he has a dog along with him.

We sold the racing editions of the papers. It was before radio. The papers were grabbed by the horse players in the saloons.

That way we got pennies. And, better, we got food. When the bartenders weren't looking, I stood on my toes and reached up for the baloney and liverwurst on the free-lunch counter. Nelly sat outside and waited for me.

We learned that that was the way to do it. At first she went in with me, but the bartenders formed the habit of throwing ice at her. So she waited under the swinging doors, looking in. And I would come out and give her all I could snatch.

After the third or fourth saloon Nelly began to feel that she had dined well. Usually she ended with a piece of store cheese, making funny faces as she chewed, because the cheese stuck to the roof of her mouth. I had to stick my finger in to dislodge it so she could get it down. We were happy.

Saturday night was the big night. The saloons were crowded. But after my clients had read everything they wanted to know, business was dull. Then one Saturday night my life suddenly took a new turn.

In our neighborhood wandering quartets sang the popular songs on the street corners. I knew the tunes. For two cents a copy I got the lyrics. And with my soprano voice—I was a member of the choir at St. Jerome's Church—I broke out one night, all alone with "My Wild Irish Rose." It went all right.

By request, I followed it with the rest of my repertory— "The Man with the Ladder and the Hose," "In a Village by the Sea," and "That's How to Spell Chicken."

There were more requests, but my repertory was exhausted. I had to build it up, and I learned "Wait Till the Sun Shines, Nelly." It became my big number, the one I always had to sing, like "River, Stay 'Way from My Door" now, or "One Meat Ball."

When I got through singing, I would pass my hat, collecting pennies.

Some time later I learned from the wandering quartets about amateur nights and that prizes were given, gold watches!

So on a Friday night, Nelly and I went to a theater on 129th Street called the Olympic, an upstairs vaudeville house.

The stage-door man stopped me.

"What do you do?"

"I sing a song."

"You can't take that mutt in with you," he said.

"Then I can't sing, because I don't want to lose her."

The man smiled and said, "Go in, but don't let her go on the stage."

Backstage, just before I was to go on, I told Nelly to sit down and not move. Then it was my turn and I went on.

It was my stage debut.

I had a couple of newspapers under my arm that I still had to sell. The pants I wore had holes in the knees from playing marbles, and on the seat was a big patch. I had a black sweater with a turtle neck that looked like a horse collar pulled up around my head, and I hadn't had a haircut in six months.

I was seven then.

I walked out on the stage.

"Where's your music?" the orchestra leader asked me.

"I haven't got any."

"What song do you sing?"

" 'Wait Till the Sun Shines, Nelly.' "

When Nelly heard me say Nelly, she thought I was talking to her and she came out on the stage and sat right down alongside me. The people, the first theater audience I ever saw, started to whistle at her.

"What key do you sing in?" the leader asked, and I said, "I don't know what you mean."

The people laughed. So, confused, I started to sing and the orchestra played along. It went something like this:

"*Wait till the sun shines, Nelly,*" I sang, and Nelly looked up and wagged her tail at the sound of her name.

"*And the clouds go drifting by* . . .

"*We will be together, Nelly* . . ."

She wagged again.

"*By and by* . . .

"*Long through the lane we wander,*

"*Sweethearts, you and I* . . .

"*Wait till the sun shines, Nelly* . . .

"*By and by* . . ."

I hit a very high note on that last one, and it must have hurt Nelly's ear drums, because she joined me with a loud moaning sound and we both ended together:

"*By and b . . . ow . . . ow . . . ow.*"

When Nelly and I got through singing there was a riot.

I took my hat off, went to the boxes that were close to the

stage, just as if I were on a street corner or in one of our saloons, and held out my hat to the nearest people. Someone put a dollar bill in it. That was the dollar I spoke of.

The manager said, "Stay and line up for the prizes."

We all formed a line on the stage, but everybody in the audience shouted, "Give it to the boy with Nelly!"

And Nelly, hearing her name called by so many people, wagged her tail again and looked expectant.

The announcer led me downstage and gave me the watch. He said it was a genuine gold-plated watch, guaranteed for 20 years not to turn green.

"I can't tell the time, but I'll give it to my father," I said to him.

It was sunshine for Nelly and me that night. We went into a lunch wagon to celebrate. We used some of the money I had collected. But we wouldn't break that dollar bill. I ordered pork and kidney beans and Nelly settled for a frankfurter.

We went home. I climbed into my bed and I heard Nelly scratching the floor under it, moving in circles. She felt pretty good. It took us both a long time to fall asleep.

Nelly lived to be 21 years old, and when she died I had been a regular professional actor for quite a few years. I had to go off on tour many times and leave her behind. We both worried when I was away from her.

Then one day I came back to my father's house to find her very sick. She died the day after.

I took her to little St. Mary's Park in the Bronx and buried her there. Over her grave I put a little stick in the shape of a cross and on it a sign on which I had printed the words "I Love Nelly."

For a long while after that it was a lonely world for me.

SUGGESTIONS FOR STUDY:

1. Do you agree with Savo that a dog can bring a necessary feeling of security to a child and thus influence the adult?
2. Are the frequent short sentences appropriate? Could some be profitably joined by means of subordinating devices?

3. Does Savo select the right details about his first stage appearance to gain the double effect he wants?
4. Is there a singular appropriateness in the sentence, "It was sunshine for Nelly and me that night"? What is the reference?
5. What is the meaning of *pamper, repertory?* Why is it appropriate that most of the words in this account are familiar?
6. Write a theme about a pet, an early stage appearance, or an incident that combines the comic and the pathetic.

....

Christmases are a common experience; disappointments are too. Sometimes they overlap, as in this selection from one of the great American autobiographies, by the crusading journalist and editor who made muck-raking a household term.

A MISERABLE, MERRY CHRISTMAS
by Lincoln Steffens

WHAT INTERESTED ME in our new neighborhood was not the school, nor the room I was to have in the house all to myself, but the stable which was built back of the house. My father let me direct the making of a stall, a little smaller than the other stalls, for my pony, and I prayed and hoped and my sister Lou believed that that meant that I would get the pony, perhaps for Christmas. I pointed out to her that there were three other stalls and no horses at all. This I said in order that she should answer it. She could not. My father, sounded, said that some day we might have horses

....
From *THE AUTOBIOGRAPHY OF LINCOLN STEFFENS*, copyright, 1931, by Harcourt, Brace and Company, Inc.

and a cow; meanwhile a stable added to the value of a house. "Some day" is a pain to a boy who lives in and knows only "now." My good little sisters, to comfort me, remarked that Christmas was coming, but Christmas was always coming and grown-ups were always talking about it, asking you what you wanted and then giving you what they wanted you to have. Though everybody knew what I wanted, I told them all again. My mother knew that I told God, too, every night. I wanted a pony, and to make sure that they understood, I declared that I wanted nothing else.

"Nothing but a pony?" my father asked.

"Nothing," I said.

"Not even a pair of high boots?"

That was hard. I did want boots, but I stuck to the pony. "No, not even boots."

"Nor candy? There ought to be something to fill your stocking with, and Santa Claus can't put a pony into a stocking."

That was true, and he couldn't lead a pony down the chimney either. But no. "All I want is a pony," I said. "If I can't have a pony, give me nothing, nothing."

Now I had been looking myself for the pony I wanted, going to sales stables, inquiring of horsemen, and I had seen several that would do. My father let me "try" them. I chose several, but my father always found some fault with them. I was in despair. When Christmas was at hand I had given up all hope of a pony, and on Christmas Eve I hung up my stocking along with my sisters', of whom, by the way, I now had three. I haven't mentioned them or their coming because, you understand, they were girls, and girls, young girls, counted for nothing in my manly life. They did not mind me either; they were so happy that Christmas Eve that I caught some of their merriment. I speculated on what I'd get; I hung up the biggest stocking I had, and we all went reluctantly to bed to wait till morning. Not to sleep; not right away. We were told that we must not only sleep promptly, we must not wake up till seven-thirty the next morning—or if we did, we must not go to the fireplace for our Christmas. Impossible.

We did sleep that night, but we woke up at six A.M. We lay in our beds and debated through the open doors whether to obey till, say, half-past six. Then we bolted. I don't know who started it, but there was a rush. We all disobeyed; we raced to disobey and get first to the fireplace in the front room downstairs. And there they were, the gifts, all sorts of wonderful things, mixed-up piles of presents; only, as I disentangled the mess, I saw that my stocking was empty; it hung limp; not a thing in it; and under and around it—nothing. My sisters had knelt down, each by her pile of gifts; they were squealing with delight, till they looked up and saw me standing there in my nightgown with nothing. They left their piles to come to me and look with me at my empty place. Nothing. They felt my stocking: nothing.

I don't remember whether I cried at that moment, but my sisters did. They ran with me back to my bed, and there we all cried till I became indignant. That helped some. I got up, dressed, and driving my sisters away, I went alone out into the yard, down to the stable, and there, all by myself, I wept. My mother came out to me by and by; she found me in my pony stall, sobbing on the floor, and she tried to comfort me. But I heard my father outside; he had come part way with her, and she was having some sort of angry quarrel with him. She tried to comfort me; besought me to come to breakfast. I could not; I wanted no comfort and no breakfast. She left me and went on into the house with sharp words for my father.

I don't know what kind of a breakfast the family had. My sisters said it was "awful." They were ashamed to enjoy their own toys. They came to me, and I was rude. I ran away from them. I went around to the front of the house, sat down on the steps, and, the crying over, I ached. I was wronged, I was hurt—I can feel now what I felt then, and I am sure that if one could see the wounds upon our hearts, there would be found still upon mine a scar from that terrible Christmas morning. And my father, the practical joker, he must have been hurt, too, a little. I saw him looking out of the window. He was watching me or something for an hour or two, drawing back the curtain ever so little lest I catch him, but I saw his face, and I think I can see now the anxiety upon it, the worried impatience.

After—I don't know how long—surely an hour or two—I was brought to the climax of my agony by the sight of a man riding a pony down the street, a pony and a brand-new saddle; the most beautiful saddle I ever saw, and it was a boy's saddle; the man's feet were not in the stirrups; his legs were too long. The outfit was perfect; it was the realization of all my dreams, the answer to all my prayers. A fine new bridle, with a light curb bit. And the pony! As he drew near, I saw that the pony was really a small horse, what we called an Indian pony, a bay, with black mane and tail, and one white foot and a white star on his forehead. For such a horse as that I would have given, I could have forgiven, anything.

But the man, a disheveled fellow with a blackened eye and a fresh-cut face, came along, reading the numbers on the houses, and, as my hopes—my impossible hopes—rose, he looked at our door and passed by, he and the pony, and the saddle and the bridle. Too much. I fell upon the steps, and having wept before, I broke now into such a flood of tears that I was a floating wreck when I heard a voice.

"Say, kid," it said, "do you know a boy named Lennie Steffens?"

I looked up. It was the man on the pony, back again, at our horse block.

"Yes," I spluttered through my tears. "That's me."

"Well," he said, "then this is your horse. I've been looking all over for you and your house. Why don't you put your number where it can be seen?"

"Get down," I said, running out to him.

He went on saying something about "ought to have got here at seven o'clock; told me to bring the nag here and tie him to your post and leave him for you. But, hell, I got into a drunk—and a fight—and a hospital, and—"

"Get down," I said.

He got down, and he boosted me up to the saddle. He offered to fit the stirrups to me, but I didn't want him to. I wanted to ride.

A Miserable, Merry Christmas

"What's the matter with you?" he said, angrily. "What you crying for? Don't you like the horse? He's a dandy, this horse. I know him of old. He's fine at cattle; he'll drive 'em alone."

I hardly heard, I could scarcely wait, but he persisted. He adjusted the stirrups, and then, finally, off I rode, slowly, at a walk, so happy, so thrilled, that I did not know what I was doing. I did not look back at the house or the man, I rode off up the street, taking note of everything—of the reins, of the pony's long mane, of the carved leather saddle. I had never seen anything so beautiful. And mine! I was going to ride up past Miss Kay's house. But I noticed on the horn of the saddle some stains like rain-drops, so I turned and trotted home, not to the house but to the stable. There was the family, father, mother, sisters, all working for me, all happy. They had been putting in place the tools of my new business: blankets, currycomb, brush, pitchfork—everything, and there was hay in the loft.

"What did you come back so soon for?" somebody asked. "Why didn't you go on riding?"

I pointed to the stains. "I wasn't going to get my new saddle rained on," I said. And my father laughed. "It isn't raining," he said. "Those are not rain-drops."

"They are tears," my mother gasped, and she gave my father a look which sent him off to the house. Worse still, my mother offered to wipe away the tears still running out of my eyes. I gave her such a look as she had given him, and she went off after my father, drying her own tears. My sisters remained and we all unsaddled the pony, put on his halter, led him to his stall, tied and fed him. It began really to rain; so all the rest of that memorable day we curried and combed that pony. The girls plaited his mane, forelock, and tail, while I pitch-forked hay to him and curried and brushed, curried and brushed. For a change we brought him out to drink; we led him up and down, blanketed like a race-horse; we took turns at that. But the best, the most inexhaustible fun, was to clean him. When we went reluctantly to our midday Christmas dinner, we all smelt of horse, and my sisters had to wash their faces and hands. I was asked to, but I wouldn't, till my mother bade me look in the mirror. Then I washed up —quick. My face was caked with the muddy lines of tears that had coursed over my cheeks to my mouth. Having washed away that shame, I ate my dinner, and as I ate I grew hungrier and hungrier. It was my first meal that day, and as I filled up on the turkey and the stuffing, the cranberries and the pies, the fruit and the nuts—as I swelled, I could laugh. My mother said I still choked and sobbed now and then, but I laughed, too; I saw and enjoyed my sisters' presents till—I had to go out and attend to my pony, who was there, really and truly there, the promise, the beginning, of a happy double life. And—I went and looked to make sure—there was the saddle, too, and the bridle.

But that Christmas, which my father had planned so carefully, was it the best or the worst I ever knew? He often asked me that; I never could answer as a boy. I think now that it was both. It covered the whole distance from brokenhearted misery to bursting happiness—too fast. A grown-up could hardly have stood it.

SUGGESTIONS FOR STUDY:

1. Is the child or the adult superior in the implied comparison in the last sentence?
2. Does the first paragraph indicate that Steffens remembers his boyish feelings and describes them with precision?
3. What reactions of Lennie's strike you most forcefully as genuine?
4. What is the main idea? Is it directly stated? If so, where?
5. What word is being repeated in the first dialog? Is this word repeated later in the essay? Effectively? Can you cite other examples of effective repetition?
6. Do sentences like "I was in despair" or sentences like "Then we bolted" predominate?
7. Does Steffens vary his sentence length and structure? Does he have any sentences climactically arranged?
8. Does Steffens become melodramatic or remain factual in telling of the climactic end to Lennie's misery?
9. What is the meaning of *disheveled, horn, curried*. Is the level of diction here similar to Savo's? Why?
10. Write a theme about a Christmas or other holiday, or about some especially moving childhood experience.

Initiation, whether for dogs, coon hunters, or college students, is a rite to be remembered. It is a highly personal experience, and E. B. White, who has refined the art of personal commentary, writes of it with wisdom and sympathy.

COON HUNT
by E. B. White

THERE WERE two dogs with us the night we went coon hunting. One was an old hound, veteran of a thousand campaigns, who knew what we were up to and who wasted no time in idle diversions. The other was a puppy, brought along to observe and learn; to him the star-sprinkled sky and the deep dark woods and the myriad scents and the lateness of the hour and the frost ground were intoxicating. The excitement of our departure was too much for his bowels. Tied in the truck, he was purged all the way over to Winkumpaw Brook and was hollow as a rotten log before the night was well under way. This may have had something to do with what happened.

It was great hunting that night, perfect for man and beast, a fateful night for coon. The stars leaned close, and some lost their hold and fell. I was amazed at how quickly and easily the men moved through the woods in strange country, guided by hunches and a bit of lantern gleam. The woods hit back at you if you let your guard down.

We were an odd lot. A couple of the men were in coveralls

From *One Man's Meat* by E. B. White. Copyright 1941, by E. B. White. Reprinted by permission of Harper & Brothers.

—those bunny suits garage mechanics wear. One old fellow had been all stove to pieces in a car accident; another was down with a hard cold and a racking cough; another had broken two ribs the day before and had been strapped up that afternoon by a doctor. He had killed the pain with a few shots of whisky and the spirits had evidently reminded him of coon hunting. This fellow had a terrible thirst for water all during the night and he had a way of straying off from the main party and hugging the water courses where he could kneel and drink when the need was great. We could sometimes follow the progress of his thirst in the winking of his buglight, in some faraway valley. After a bit he would rejoin us. "I'm drier'n a covered bridge," he would say disconsolately.

I felt a strong affinity for the puppy because he and I were the new ones to this strange game, and somehow it seemed to me we were sharing the same excitement and mystery of a night in the woods. I had begun to feel the excitement back in the kitchen of the farmhouse, where the hunters had gathered, dropping in and standing about against the walls of the room. The talk began right away, all the cooning lore, the tales of being lost from three in the morning until six, and the tricks a coon would play on a dog. There was a woman in the room, wife of the owner of the old dog, and she was the only one for whom the night held no special allure. She sat knitting a huge mitten. Mostly, the hunters paid no attention to her. Only one remark went her way. One of the men, observing the mitten, asked:

"Gettin' that man o' yours ready for winter?"

She nodded.

"I should kill him before winter if he was mine—he's no good for anything else," the fellow continued, pleasantly.

The woman raised a grudging smile to this sure-fire witticism. She plied the needles without interruption. This obviously was not the first time she had been left at home while men and dogs went about their business, and it wasn't going to be the last time either. For her it was just one night in a long succession of nights. This was the fall and in the fall the men hunted coon. They left after sundown and returned before sunup. That was all there was to that.

The best coon country is always far away. Men are roamers, and getting a long way from home is part of the sport. Our motorcade consisted of two vehicles, a truck for the dogs and owners, and a sedan for the hangers-on, lantern-bearers, and advisory committee. The old dog jumped into place the minute he was let out of the barn; the puppy was hoisted in and tied. The two of them sat on a pile of straw just behind the cab. The man with the broken ribs got into the sedan. Nobody seemed to think it was in the least odd that he was going coon hunting, to walk twelve or fifteen miles in rough country. He said the adhesive tape held everything O.K. and anyway, he said, the only time his chest hurt was when he breathed.

We advanced without stealth, the truck leading. The headlights of our car shone directly in the faces of the dogs. The old dog leaned back craftily against the sideboards, to steady himself against the motion. He half closed his eyes and was as quiet on the journey as a middle-aged drummer on a way train. The pup crouched uneasily and was frequently thrown. He would rare up and sniff, then crouch again, then a curve would throw him and he would lose his balance and go down. He found a hole in the sideboards and occasionally would press his nose through to sniff the air. Then the excitement would attack his bowels and he would let go all over everything—with some difficulty because of the violent motion of the truck. The old dog observed this untidiness with profound contempt.

We got away from the highway after a while and followed a rough back road up into some country I had never been into. At last we got out and let the old hound go. He went to work instantly, dropping downhill out of sight. We could hear his little bell tinkling as he ranged about in the dim valley between us and a night-struck lake. When he picked up a scent, suddenly his full round tones went through you, and the night was a gong that had been struck. The old dog knew his business. The men, waiting around, would discuss in great detail his hunting and would describe what he was doing off there, and what the coon was doing; but I doubted that they knew, and they just kept making things up the way children do. As soon as the hound barked tree, which is a slightly different sound than the sound of the running, we followed his voice and shot the coon.

Once the dog led us to an old apple tree in an almost impenetrable thicket, and when the flashlights were shined up into the topmost branches no coon was there. The owner was puzzled and embarrassed. Nothing like this had ever happened before, he said. There was a long period of consultation and speculation, all sorts of theories were advanced. The most popular was that the coon had climbed the apple tree, then crossed, squirrel-like, into the branches of a nearby hackmatack, then descended, fooling the hound. Either this was the case or the dog had made an error. Upward of an hour was spent trying every angle of this delicious contretemps.

The puppy was held in leash most of the time, but when the first coon was treed he was allowed to watch the kill. Lights from half a dozen flashlights swept the tree top and converged to make a halo, with the coon's bright little sharp face in the center of the luminous ring. Our host lethargically drew his pistol, prolonging the climax with a legitimate sense of the theater. No one spoke while he drew a bead. The shot seemed to puncture first the night, then the coon. The coon lost his grip and landed with a thud, still alive and fighting. The old hound rushed in savagely, to grab him by the throat and finish him off. It was a big bull coon; he died bravely and swiftly, and the hound worked with silent fury. Then the puppy, in leash, was allowed to advance and sniff. He was trembling in every muscle, and was all eyes and ears and nose —like a child being allowed to see something meant only for grownups. (I felt a little that way myself.) As he stretched his nose forward timidly to inhale the heady smell of warm coon the old hound, jealous, snarled and leaped. The owner jerked back. The puppy yelped in terror. Everyone laughed. It was a youngster, getting burned by life—that sort of sight. Made you laugh.

After midnight we moved into easier country about ten miles away. Here the going was better—old fields and orchards, where the little wild apples lay in thick clusters under the trees. Old stone walls ran into the woods, and now and then there would be an empty barn as a ghostly landmark. The night grew frosty and the ground underfoot was slippery with rime. The bare birches wore the stars on their fingers, and the world rolled seductively, a dark symphony of brooding groves and plains. Things had gone well, and everyone was content just to be out in the small hours, following the musical directions of a wise and busy dog.

The puppy's owner had slipped the leash and allowed his charge to range about a bit. Nobody was paying much attention to him. The pup stayed with the party mostly, and although he was aware of the long-range operations of the older dog, he seemed to know that this was out of his class; he seemed timid of the woods and tended to stay close, contenting himself with sniffing about and occasionally jumping up to kiss someone's face. We were stepping along through the woods, the old hound near at hand, when the thing happened. Suddenly the puppy (who had not made a sound up to this point) let out a loud whoop and went charging off on a tangent. Everybody stopped dead in surprise.

"What goes on here anyway?" said somebody quietly.

The old hound was as mystified as the rest of us. This was a show-off stunt apparently, this puppy trying to bark coon. Nobody could make it out. Obviously there was no coon scent or the old dog would have picked it up instantly and been at his work.

"What in *the* devil?" asked somebody.

The puppy was howling unmercifully as though possessed. He charged here and there and came back along his own track passing us at a crazy mad pace, and diving into the woods on the other side of the trail. The yelps sounded hysterical now. Again the puppy charged back. This time as he passed we could see that he had a queer look in his eye and that his movements were erratic. He would dive one way at a terrible clip, then stop and back off as though ducking an enemy, half cringing; but he kept putting up this terrible holler and commotion. Once he came straight at me. I stepped aside and he went by screaming.

"Runnin' fit," said his owner. "That's the trouble. I can tell now by the way he acts. He's took with cramps in his bowwils and he don't know anythin' to do 'cept run and holler. C'mon, Dusty, c'mon, boy!"

He kept calling him softly. But Dusty was in another world and the shapes were after him. It was an eerie business, this crazy dog tearing around in the dark woods, half coming at you, half running from you. Even the old dog seemed disturbed and worried, as though to say: "You see—you *will* bring a child along, after his bedtime."

The men were patient, sympathetic now.

"That's all it is, he's took with a fit."

Dusty charged into the midst of us, scattering us. He stopped, bristling, his eyes too bright, a trace of froth at his mouth. He seemed half angry, half scared and wanting comfort. "Nothing much you can do, he'll run it off," they said.

And Dusty ran it off, in the deep dark woods, big with imaginary coons and enormous jealous old hounds, alive with the beautiful smells of the wild. His evening had been too much for him; for the time being he was as crazy as a loon. Someone suggested we go home.

We started moving up toward the cars, which were two or three fields away over where you could see the elms black against the sky. The thought of home wasn't popular. A counter suggestion was made to prolong the hunting, and we separated off into two parties, one to return to the cars, the other to cut across country with the old dog and intercept the main body where a certain woods road met the highway. I walked several more miles, and for the first time began to feel cold. It was another hour before I saw Dusty again. He was all right. All he needed was to be held in somebody's arms. He was very, very sleepy. He and I were both sleepy. I think we will both remember the first night we ever went coon hunting.

SUGGESTIONS FOR STUDY:

1. Who alone is named?
2. Would the sketch be improved if all the hunters were identified by name? Why? Why not?
3. Are the hunters individualized at all? How?

4. How many times does White compare himself to the puppy? Where? Why?
5. What is the purpose of introducing the knitting woman?
6. What tone is suggested by *all stove to pieces, hackmatack,* "*drier'n a covered bridge,*" *terrible holler and commotion?*
7. What tone is suggested by "The stars leaned close, and some lost their hold and fell," and "The bare birches wore the stars on their fingers"?
8. What tone is suggested by a strong *affinity,* delicious *contretemps, lethargically* drew, *eerie* business, a *counter* suggestion, said *disconsolately?* What do the words mean?
9. Has the writer successfully blended the kinds of diction cited above?
10. Write a theme in which a natural background plays a large part.

....

America's most famous humorist recounts his initiation into the trade from which he took his penname.

A CUB-PILOT'S EXPERIENCE
by *Samuel L. Clemens*

WHAT WITH lying on the rocks four days at Louisville, and some other delays, the poor old *Paul Jones* fooled away about two weeks in making the voyage from Cincinnati to New Orleans. This gave me a chance to get acquainted with one of the pilots, and he taught me how to steer the boat, and thus made the fascination of river life more potent than ever for me.

It also gave me a chance to get acquainted with a youth
....
Reprinted from *Life on the Mississippi,* by Samuel L. Clemens.

who had taken deck passage—more's the pity; for he easily borrowed six dollars of me on a promise to return to the boat and pay it back to me the day after we should arrive. But he probably died or forgot, for he never came. It was doubtless the former, since he had said his parents were wealthy, and he only travelled deck passage because it was cooler.

I soon discovered two things. One was that a vessel would not be likely to sail for the mouth of the Amazon under ten or twelve years; and the other was that the nine or ten dollars still left in my pocket would not suffice for so impossible an exploration as I had planned, even if I could afford to wait for a ship. Therefore it followed that I must contrive a new career. The *Paul Jones* was now bound for St. Louis. I planned a siege against my pilot, and at the end of three hard days he surrendered. He agreed to teach me the Mississippi River from New Orleans to St. Louis for five hundred dollars, payable out of the first wages I should receive after graduating. I entered upon the small enterprise of "learning" twelve or thirteen hundred miles of the great Mississippi River with the easy confidence of my time of life. If I had really known what I was about to require of my faculties, I should not have had the courage to begin. I supposed that all a pilot had to do was to keep his boat in the river, and I did not consider that that could be much of a trick, since it was so wide.

The boat backed out from New Orleans at four in the afternoon, and it was "our watch" until eight. Mr. Bixby, my chief, "straightened her up," ploughed her along past the sterns of the other boats that lay at the Levee, and then said, "Here, take her; shave those steamships as close as you'd peel an apple." I took the wheel, and my heart-beat fluttered up into the hundreds; for it seemed to me that we were about to scrape the side off every ship in the line, we were so close. I held my breath and began to claw the boat away from the danger; and I had my own opinion of the pilot who had known no better than to get us into such peril, but I was too wise to express it. In half a minute I had a wide margin of safety intervening between the *Paul Jones* and the ships; and within ten seconds more I was set aside in disgrace, and Mr. Bixby was going into danger again and flaying me alive with abuse of my cowardice. I was stung, but I was obliged to admire the easy confidence with which my chief loafed from side to side of his wheel, and trimmed the ships so closely that disaster seemed ceaselessly imminent. When he had cooled a little he told me that the easy water was close ashore and the current outside, and therefore we must hug the bank, upstream, to get the benefit of the former, and stay well out, down-stream, to take advantage of the latter. In my own mind I resolved to be a down-stream pilot and leave the up-streaming to people dead to prudence.

Now and then Mr. Bixby called my attention to certain things. Said he, "This is Six-Mile Point." I assented. It was pleasant enough information, but I could not see the bearing of it. I was not conscious that it was a matter of any interest to me. Another time he said, "This is Nine-Mile Point." Later he said, "This is Twelve-Mile Point." They were all about level with the water's edge; they all looked about alike to me; they were monotonously unpicturesque. I hoped Mr. Bixby would change the subject. But no; he would crowd up around a point, hugging the shore with affection, and then say: "The slack water ends here, abreast this bunch of China-trees; now we cross over." So he crossed over. He gave me the wheel once or twice, but I had no luck. I either came near clipping off the edge of a sugar plantation, or I yawed too far from shore, and so dropped back into disgrace again and got abused.

The watch was ended at last, and we took supper and went to bed. At midnight the glare of a lantern shone in my eyes, and the night watchman said: "Come, turn out!"

And then he left. I could not understand this extraordinary procedure; so I presently gave up trying to, and dozed off to sleep. Pretty soon the watchman was back again, and this time he was gruff. I was annoyed. I said:

"What do you want to come bothering around here in the middle of the night for? Now, as like as not, I'll not get to sleep again to-night."

The watchman said:

"Well, if this ain't good, I'm blessed."

The "off-watch" was just turning in, and I heard some brutal laughter from them, and such remarks as "Hello, watchman! an't the new cub turned out yet? He's delicate, likely. Give him some sugar in a rag, and send for the chambermaid to sing 'Rock-a-by, Baby,' to him."

About this time Mr. Bixby appeared on the scene. Something like a minute later I was climbing the pilothouse steps with some of my clothes on and the rest in my arms. Mr. Bixby was close behind, commenting. Here was something fresh—this thing of getting up in the middle of the night to go to work. It was a detail in piloting that had never occurred to me at all. I knew that boats ran all night, but somehow I had never happened to reflect that somebody had to get up out of a warm bed to run them. I began to fear that piloting was not quite so romantic as I had imagined it was; there was something very real and worklike about this new phase of it.

It was a rather dingy night, although a fair number of stars were out. The big mate was at the wheel, and he had the old tub pointed at a star and was holding her straight up the middle of the river. The shores on either hand were not much more than half a mile apart, but they seemed wonderfully far away and ever so vague and indistinct. The mate said:

"We've got to land at Jones's plantation, sir."

The vengeful spirit in me exulted. I said to myself, "I wish you joy of your job, Mr. Bixby; you'll have a good time finding Mr. Jones's plantation such a night as this; and I hope you never *will* find it as long as you live."

Mr. Bixby said to the mate:

"Upper end of the plantation, or the lower?"

"Upper."

"I can't do it. The stumps there are out of water at this stage. It's no great distance to the lower, and you'll have to get along with that."

"All right, sir. If Jones don't like it, he'll have to lump it, I reckon."

And then the mate left. My exultation began to cool and my wonder to come up. Here was a man who not only proposed to find this plantation on such a night, but to find either end of it you preferred. I dreadfully wanted to ask a question, but I was carrying about as many short answers as my cargo-room would admit of, so I held my peace. All I desired to ask Mr. Bixby was the simple question whether he was ass enough to really imagine he was going to find that plantation on a night when all plantations were exactly alike and all of the same color. But I held in. I used to have fine inspirations of prudence in those days.

Mr. Bixby made for the shore and soon was scraping it, just the same as if it had been daylight. And not only that, but singing:

"Father in heaven, the day is declining," etc.

It seemed to me that I had put my life in the keeping of a peculiarly reckless outcast. Presently he turned on me and said:

"What's the name of the first point above New Orleans?"

I was gratified to be able to answer promptly, and I did. I said I didn't know.

"Don't *know?*"

This manner jolted me. I was down at the foot again, in a moment. But I had to say just what I had said before.

"Well, you're a smart one!" said Mr. Bixby. "What's the name of the *next* point?"

Once more I didn't know.

"Well, this beats any thing. Tell me the name of *any* point or place I told you."

I studied a while and decided that I couldn't.

"Look here! What do you start out from, above Twelve-Mile Point, to cross over?"

"I—I—don't know."

"You—you—don't know?" mimicking my drawling manner of speech. "What *do* you know?"

"I—I—nothing, for certain."

"By the great Caesar's ghost, I believe you! You're the stupidest dunderhead I ever saw or ever heard of, so help me Moses! The idea of *you* being a pilot—*you!* Why, you don't know enough to pilot a cow down a lane."

Oh, but his wrath was up! He was a nervous man, and he

shuffled from one side of his wheel to the other as if the floor was hot. He would boil a while to himself, and then overflow and scald me again.

"Look here! What do you suppose I told you the names of those points for?"

I tremblingly considered a moment, and then the devil of temptation provoked me to say:

"Well—to—to—be entertaining, I thought."

This was a red rag to the bull. He raged and stormed so (he was crossing the river at the time) that I judge it made him blind, because he ran over the steering-oar of a trading-scow. Of course the traders sent up a volley of red-hot profanity. Never was a man so grateful as Mr. Bixby was; because he was brimful, and here were subjects who could *talk back*. He threw open a window, thrust his head out, and such an irruption followed as I never had heard before. The fainter and farther away the scowmen's curses drifted, the higher Mr. Bixby lifted his voice and the weightier his adjectives grew. When he closed the window he was empty. You could have drawn a seine through his system and not caught curses enough to disturb your mother with. Presently he said to me in the gentlest way:

"My boy, you must get a little memorandum-book; and every time I tell you a thing, put it down right away. There's only one way to be a pilot, and that is to get this entire river by heart. You have to know it just like A B C."

This was a dismal revelation to me; for my memory was never loaded with anything but blank cartridges. However, I did not feel discouraged long. I judged that it was best to make some allowances, for doubtless Mr. Bixby was "stretching." Presently he pulled a rope and struck a few strokes on the big bell. The stars were all gone now, and the night was as black as ink. I could hear the wheels churn along the bank, but I was not entirely certain that I could see the shore. The voice of the invisible watchman called up from the hurricane desk:

"What's this, sir?"

"Jones's plantation."

I said to myself, "I wish I might venture to offer a small

bet that it isn't." But I did not chirp. I only waited to see. Mr. Bixby handled the engine-bells, and in due time the boat's nose came to the land, a torch glowed from the forecastle, a man skipped ashore, a darky's voice on the bank said, "Gimme de k'yarpetbag, Mass' Jones," and the next moment we were standing up the river again, all serene. I reflected deeply a while and then said—but not aloud—"Well, the finding of that plantation was the luckiest accident that ever happened; but it couldn't happen again in a hundred years." And I fully believed it *was* an accident, too.

By the time we had gone seven or eight hundred miles up the river, I had learned to be a tolerably plucky up-stream steersman, in daylight, and before we reached St. Louis I had made a trifle of progress in night-work, but only a trifle. I had a note-book that fairly bristled with the names of towns, "points," bars, islands, bends, reaches, etc.; but the information was to be found only in the note-book—none of it was in my head. It made my heart ache to think I had only got half of the river set down; for as our watch was four hours off and four hours on, day and night, there was a long four-hour gap in my book for every time I had slept since the voyage began.

My chief was presently hired to go on a big New Orleans boat, and I packed my satchel and went with him. She was a grand affair. When I stood in her pilot-house I was so far above the water that I seemed perched on a mountain; and her decks stretched so far away, fore and aft, below me, that I wondered how I could ever have considered the little *Paul Jones* a large craft. There were other differences, too. The *Paul Jones*'s pilot-house was a cheap, dingy, battered rattle-trap, cramped for room; but here was a sumptuous glass temple; room enough to have a dance in; showy red and gold window curtains; an imposing sofa; leather cushions and a back to the high bench where visiting pilots sit, to spin yarns and "look at the river"; bright, fanciful "cuspadores," instead of a broad wooden box filled with sawdust; nice new oilcloth on the floor; a hospitable big stove for winter; a wheel as high as my head, costly with inlaid work; a wire tiller-rope; bright brass knobs for the bells; and a tidy, white-aproned, black "texas-tender," to bring up tarts and ices and coffee during mid-watch, day and night. Now this was "something like"; and so I began to take heart once more to believe that piloting was a romantic sort of occupation after all. The moment we were under way I began to prowl about the great steamer and fill myself with joy. She was as clean and as dainty as a drawing-room; when I looked down her long, gilded saloon, it was like gazing through a splendid tunnel; she had an oil-picture, by some gifted sign-painter, on every state-room door; she glittered with no end of prism-fringed chandeliers; the clerk's office was elegant, the bar was marvellous, and the barkeeper had been barbered and upholstered at incredible cost. The boiler-deck (*i.e.*, the second story of the boat, so to speak) was as spacious as a church, it seemed to me; so with the forecastle; and there was no pitiful handful of deck-hands, firemen, and roustabouts down there, but a whole battalion of men. The fires were fiercely glaring from a long row of furnaces, and over them were eight huge boilers! This was unutterable pomp. The mighty engines—but enough of this. I had never felt so fine before. And when I found that the regiment of natty servants respectfully "sir'd" me, my satisfaction was complete.

SUGGESTIONS FOR STUDY:

1. Is Clemens' purpose narrative or expository? Is exposition present? Where?
2. Are the details in the description of the New Orleans boat arranged in a logical order?
3. Does the comparison with the *Paul Jones* help to make the last sentence convincing?
4. Does the remark about Mr. Bixby's gratitude at having someone to talk back to him testify to the writer's observation and understanding of people?
5. Is Bixby's gentleness after the storm of profanity credible?
6. What figure does Clemens use to indicate Bixby is purged of profanity? Is it appropriate?
7. Does Clemens use figurative language elsewhere? Where? Much?
8. What is basic to the humor in "I was gratified to be able to answer promptly, and I did"? Is there similar humor elsewhere?

9. What is the meaning of *ceaselessly imminent, irruption, pomp, natty?*
10. Write a theme about an experience of your own paralleling Clemens'; that is, you learn to get along with a person or situation not altogether congenial to you.

The campers mean trouble but old Joe Bessom will be glad to see them just the same.

THE CAMPERS ARE COMING
by *William Chapman White*

THE LAST T-shirt is bought, the last suitcase packed. In a day or so Junior and his sister will be heading north to summer camps. In good time. Their mother is probably near collapse from the combination of shopping, packing and sitting on Junior's impatience and hour counting. She can soon get a good rest. Junior and sister won't be back until the end of August.

If the parents of all the kids heading north are exhausted by camping preparations they ought to know what has been going on up in Michigan, in the Adirondacks and in New England, where things have to be done to get the camps ready for the kids. A city mother worn out preparing for one child ought to know old Joe Bessom, handyman at a camp for twenty years, as he gets ready for a hundred children.

A month ago Joe and his helpers started to repair the winter damage. They patched holes in roofs that were hit by falling branches and rebuilt the corner of the dock that the

Copyright 1952, The New York Herald Tribune, Inc.

winter ice had wrecked. They removed fallen trees. They split firewood and piled it. They painted boats, put out the safety floats in the water, set up new diving boards, cut the weeds, cleaned up the tennis courts and repaired tables, chairs and bunks.

At the same time Joe helped the camp director make arrangements with grocers, dairies and vegetable growers. He helped find a replacement for Mrs. Random, who did the camp laundry for the last ten years but doesn't feel up to it this season. He helped find a new cook to take the place of Mrs. Grey, whose daughter is having a baby and who will have to stay home. In odd moments Joe fixes the camp truck, the kitchen stove, the flagpole, and chases chipmunks from the bunkhouses. He isn't the slightest bit worn out. On the contrary, he's eager for the campers to arrive.

In all the many jobs there is a sense of things about to happen. The lake shores that have long been silent will soon echo the calls of a hundred kids. The lake waters, unbroken by a diving body or a canoe paddle, will begin to foam and splash. Back roads where no foot has trod since last autumn will soon be rutted by the camp truck, and a familiar cry will sound in the brush: "Johnny, the mail's in and there's a parcel from home for you, as big as a cake." Local characters are brushing up their dialect for the campfire tales of the Indians that never were and of the wild animals that never could have been. As for the animals themselves, the frogs, toads and garter snakes in the neighborhood, they seem to be making themselves scarce as if they sensed what was coming. The yellow perch and sunnies in the lake still swim about, little knowing what is soon to be dangled in front of their eyes. There seem to be plenty of angle worms, as witless as ever.

As Joe, the handyman, does a last paint job, he talks to his helpers about the kids of last year. "Remember that boy who learned to hoot like an owl and used to wake up the whole camp at 2 every morning? And that one from New York who ate enough for six men—I remember he used to put maple syrup and sugar on his baked beans. And the girl who got a rope around a porcupine and wanted to take it home for her baby brother? And the boy who put bullfrogs in every bed? And the one who covered himself with catsup and howled for help because a bear had attacked him? And the one who put water in the truck's gas tank on the last day because he didn't want to be driven to the railroad station? Oh, brother, were they something! I wonder if they're all coming back this season."

Joe puts down his paint brush for a moment and looks across the lake. "Yet, you know, it'll be good to have 'em, every one of 'em. Things have been peaceful around here for nine months now and that's long enough."

SUGGESTIONS FOR STUDY:

1. What is White's purpose?
2. What does he accomplish in the first two paragraphs?
3. Are the main divisions of the selection clearcut?
4. Is this generalized description characterized by specific detail? For example?
5. What is characteristic of the verbs?
6. Write a theme describing a general institution in specific terms.

Things are not always what they seem.

MAINE GUIDE
by Louise Dickinson Rich

MY SISTER and I used to play a game called "Husband's Occupation?" It was a simple-minded game that we made up off application blanks of various sorts. One of us

From *WE TOOK TO THE WOODS* by Louise Dickinson Rich. Copyright, 1942, by Louise Dickinson Rich, published by J. B. Lippincott Company.

would ask suddenly, "Husband's Occupation?" and the other had to think up a possible but not very probable answer. "Flea trainer," for example. Or "Percheron Faulter." Or "Sealer of Weights and Measures." I guess we were easily entertained.

I guess we still are, because I am amused, spasmodically, at being married to a Maine guide. Oh, yes, Ralph's a guide, too, although he doesn't work at it much.

Of course a guide has to be a good woodsman and canoeman and camp cook and emergency doctor, and the State of Maine ascertains that he is, before issuing him a license to guide. But he could never earn a living if he didn't also make the grade with the sports—same as dudes of the West—as "quite a character." He has to be laconic. He has to be picturesque. Maine guides have a legend of quaintness to uphold, and, boy! do they uphold it. They're so quaint that they creak. They ought to be. They work hard enough at it.

Here's the Maine guide. He wears what amounts to a uniform. It consists of a wool shirt, preferably plaid, nicely faded to soft, warm tones; dark pants, either plus-fours, for some unknown reason, or riding breeches; wool socks and the soleless, Indian-type moccasin, or high laced boots. He carries a bandanna in his hip pocket and may or may not wear another knotted around his neck. But he must wear a battered felt hat, with a collection of salmon flies stuck in the band, and he must wear it with an air; and he must wear a hunting knife day and night; and he must look tough and efficient. If he has high cheek bones and tans easily, that is his good luck. He can then admit to part-Indian ancestry, accurately or not. Indian blood is an item highly esteemed by sports. Naturally he could do his work as well in mail-order slacks, or in a tuxedo, for that matter; but the sports wouldn't think so. Sports are funny.

"That fellow there," the sport is supposed to say, showing his vacation movies in his Westchester rumpus room, "was my quarter-breed guide. He's quite a character. Never had any education beyond the seventh grade, but I don't know anyone I'd rather spend a week alone with. That's the real test. He's a genuine natural philosopher. For instance, we were talking about the War, and he said—and I never thought of it this way before—." What the guide said he probably lifted from Shirer's book, but translated into Down East, it wouldn't be recognizable.

A few livid scars are a great asset to a guide. It doesn't matter how he got them. Maybe as a barefoot boy he stepped on a rake. The holes make swell bear-trap scars, acquired one night up in the Allagash, when the thermometer was at thirty below and the nearest settlement was fifty miles away. Maybe he cut his hand peeling potatoes. It sounds much better to say a beaver bit him. Maybe he fell downstairs and gashed his forehead. When asked—and he'll be asked all right—he can tell all about his big fight with the lynx. They all make good stories to tell around the evening camp-fire.

Oh, those evening camp-fires! That's when the good guide gets in his dirty work. That's when he sows the seed for a re-engagement next year.

This is the set-up:—Supper—fresh-caught trout with bacon curls, potatoes baked in the coals and slathered with butter, a kind of biscuit cooked in a frying pan and resembling Yorkshire pudding, canned peas and fruit—is over. The sports, pleasantly stuffed and mildly weary from having "helped" paddle for ten or twelve miles, stretch out around the fire. Down on the shingle that natural philosopher, that real character, Bobcat Bill, washes the dishes. The water glows like blood-stained ebony in the leaping light, and the firs stand up behind, black and motionless. Back in the bush a fox barks and a deer crashes away from the scent of woodsmoke. All around lies the wilderness, dark and unknown and sinister. Inside the little pool of light is all that is left of the safe and familiar—the canoes drawn up on the shore, the piled packsacks and blanket rolls, the forms and faces of friends. A loon sends its lost-soul lament over the darkling water, and a shiver runs around the fire. Then Bobcat Bill strolls up from the lake, throws an armful of dry-ki onto the blaze, and begins tossing blankets toward the group. In the flash of a buck's tail the old magic begins to work. The tight little fire-hearted circle of fellowship is formed. We're all brothers here, united by our common cause against the power of the black beyond. We're all valiant, noble renegades from civilization's chafing bonds. We're dangerous and free!

The loon throws its blood-curdling cry against the mountains once more, and laughs its crazy laughter.

"Never hear one of them critters a-hollerin'," Bobcat Bill drifts easily into his act, "but what it 'minds me of one time I was lost up on them big caribou barrens across the lake. That's how I come by this here scar on my shoulder. Reason I was up in there, a feller had met foul play—"

I'm making guides sound like a bunch of frauds, and I don't mean to. They work hard and they're in a difficult position. Like all merchandisers, they're obliged to give the customer what he wants, and it's their tough luck that the customer wants adventure. Adventure, free of actual risk, is hard to produce; and the state frowns on the actual killing off of sports, even by accident. So the guide has to make the customer believe himself Daniel Boone's contemporary equivalent, without actually letting him stick his neck out too far. A little discomfort, yes. That'll make fine telling back in Westchester. Too much discomfort, no. Actual danger, a thousand times no, not even if he insists with tears and pleading that he really wants to rough it, to get off the beaten track into tough country, to pit his own brains and brawn against death by violence or starvation. It's too easy to meet trouble in this country without deliberately looking for it.

So what's the answer? The answer is atmosphere:—tall tales around the camp-fire, a perpetually grim and watchful bearing, a knife and revolver worn always at the ready. The answer is illusion:—jam into bear's blood, bobcat into Canada lynx, vaccination scar into dagger wound.

SUGGESTIONS FOR STUDY:

1. What is the purpose of the first two paragraphs?
2. What is the purpose of the third paragraph?
3. How many main divisions are there in this character sketch?
4. What contributes to the satire in the description of the evening campfire? Is the satire effective?
5. What is the meaning of *laconic, livid, slathered?*

6. Write a character sketch of a type; try to keep it as specific as Mrs. Rich's sketch.

A philosophic farmer upsets Nature's plan and finds reason to lament what man has made of chickens.

CLUCKS AND QUACKS
by John Gould

      SETTING A HEN on duck eggs is a mean and contemptible trick. Every time I do it, I am sorry. I promise myself I shall never do it again. And then every year I do it—for a practical reason.

You see, mallard ducks start laying early in the season, and each of the girls will drop eight or ten eggs around the edge of the pond before she realizes it's time to go broody. I wade out in my rubber boots and gather these eggs in, and inside of a week, I'll have a bowl of duck eggs. Duck eggs are good to eat, and we use them, but the family is only so big, and the hens are all laying, too.

So I find myself turning to the hens for an answer, because one of them is generally of a maternal turn of mind about that time and doesn't seem to have anything else to do. I fix up a nest in a hidden corner, arrange a dozen or so duck eggs, and clap a hot hen on them—just so we can have cunning little ducklings in the pond that much the sooner.

A hen is not overbright when she is at peak condition, but when she goes broody she loses all rational contacts. The

------

Reprinted from The Christian Science Monitor, June 26, 1952.

first thing you notice is her complete indifference to time. The incubation period for her own eggs is 21 days, but the duck eggs will take four weeks, perhaps even 30 days, and she doesn't know the difference. The best proof of this lies in the obvious—that if she had any inkling of what she was in for, she would quit exactly 21 days and one minute from the first involvement. But she doesn't. She sits there gazing intently at a crack in a board, and attends the fourth week as patiently as she nurtured the first. This shows you what to expect.

The next giveaway comes when the eggs hatch. A duckling may appear to peep like a chick, but an attentive ear can detect a distinct difference. A hen should notice this at once. But she doesn't. She assumes the full role of motherhood with every expectation that her web-footed young will be mostly whitemeat, which they will not. Her entire conduct shows she is 100 per cent misled, and believes blindly that all is well.

Baby ducks eat and drink after their own style, and are not like chicks. Mother doesn't notice this. It seems the alimentary tract of waterfowl differs from landlocked poultry, and ducks feed periodically to accommodate this difference. So when Mother gathers her babies under her, to hover them like chicks, the expectation of a lengthy lullaby is interrupted by the sudden sallying forth of the ducklings after more provender. The hen never really gets either up or down.

Water is another thing—baby chicks have to be dried off if they get wet, and a careful proprietor will provide a drinking fountain that minimizes moisture. But for ducks you can have a pan ten feet deep if you wish, and none of them has ever drowned yet. So Mother spends a great part of her time trying to coax her babies into the drier, and they splash all the more. Disintegration of the relationship is now well begun.

Another sad sight is to see Mother picking up shreds of goodies and offering them to the little ones, as good hens do. She will cluck about it, and mouth the kernel, and then drop it so a smaller beak can have it. But ducks don't speak her language, and while she is off by herself doing this, the ducklings are swizzling and guzzling and recking not. They do run under her at times, but the things baby ducks do under a hen keep a startled look in the old hen's eyes, and she looks like a steeplejack who is convinced the flue is about to collapse under him.

One of the things they do is to flip their bills. Ducks seem to wipe their bills on the wind they create by waggling their heads. If you should attempt the same maneuver, you would forthwith flop your own ears off, but a duck does it naturally, and appears to have a bill about six inches wide for the moment.

When a duckling does this in under a hen, it must make her think she has just found a hot electric circuit. Her face takes on a bewildered note, as if she felt it, but still doesn't believe it. You can see that she has been astonished in some way, and if you don't know about ducks' flipping their bills, you'd think she has just received some bad news.

Hens put up with these outrages because they are good mothers, and know their duty. But ducklings grow faster than chicks, and in about a week they are rather high-posted for hen accommodations. By this time, if you approach the pen and make a noise like a dish of wet bran, the brooding ducklings will all stand up and peep, hoisting their dame into the air, and they will come rushing toward you like a victorious football team escorting the coach off the field. The hen, about now, is ready to give up.

She gives up the day you let the little ones go to the pond. They sail away and leave her pacing the bank and calling to them not to get wet. This is definitely the end. Beaten and defeated, she shortly retires and forgets the whole sad affair. By nightfall she is ready to go back on a roost, and when I carry her into the henhouse I always apologize and promise never to do it again.

SUGGESTIONS FOR STUDY:

1. Is the final paragraph a return to the first?
2. Is Gould's expressed main idea to be taken completely seriously? Why?
3. What tone is suggested in the second paragraph by the phrase "each of the girls"?

232   Current Prose

4. Does Gould maintain this tone throughout?
5. What is the basis of the humor in "ducklings are swizzling and guzzling and recking not" or "ducklings . . . are rather high-posted for hen accommodations"?
6. Write a theme built around an incident which suggests an idea.

***

A reporter visits an American institution and paints a picture most of us will recognize.

JERSEY FAIR
by Bernard Peyton, Jr.

AT 9 A.M. the man in the purple shirt began his spiel: "Crowds! Crowds! Here's the largest thrill on the North American continent—those crazy, zany maniacs of speed, risking life and limb with only the turn of the wheel in open convertibles, sliding, smashing, twisting, turning, braiding autos like you braid long hair. . . ."

Up and down the midway, the chants picked up, drowsily, but then with staccato frenzy. Stout women troweled mounds of white popcorn. Farmers set pumpkins and eggplants in beds of kale as symmetrically as jeweled brooches. Ancient men with gnarled arms hoisted signs modestly promising "Sadistic Satisfaction—Korean Torture—The Coolie and the Mandarin's Daughter—Hear Them Moan—See Them Suffer." The 207th annual New Jersey State Fair had opened its eight-day stand.

A young girl from Freehold vigorously combed the bush of her cow's tail at the livestock exhibit. "She's got straight

Copyright 1952, The New York Herald Tribune, Inc.

legs and a good udder and a good back," the girl beamed, patting the Guernsey, "and she's got a good barrow—it doesn't thin out around the pins. I think she'll come in no worse than fourth in the judging on Wednesday." The girl said the cow's name was Landhome Rangers Beeswax, and her own, Betty Lou Maghan.

Then the people came, 75,000 of them, by the early afternoon. The spieler kept harassing them. "You'll see the human bomb," he thundered, "the man who blows himself up into smithereens in a coffin filled with ten sticks of dynamite" . . .

Out on the field, the bomb sourly turned down a photographer's request for a trial detonation. "Get paid for one bump a day," he muttered. Mollified, the bomb introduced himself as Capt. F. F. Frakes. "I don't drink liquor," he said, "and I'm a deacon in the Presbyterian Church. I was born two miles from Rabbittown, down Willow Branch of Happy Hollow on the side of Kilbuck Knob, Tennessee."

He pulled a wire threaded to a dynamite cap from his breast pocket and stuffed the ten sticks and a five-pound bag of flour at the base of a V-shaped steel shield inside the flimsy coffin. "That's what saves me," he said. "I just prop myself in a stoopin' position behind it, stuff my ears with cotton, touch the wire to the battery, and whoom, I go like a ball with the concussion.

"I used to crack Jenny flying machines into houses, water, trees—anything they put their money on the line for," he said, "but now I do the flying coffin. I tried it with a chicken hen first, and it didn't kill her, so I did it. In Langhorn, Pa., somebody moved the shield and the dynamite chewed up my hand and wrecked the $350 sound system.

"I got this box under control now, but the old one used to blow like a cracker box. Once a nail stuck in a man's head 300 feet away. They took him to the hospital, and the nail was only half a nail, but they took X-rays anyway to find the other half and charged me more than was necessary."

Capt. Frakes said he has donned his black-and-white football helmet 300 times now and exploded himself in the coffin, and he is no longer afraid. "I'm just living Monday, Tuesday, Wednesday, Thursday, Friday and Saturday like a lot of people pretend they live Sunday," he said. "I had a wonderful life, really."

SUGGESTIONS FOR STUDY:

1. What is Peyton's main idea? Is it expressed in any one sentence?
2. Is the man in the purple shirt an effective introduction? Why?
3. What aspect of the fair is Peyton most interested in?
4. Is Capt. Frakes clearly described? How?
5. What do the verbs of paragraph 2 have in common?
6. Describe a fair, carnival, convention, pep rally, basketball crowd, or other gathering; develop by means of the specific elements in the total impression.

*****

The American tourist has been called the greatest international shopper in history. Nowhere does our national mania for acquisition reveal itself more than in our passion for souvenirs. Bernard Kalb suggests that our enthusiasm often outruns our good sense.

SOUVENIR SHOPPING
by Bernard Kalb

SOME AMERICAN tourists abroad would rather die than come home empty-handed. Europe to them is a vast, roofless department store, with liqueurs sold at the French counter, tweeds at the English, and Borsalino hats at the

*****
Reprinted by permission from The New York Times, June 1, 1952.

Italian. Yet there are tourists who, turning up their noses at these highly advertised offerings, indulge in items like a chandelier that, somehow, looks just right in the flea market in Paris. It's the chandelier, they say, or nothing. So, to the chandelier salesman in the flea market, it will no doubt come as a surprise to learn that the objet d'art is still in its original wrapper.

For Americans are perhaps the most souvenir-happy of the globe-trotters and they soak up the world's odds and ends, often without any idea of what to do with them back home. Why a tourist in, say, Haiti will stop short at the sight of a voodoo drum up for sale is not difficult to understand. It is an arresting piece of furniture—a yard high, a foot in diameter, brilliantly colored. Not only is it different from the bric-a-brac sold anywhere else, it looks as if it will be a lot of fun to play in the living room Saturday nights. It is evocative, too, the root of the rhythmic da-da-da that comes down from the Haitian hills nightly like an endless rain. Anyway, there it is, on a shelf in a souvenir shoppe in Port-au-Prince, a sprawling store mostly full of mahogany bowls and straw sandals. The price: $20. It is irresistible.

When I was in Haiti recently I bought this drum. First time I stopped in at the shoppe I saw it, something of an abbreviated obelisk of color off in the corner. I strolled over casually, tapped it. Boom. In a flash the proprietor was at my side, whispering with enormous conviction that I didn't look like the sort of tourist who went in for mahogany spoons and forks. "A drum," he muttered hypnotically. "A drum." Still, it was much too impractical to snap up on the spot. Drumless, I stepped out into the clinging sunshine, but I found myself coming back all week, to run my fingers once or twice over the drumhead.

The boom kept getting better, and, finally, I succumbed. By that time, the price was $13.25. The drum was much too heavy to fly back on my airplane ticket, but the proprietor, detecting my impatience, said not to worry about it. He'd worry about it. He'd send it air freight, he said. Much cheaper that way. It would reach New York in a week—two, at the most—after I returned. Idlewild Airport would telephone. "Carve your initials in it," the proprietor said merrily, handing me a jackknife. "You'll have it in a week."

For one reason or another the drum did not arrive the first week, nor the second, so I dispatched a nasty letter to the shoppe. No reply. I telephoned Idlewild, asking if by any chance———. No, no chance. New York was unbearable without the drum.

A month later Idlewild called. I discovered at the airport that the drum was trussed up in a long sisal jacket. The customs man wanted to check on it, so we cut open the jacket. There stood the voodoo drum at last, unsheathed—a yard high, a foot in diameter, brilliantly colored. It looked exactly as it had on a shelf in the souvenir shoppe, except that on the customs counter at Idlewild it looked awful. As a matter of fact, it looked terrible. The trunk suddenly looked warped, the colors lurid, the sound hollow, the drumhead stained. I quickly searched for my initials, certain that———. They were there. The customs man had only one comment: "There's a six-dollar freight charge, too, son."

The drum looked even worse at home. Once or twice I tried a sharp tattoo of sound, but I had done better at 6 with a spoon and a kettle. I slowly lowered the drum into its jacket, and, as I was about to entomb it in the cellar, several of my friends stopped in. "Is that it?" they asked incredulously.

My only compensation is that lately I have taken to dropping in at their homes to see what they picked up when they were abroad. Here's the full list of what I uncovered in the course of a single week's investigation:

A bamboo bird cage, from Fortin, Mexico. "I thought I'd put a bird, or a flower pot, in it." He did neither. The cage is in the closet, has been for five years.

A burnoose, from Nazareth, Israel. "I thought I'd use it on the beach to protect my head from the sun." He hasn't, thinks it's too ostentatious.

A goat-skin milk bag, from Tunis. "I thought it would be just the thing to run down to the corner grocer and pick up two, three quarts of milk." He's just scared to use it, afraid it's contaminated.

An unstuffed hassock, made of goat skin, from Morocco. "I thought it would be fine to sit on in front of the television set." He tried it once, found his blue suit covered with goat hairs.

A little porcelain brandy barrel, from Perpignan, France. "I never saw brandy come out of a barrel before, like beer." She still hasn't.

A pair of peon's white trousers, from Guatemala. "I thought they would be wonderful for driving in the summer." He found a pair of slacks on Madison Avenue the other day that he likes a lot more, he says.

An ex-souvenir buyer summed up the situation philosophically the other day. "A serape I bought in some muddy market place in Texcoco, Mexico," he said, "looks about as good in my eighteenth century English parlor as my eighteenth century English parlor would look in Texcoco."

SUGGESTIONS FOR STUDY:

1. What is Kalb's main idea, and where is it expressed?
2. How many main divisions are there?
3. Is the original description of the voodoo drum paralleled later? Effectively?
4. What is the effect of the sentence fragments in the paragraphs about the voodoo drum?
5. How does the discussion of the friends' souvenirs contrast with that of the voodoo drum?
6. Are the final sentences of the paragraphs on the bird cage, burnoose, milk bag, and hassock constructed similarly? What is Kalb's purpose in this construction?
7. Are the direct quotations effective? Is the final one a good ending?
8. What is the meaning of *objet d'art, obelisk, evocative, sisal, incredulous, ostentatious, serape?*
9. Can you cite any words that suggest a less formal tone than the words above?
10. In a theme discuss a family possession that you consider ludicrous, or analyze a current mania.

An editorial writer for the New York Herald Tribune *muses on violence and its consequences.*

THE MURDERED TV SET

IT OBVIOUSLY is news when a man shoots a television set. Mr. Frank Walsh, the West Hempstead marksman who put a bullet through his large-sized screen, may not have been aware that he was making history. But he certainly has demonstrated a completely novel, as well as highly effective way of shutting off a TV set. His wife, understandably disturbed, called in the police after Mr. Walsh took dead aim and fired. But there is nothing about shooting television sets in the law books. The result is that Mr. Walsh today faces no recriminations except, of course, those offered by Mrs. Walsh.

Was it an act of unprovoked assault, or was it self-defense? This is a question that thoughtful citizens may well ponder. The answer depends in large part on what was on the screen at the time. Was it a politician? A comedian? A soap opera? A commercial? All of these have been known, at various times, to provoke listeners to stern action. Another key factor is, what was Mr. Walsh doing at the time? Was he watching the screen? Was he—one hesitates to suggest it—reading? Or—most likely of all—was he trying to get some sleep?

Without the answers to these and similar queries, it is impossible to judge the enormity of his crime, if crime it was.

Reprinted by permission from The New York Herald Tribune, October 22, 1952.

But let Mr. Walsh and others who share his feelings beware. Technology will not stand still. One of these days, some one is going to invent a television set that can shoot back.

SUGGESTIONS FOR STUDY:

1. Is this editorial serious in purpose?
2. Is the tone formal?
3. Is the contrast between purpose and tone effective?
4. What are the main divisions of the editorial?
5. Write a two-part theme—the first part to be the description of an incident, the second part to be a discussion of ideas involved in or suggested by the incident.

Proving that recipes can be more than just entries in a cookbook.

SALT OF THE EARTH
by Mabel Slack Shelton

I AM a slave to cookbooks. I admit it. And never am I more conscious of it than when I sit in the Zaugg's homey kitchen and watch Emmaline and her girls as they whizz gaily through a "baking day." Never once do they resort to a cookbook, as they turn out angel food cakes, rolls, pies, bread, and that delicious Pennsylvania Dutch goody they call "butter lemmels."

My mouth never fails to water when I so much as think of butter lemmels. They are light, delicately golden squares

----
Reprinted from The Christian Science Monitor, March 17, 1952.

of flaky dough folded over a center of butter and sugar, and simply dripping with goodness.

"How do you remember all your recipes so well?" I asked humbly, the first time I saw the three of them, mother and two flaxen-haired, rosy-cheeked daughters, working in perfectly synchronized harmony as they stirred, sifted, tasted, and handed buttered and floured pans to each other with split-second precision. Just like an assembly line!

"Recipes?" Emmaline paused, with her floury arms in her huge, yellow mixing bowl, a bewildered look in her china-blue eyes. Then the light dawned. "Ach, you mean receipts! In our head we keep them yet. It's no trouble."

"No trouble! But Emmaline, you cook dozens of things that are complicated, to say the least. Do you mean you have none of them written down?"

"I mean."

Well, I simply had to learn the secret of making butter lemmels and shoofly pie, so I undertook to get some of the "receipts" down on paper, though it turned out to be a complicated and long-drawn out process.

Amos Zaugg adores his brisk, competent Emmaline, even if the Amish do frown on any display of tender emotions. It is written large on his face as he watches her flit about their kitchen, heavy of waistline, but light of foot, bubbling over with her love of life and family. Eli, too, thinks "momma" a cut above all other women. (Especially a "dumkopf" like me, I fear.) But the eyes of father and son often meet in vast but tender amusement as Emmaline struggles with the English language, especially when she is instructing me in some household art, such as cooking.

Our first struggle was with dandelion salad, away last spring.

I had driven Emmaline and Hilda to the local tin shop, along with some pans and pails Emmaline wanted "re-bottomed." Dan Beiler, the tinner, was out and we sat in the cluttered little shop surrounded by other people's pans and pails until he came back. Dan is a cheery little grasshopper of a man, and only the fringe of snowy hair under his black Amish hat bespeaks his age.

"It's late I am," he greeted us, rattling up out in front

in an ancient coupé, which he can drive without being accused of "worldliness," since it is for business and not pleasure, "but my 'excuse-me' is goot." He extended the fingers of his right hand, which were stained an earthy green, and he and Emmaline exchanged smiles.

"Picking dandelion," she said, and then their talk ran on about how dandelion could "pep you up something wonderful," while he pegged away on the pans.

"Where do you buy this all-powerful dandelion?" I asked Emmaline on the way home. She pointed one stubby finger toward the yellow-dotted shoulder of the highway. "You don't buy dandelion; you pick."

"But those are weeds," I insisted.

Emmaline wagged her bonneted head. "All the same, it's dandelion. To get goot ones though, you wouldn't pick by the side of the road. It's dusty here. Down by the springhouse they grow better."

I was skeptical until I ate dandelion salad at the bountiful Zaugg table, where the salad, with its hot, sweet-sour dressing was a noble accompaniment to a nobler meal of plump spring chicken in a rolled pot pie, mashed potatoes, rich gravy, "red beets," two kinds of hot bread, plum cobbler, and yellow country butter and big goblets of cream-flecked milk.

"I must have the dandelion salad recipe," I told my smiling Dutch neighbors, "for even if it doesn't pep me up it tastes too good to resist."

It sounded simple enough, the getting of a recipe down on paper. And since twelve-year-old Anna had made the salad for supper that evening, I anticipated no difficulties, but that was before I started writing.

"First off, you pick your dandelion," Emmaline said. I thought of the old recipe for braised hare which starts out, "First, catch a hare," and looked to see if she could possibly be teasing. She was in dead earnest, her blue eyes "squiged" up tight, the way they are when concentrating.

The recipe progressed slowly, with Anna finally being called away from the dishpan to lend her assistance.

The recipe for dandelion salad: Wash and dry one pound of young dandelion. Place in bowl and let stand in warm place, after greens have been chopped. Mix two tablespoons butter and one-half cup cream. Beat two eggs, add one teaspoon salt and one-half teaspoon paprika, four tablespoons vinegar and one tablespoon sugar. Cook dressing to a soft custard and pour over greens hot. Add diced, boiled egg if desired.

"And the gritzel-grotzels you must not leave out," Emmaline warned.

Here was surely something new under the sun! I was positive I would have noticed anything as unusual as a gritzel-grotzel if I had ever eaten one.

"It's the little dices of bacon still," Anna contributed shyly, noting my bewilderment.

Ah, the little dices of bacon! I had indeed noticed them, thought how they complemented the dish. Anna had diced her bacon finely, fried it very crisp in the pan, then drained it on paper before adding it to the tangy, hot, delicious salad. So diced bacon makes gritzel-grotzels in Amishland. And my Dutch friends are the kindest, most lovable people extant or they would not bother with a dopple such as I. But I am slowly learning their ways, and as my knowledge increases my respect keeps pace with it, for these are frugal, kindly, hard-working folk who are indeed the salt of the earth.

SUGGESTIONS FOR STUDY:

1. Is Mrs. Shelton more concerned with food as food or food as a means of characterizing people?
2. Do the characters in the sketch speak? Do they act? Does Mrs. Shelton describe them?
3. How much analysis or labeling of characters does the writer engage in?
4. Would you say that Mrs. Shelton's attitude toward her subject is that of Amos and Eli toward Emmaline?
5. Have you ever heard anyone say *receipt* for *recipe*? Is it "correct"?
6. Are *dumkopf* and *gritzel-grotzel* English? Is *squiged*?
7. Who are the Amish?
8. Write a theme about a class or group of people whose customs in speech or dress or interests differ from your own; or write about an unusual individual.

In our well-fed country, we reputedly eat ourselves into the grave with considerable frequency. Here a well-fed country philosopher enters a dissenting opinion on the virtues of dieting.

IN PRAISE OF SALT PORK
by William Chapman White

UP IN the Adirondack hamlet of Sugarbush, where Virgil Lissom has been watching the scarlet maples fade to gold for the seventieth time, Virgil has also made his autumnal change. For him it isn't leaves, it's breakfasts. All summer long he's content to stick to things like bacon and sausage but come autumn the staff of life, as far as he is concerned, is salt pork fried to a crisp brown and served with cream gravy. Not every morning, maybe, but most mornings. Virgil has always scorned the light eater, particularly the light breakfaster. "What's the good of keepin' your figure," he used to ask, "if you ain't got the strength to move it around?"

Salt pork comes from pretty low down on the hog. It's a favorite Adirondack dish and goes back to the time when there was no fresh meat to be had in winter and when farmers butchered and cured their own meat and ate up every scrap. Today it gets snooted in the stores for fancier cuts but in Virgil's mind that only shows that the sons are not the men their fathers were—how could they be when they won't

Copyright 1952, The New York Herald Tribune, Inc.

even eat the same foods? Later decadent generations may sit around counting calories: the earlier generations didn't bother—they went out and worked 'em off. Virgil's not one for crying down the younger generation just because they're young—they have more serious faults than that—but he sometimes wonders whether the light breakfast hasn't much to do with the apparent decline of civilization.

Every time Virgil hears about the light breakfast he remembers old Joe Magee up on the Owlshead road. Joe went out to look for work one summer against his better judgment and took a job on a city fellow's place. Board, lodging and $10 a week. When the household breakfast of toast, butter and coffee was set in front of him, Joe couldn't believe his eyes. "You call that board, mister?" he asked. "That ain't even a decent-sized splinter." Whereupon he quit and went back to his regular summer profession of catching short trout out of Alder Brook and frying them on the spot with a slice of salt pork in the pan. The game warden caught up with him for that and fined him $25. Joe always blamed that on the city fellow. "He drove me to it," Joe explained. "You eat light breakfasts, you're going to get into trouble some time."

On these days in the farmhouse at Sugarbush the smells of autumn and of frying salt pork are alive and rich. Yet Virgil rarely gets anything as choice as that for breakfast without trouble. Even as his wife, Ithaca, freshens the meat in boiling water, dips it in breadcrumbs and gets the cream ready for the gravy, she's liable to argue that this is too heavy a diet for Virgil. That argument's been chronic ever since Ithaca read a magazine piece about calorie counting. Virgil's inclined to agree but he says: "Sure, salt pork's got calories but it's also got vitameens and any doctor'll tell you that a man's got to have vitameens."

Then Ithaca read somewhere that salt pork's liable to be bad for the heart. "Maybe so," Virgil agrees, helping himself to a fourth browned slice. "But that sort of depends on the kind of heart you got. That's what the doctors forget. I just ain't got the kind of heart that salt pork troubles."

Ithaca makes one more try and points out that some doctors say that a diet like that might shorten life. Virgil agrees with that, too. "Could be possible," he says. "I got seventy years behind me already. Just when do the doctors say this life shortenin's going to begin? I got to be ready for it."

Ithaca herself never eats enough breakfast, according to Virgil, to satisfy a dyspeptic chipmunk. But the other morning, after a long argument over the merits of salt pork because Virgil had eaten six slices, he went out to sort his potatoes. When he came back to the kitchen in mid-morning there was Ithaca, frying up a batch of salt pork. Virgil asked if she wasn't getting lunch ready a mite early. " 'Taint for you," Ithaca said. "You ain't the only one that needs sustenance around here. I'm just plumb worn out arguing with you and I just got to eat something to build up my strength if I'm going on trying to make you see the errors of your ways."

SUGGESTIONS FOR STUDY:

1. The Adirondack hamlet of Sugarbush and its inhabitants are a recurrent feature of William Chapman White's newspaper columns. Do Virgil and his wife seem real people? Why?
2. What is the main idea of this selection? Is it stated anywhere?
3. Is the last paragraph useful in developing the main idea, or is it just a "twist"? Explain.
4. Is the dialog effective? Why?
5. What is the meaning of *hamlet, sugarbush, decadent, dyspeptic?*
6. Write a theme using a series of incidents and a narrative framework to develop an idea you do not explicitly state.

This piece of organized confusion by a feature writer for the European edition of the New York Herald Tribune suggests that the art of not listening is not confined to college students.

THE COCKTAIL PARTY
by Art Buchwald

THE ONE place where a tourist finds little difference between Paris and New York is at a cocktail party. Take a friend of ours, for instance, who reports on a recent party he attended in Paris.

"Harry, you old son of a gun. When did you get to Paris? It's great to see you, Harry, just great. How is everything?"

"My grandmother just died."

"Wonderful, Harry, that's just wonderful. Come on over and meet some people. Harry, this is Mrs. Pennysnither."

"How do you do, Harry."

"Not so good, my grandmother just died."

"Now isn't that nice. Isn't this a lovely party? Here's Mrs. Martini. I'll introduce you to her. Mrs. Martini, this is Harry Uhuhuh."

"Hello, Mr. Uhuhuh. You remind me of some one I know in Pittsburgh. Have you ever been in Pittsburgh?"

"No, I have never been in Pittsburgh. I'm from New York. I have to go there tomorrow because my grandmother died."

Copyright 1952, The New York Herald Tribune, Inc.

"Isn't that exciting. So you're going to New York. Will you take in any shows? I love New York and love the Broadway shows. Of course, it's hot now. But I love it in the fall. Don't you love it in the fall?"

"I would except my grandmother died."

"Yes, that's exactly what I mean. The honking of taxicabs, the hustle and the bustle. My, I'm homesick just talking about it. Oh, Mr. Imbiber, this is Mr. Harry Uhuhuh. He's from New York and an expert on show business."

"Show business, huh. I'm sort of in show business too. Back a show almost every season. No big hits, but I still get a bang out of it. Great business, show business. No business like it. Here's my wife. Honey, this is Harry Uhuhuh. He's a Broadway producer. He could tell you anything you want about the theater."

"Oh, the theater, the theater. I love the theater. Do you know the Lunts? I adore the Lunts, I just adore them. Have you ever seen the Lunts?"

"No, I never did, but my grandmother did. She just died."

"Oh you lucky man. To work in the theater, to smell the fragrance of grease paint and hear the thundering applause from the wings. Won't you have a drink?"

"No, I can't out of respect to my grandmother who just died."

"That's all right, don't you apologize. I understand many people in the theater don't drink. And then again, I understand many people do. Mr. Harry Uhuhuh . . . Mrs. Savories. Mr. Uhuhuh is a producer."

"Movies I expect. It is so wonderful to meet a Hollywood producer face to face. When on earth are you going to use Montgomery Clift again? I adore Montgomery Clift. If you have an opportunity, I wish you would star him in a picture. Oh, by the way there is some one here I'd like you to meet. He's got a wonderful idea for a story. It's perfect for Marlon Brando and Gloria Swanson. There he is! Gerald come here. Meet Mr. Uhuhuh, a Hollywood producer, Gerald."

"He looksh like a bum to me."

"Gerald, you've had too much to drink."

"Sho you're the greatsh Harry Uhuhuh. I shent you a shcrip, you bum, and you shent it back. You don't know talent when ish walks up to you, you bum. Lemme tell you shummin, you think just because you got a Rollsh Roysh you can treat me like a bum. Well you gotta anoth' thinksh coming."

"Harry, you old son of a gun, how come you're leaving so soon?"

"I got to catch a plane for New York. My grandmother died."

"Swell, swell. If you gotta go, you gotta go. But let's have lunch some time in the next two weeks. Call me, Harry, just call me. If I'm not at home leave a message. Glad everything's going so well for you, Harry, I really am."

SUGGESTIONS FOR STUDY:

1. Does the first sentence announce the topic?
2. Does any sentence definitely state the main idea? What is the main idea?
3. What phrase is repeated to achieve the ludicrous?
4. Is this static repetition balanced by any forward progress?
5. What variation do you find in speakers?
6. Who is the last speaker? Do his words give symmetry to the composition?
7. Write a dialog or conversation that makes a point without reducing the point to an expository sentence.

Despite man's tragic sins and stupidities, we are not required to take the pessimistic view.

I ADMIRE THE HUMAN RACE
by Roger William Riis

I ADMIRE the human race. I do, indeed. Everybody is busy running us down, these days, for the mess they say we have made here and there and everywhere. Pshaw! That's short-range stuff, a worm's-eye view of our world. Over the marching and abundant centuries, we haven't made any mess. Far from it!

We have done and are doing a better job than anyone has any right to expect. We're all right!

From the beginning, we found ourselves alone in a vast universe, and not only alone but the only living thing on this planet which could realize its loneness. We realized it, gave it a good close look, and then turned our attention to making something practical and useful out of an unprecedented situation.

First of all, we found for ourselves a Light, a God, and we got a sense of direction, a goal to work toward. This was pretty clever of us, if you think of it carefully.

We proceeded to set up standards for our living together. Early in our experience we made the revolutionary discovery that gentleness and kindliness were more practical than brute strength. No other species has ever found that out and used it as a model and practical code of conduct.

Reprinted by permission of The Book of the Month Club, Inc.

We have in actual fact no one we need answer to, beyond ourselves, and yet we observe our ideal standards in remarkable degree. We are honest and trustworthy one with another so that it is the exception, it is news, when we commit a theft. We are decent 99 per cent of the time, when we could easily be vile. With silence and mystery behind us and ahead of us, we make up gay little songs and whistle them, and our feet keep jig time to them. We look life and fate in the eye, and smile. I like that, and I admire the people who do it.

Alone among all living things, we have discovered Beauty, and we cherish it, and create it for eye and ear. Alone among living things, we have the power to look at our environment and criticize it and improve it.

Finding it necessary to live together by the millions, we created for ourselves governing systems covering vast geographical spaces. Now we actually have the thrilling and terrific idea of a world government, a global government to bring justice to white and black, to Eskimo and Afrikander, rich and poor, not because any tribe is powerful and can exact justice, but because we have conceived and created the ideal of justice and plan it for all men. This is great. This is not the act of a little animal, or a mean animal. This is possible only to a great animal. We think in global terms. We inhabit a star, and we know it.

Finding that we have to work to stay alive, we work with ability beyond imagining.

Out of the earth we take food, and improve that food year by year; we take heat, and light, so that darkness which lay upon the face of the earth is dispelled by man-made light. We enjoy all the myriad products of our unparalleled ingenuity.

Every morning the necessity for the day's work faces us. And we go and do a day's work, with an overall average effectiveness and perseverance that is amazing, considering many of the jobs.

Of a persistence, a daring and ingenuity impossible to surpass, we find ways to move easily under the water and through the air. Now we speculatively eye our neighboring planets. It should astound no one if man one day begins to move among these planets. How shall I not admire such a creature? Daunted by nothing, his horizons constantly recede, the territories of his possession and use expand and expand.

Whenever he comes to an impassable obstacle, an apparantly final barrier, he goes to work at it and, in due time, surpasses it. If he has limits, I do not see where they are. I do not think he has limits. I think he is a child of the universe who inherits eternity. I think he is wonderful, I am his devoted partisan, and I am proud indeed to be one of him.

SUGGESTIONS FOR STUDY:

1. What is the main idea? Where is it expressed? How is the essay organized?
2. What tone is established by the exclamations, sentence length, and diction of the first two paragraphs? Is this tone maintained?
3. Is the fact that theft is news an effective point?
4. Study the sentence structure and length in the paragraph beginning, "Finding it necessary . . ."
5. Is the essay closely reasoned or inspirational?
6. What do the words "darkness which lay upon the face of the earth" suggest?
7. Write an essay praising something in which you sincerely believe. Try to be enthusiastic without falling into uncritical acceptance.

A famous American critic replies to a request for his views on the ultimate realities.

A LETTER TO WILL DURANT
by H. L. Mencken

YOU ASK ME, in brief, what satisfaction I get out of life, and why I go on working. I go on working for the same reason that a hen goes on laying eggs. There is in every living creature an obscure but powerful impulse to active functioning. Life demands to be lived. Inaction, save as a measure of recuperation between bursts of activity, is painful and dangerous to the healthy organism—in fact, it is almost impossible. Only the dying can be really idle.

The precise form of an individual's activity is determined, of course, by the equipment with which he came into the world. In other words, it is determined by his heredity. I do not lay eggs, as a hen does, because I was born without any equipment for it. For the same reason I do not get myself elected to Congress, or play the violoncello, or teach metaphysics in a college, or work in a steel mill. What I do is simply what lies easiest to my hand. It happens that I was born with an intense and insatiable interest in ideas, and thus like to play with them. It happens also that I was born with rather more than the average facility for putting them into words. In consequence, I am a writer and editor, which is to say, a dealer in them and concoctor of them.

From *On the Meaning of Life*, edited by Will Durant, published by Ray Long and Richard B. Smith, 1932. Reprinted by permission of Mr. Mencken.

There is very little conscious volition in all this. What I do was ordained by the inscrutable fates, not chosen by me. In my boyhood, yielding to a powerful but still subordinate interest in exact facts, I wanted to be a chemist, and at the same time my poor father tried to make me a business man. At other times, like any other relatively poor man, I have longed to make a lot of money by some easy swindle. But I became a writer all the same, and shall remain one until the end of the chapter, just as a cow goes on giving milk all her life, even though what appears to be her self-interest urges her to give gin.

I am far luckier than most men, for I have been able since boyhood to make a good living doing precisely what I have wanted to do—what I would have done for nothing, and very gladly, if there had been no reward for it. Not many men, I believe, are so fortunate. Millions of them have to make their livings at tasks which really do not interest them. As for me, I have had an extraordinarily pleasant life, despite the fact that I have had the usual share of woes. For in the midst of those woes I still enjoyed the immense satisfaction which goes with free activity. I have done, in the main, exactly what I wanted to do. Its possible effects upon other people have interested me very little. I have not written and published to please other people, but to satisfy myself, just as a cow gives milk, not to profit the dairyman, but to satisfy herself. I like to think that most of my ideas have been sound ones, but I really don't care. The world may take them or leave them. I have had my fun hatching them.

Next to agreeable work as a means of attaining happiness I put what Huxley called the domestic affections—the day to day intercourse with family and friends. My home has seen bitter sorrow, but it has never seen any serious disputes, and it has never seen poverty. I was completely happy with my mother and sister, and I am completely happy with my wife. Most of the men I commonly associate with are friends of very old standing. I have known some of them for more than thirty years. I seldom see anyone, intimately, whom I have known for less than ten years. These friends delight me. I turn to them when work is done with unfailing eagerness.

We have the same general tastes, and see the world much alike. Most of them are interested in music, as I am. It has given me more pleasure in this life than any other external thing. I love it more every year.

As for religion, I am quite devoid of it. Never in my adult life have I experienced anything that could be plausibly called a religious impulse. My father and grandfather were agnostics before me, and though I was sent to Sunday-school as a boy and exposed to the Christian theology I was never taught to believe it. My father thought that I should learn what it was, but it apparently never occurred to him that I would accept it. He was a good psychologist. What I got in Sunday-school—beside a wide acquaintance with Christian hymnology—was simply a firm conviction that the Christian faith was full of palpable absurdities, and the Christian God preposterous. Since that time I have read a great deal in theology—perhaps much more than the average clergyman—but I have never discovered any reason to change my mind.

The act of worship, as carried on by Christians, seems to me to be debasing rather than ennobling. It involves grovelling before a Being who, if He really exists, deserves to be denounced instead of respected. I see little evidence in this world of the so-called goodness of God. On the contrary, it seems to me that, on the strength of His daily acts, He must be set down a most stupid, cruel and villainous fellow. I can say this with a clear conscience, for He has treated me very well—in fact, with vast politeness. But I can't help thinking of his barbaric torture of most of the rest of humanity. I simply can't imagine revering the God of war and politics, theology and cancer.

I do not believe in immortality, and have no desire for it. The belief in it issues from the puerile egos of inferior men. In its Christian form it is little more than a device for getting revenge upon those who are having a better time on this earth. What the meaning of human life may be I don't know: I incline to suspect that it has none. All I know about it is that, to me at least, it is very amusing while it lasts. Even its troubles, indeed, can be amusing. Moreover, they tend to foster the human qualities that I admire most—courage and its analogues. The noblest man, I think, is that one who fights God, and triumphs over Him. I have had little of this to do. When I die I shall be content to vanish into nothingness. No show, however good, could conceivably be good forever.

SUGGESTIONS FOR STUDY:

1. What is the main idea and where is it expressed?
2. Does the author use topic sentences for his paragraphs?
3. Are his paragraphs readily outlined? What method of development can you recognize in the paragraphs?
4. What is the basis of humor in the remark about the cow's giving gin?
5. Indicate the means of transition—repetitions, synonyms, antecedents and pronouns, sentence modifiers—in paragraphs 4 and 5.
6. What is the meaning of *metaphysics, theology, palpable, puerile egos, analogues?*
7. Write a theme stating your beliefs about something or attacking a traditional belief.

Other lands—other customs. One of America's best sports columnists describes a custom he encountered while covering the Olympic games in Helsinki in 1952.

CO-EDUCATIONAL SOAP WORSHIP
by Red Smith

THE LADY of the bath glanced up without curiosity when four gents tottered out of the steam room of the Sauna all naked as jaybirds and broiled like proper sirloins, charred on the outside, medium rare in the middle. The lady of the bath, an old doll wearing spectacles and a long rubber apron, was busy soaping and scrubbing the tract of masculine meat on her pine board table, and the newcomers represented more work on an already crowded day.

The Sauna (pronounced "Sowna") is a Finnish bath, and a great deal more. It is a sacred rite, a form of human sacrifice in which the victim is boiled like a missionary in the cannibal islands, then baked to a turn, then beaten with sticks until he flees into the icy sea, then lathered and honed and kneaded and pummeled by the high priestess of this purgatorial pit.

Nothing relaxes a Finn like this ritual of fire-worship, water-worship and soap-worship. It is an ancient folk custom dating from forgotten times, and it explains why Finland produces so many great marathon runners. Anybody who

Copyright 1952, The New York Herald Tribune, Inc.

can survive a Sauna can run twenty-six miles barefoot over broken beer bottles.

The most gracious gesture of hospitality a Finn can make is to bathe with his guest. From an American host, a suggestion that everybody go get washed might imply that the guest was getting a trifle gamey, but Americans don't know everything. Lots of them haven't been bathed by a doll since they were six.

"A foreigner," says a pamphlet on the subject, "who leaves Finland without the intimate acquaintance of a Sauna cannot boast of having got into grips with the Finnish mentality. Through it the creature of civilization is enabled to get in touch with primal forces of nature—earth, fire and water."

Curious about primal forces, three Americans and Kai Koskimies, their Finnish keeper, had taxied out to Waskiniemi, on the outskirts of Helsinki, where a birch forest meets the blue waters of the Gulf of Finland. There they stripped to the buff, bowed cordially to the lady of the bath, and entered the steam room.

In a murky, low ceilinged cubicle recognizable to anybody who ever read Dante, several other lost souls attired in sweat sat on benches with faces buried in their hands. The room was heated—an understatement, as ever was—by a sort of Dutch oven in which cobblestones cooked over a fire of birch logs. A thermometer registered only 130 degrees fahrenheit and Kai, making a snoot of disapproval, scooped water onto the hot rocks to get up a head of steam.

The visitors were destined to discover the difference between dry heat and the steamy coziness of this inferno. The steam room is the simple, ancient type of Sauna, which is part of the humblest Finnish home. There are 400,000 of them in Finland, one for every four people. "The air gives off a slight but exhilarating aroma of smoke," says the pamphlet. "The effect of the open fireplace feels strong to sensitive people."

Four sensitive people stood it as long as any hickory-smoked ham could have done. Then they oozed out of the cell like melted tallow, and Kai led the way to another room providing dry heat. There the thermometer outraged him. It registered only 176 degrees, not even warm enough to boil an egg. The Sauna proprietor agreed that this was ridiculous.

"This is no Sauna," he said, and did something with the fireplace. "In 1, 2, 3 minutes it will be warm." In 1, 2, 3 minutes the thermometer raced up to 219 degrees. Missionaries are fricasseed at 212.

Bundles of leafy birch branches were provided as knouts so the bathers could beat themselves. Kai splashed water around to cool the wooden floor and benches but it evaporated instantly. Even with the insulation of a folded Turkish towel, the seats were like stove lids.

Relaxing Finnish style, everybody tried to avoid being fried outright. At the same time, all laid about with the birch, flogging themselves like flagellantes. After that came a refreshing dip in the sea.

The Gulf of Finland is colder than an Eskimo spinster. However, all feeling had been left behind in the stew pot. The instant a guy hit the water he turned numb; he suffered no more than a corpse.

Cleanliness was next on the schedule, and the lady of the bath was the babe to provide it. She starts with a shampoo, then works on the subject in sections—just as one eats a lobster, cleaning up one claw, laying it aside and picking up another.

Her powerful fingers probe deep, finding muscles the doctors never have charted. She is skillful, efficient and thorough. She scrapes the hull with a rough wet towel. The combination massage-and-scouring process is genuinely relaxing, easing muscles, untying knotted nerves.

That's all there is to a Sauna, except for one technicality. The technicality is that as soon as you're finished you do it all over, the heat, the swim, and the shower. In the winter, when the sea drops two degrees in temperature and freezes over, you can't swim. You go outdoors and roll in the snow instead.

On the second time around, the temperature in the dry oven had got satisfactorily cozy. It was slightly over 269 degrees. This created some excitement around the Sauna. They said it was a world record.

When it's all over you get a diploma testifying that you are alive and clean. This is partly true.

SUGGESTIONS FOR STUDY:

1. Is the essay an exposition of a process?
2. Is the tone of the essay an integral part of Smith's main idea?
3. How many *like, as,* and *than* comparisons does Smith use?
4. Does the reference to twenty-six miles over broken beer bottles suggest exaggeration as a source of humor? Do you find other evidence?
5. Does the reference to Dante find a further echo in the paragraph in which it occurs and in the next paragraph?
6. Does the diction vary markedly from the extremely informal to the essentially literary? Cite some examples.
7. What is the meaning of *primal, inferno, fricasseed, flagellantes?*
8. Write a theme explaining a process, or describing an unfamiliar custom.

In Rome, the proverb reminds us, one should do as the Romans do. In the following two selections, the anthropologist whose remarks on war appear earlier and a reporter remind us that in any society the non-conformist is in for trouble.

ON NOT CONFORMING
by Ruth Benedict

MOST ETHNOLOGISTS have had experiences in recognizing that the persons who are put outside the pale of society with contempt are not those who would be placed there by another culture. Lowie found among the Crow Indians of the plains a man of exceptional knowledge of his cultural forms. He was interested in considering these objectively and in correlating different facets. He had an interest in genealogical facts and was invaluable on points of history. Altogether he was an ideal interpreter of Crow life. These traits, however, were not those which were the password to honour among the Crow. He had a definite shrinking from physical danger, and bravado was the tribal virtue. To make matters worse he had attempted to gain recognition by claiming a war honour which was fraudulent. He was proved not to have brought in, as he claimed, a picketed horse from the enemy's camp. To lay false claim to war honours was a paramount sin among the Crow, and by the general opinion, constantly reiterated, he was regarded as irresponsible and incompetent.

From *Patterns of Culture*, by Ruth Benedict. Reprinted by permission of Houghton Mifflin Company, Publishers.

On Not Conforming 261

Such situations can be paralleled with the attitude in our civilization toward a man who does not succeed in regarding personal possessions as supremely important. Our hobo population is constantly fed by those to whom the accumulation of property is not a sufficient motivation. In case these individuals ally themselves with the hoboes, public opinion regards them as potentially vicious, as indeed because of the asocial situation into which they are thrust they readily become. In case, however, these men compensate by emphasizing their artistic temperament and become members of expatriated groups of petty artists, opinion regards them not as vicious but as silly. In any case they are unsupported by the forms of their society, and the effort to express themselves satisfactorily is ordinarily a greater task than they can achieve.

The dilemma of such an individual is often most successfully solved by doing violence to his strongest natural impulses and accepting the rôle the culture honours. In case he is a person to whom social recognition is necessary, it is ordinarily his only possible course. One of the most striking individuals in Zuñi had accepted this necessity. In a society that thoroughly distrusts authority of any sort, he had a native personal magnetism that singled him out in any group. In a society that exalts moderation and the easiest way, he was turbulent and could act violently upon occasion. In a society that praises a pliant personality that 'talks lots'—that is, that chatters in a friendly fashion—he was scornful and aloof. Zuñi's only reaction to such personalities is to brand them as witches. He was said to have been seen peering through a window from outside, and this is a sure mark of a witch. At any rate, he got drunk one day and boasted that they could not kill him. He was taken before the war priests who hung him by his thumbs from the rafters till he should confess to his witchcraft. This is the usual procedure in a charge of witchcraft. However, he dispatched a messenger to the government troops. When they came, his shoulders were already crippled for life, and the officer of the law was left with no recourse but to imprison the war priests who had been responsible for the enormity. One of these war priests was probably the most respected and important person in recent Zuñi history, and when he returned after imprisonment in the state penitentiary he never resumed his priestly offices. He regarded his power as broken. It was a revenge that is probably unique in Zuñi history. It involved, of course, a challenge to the priesthoods, against whom the witch by his act openly aligned himself.

The course of his life in the forty years that followed this defiance was not, however, what we might easily predict. A witch is not barred from his membership in cult groups because he has been condemned, and the way to recognition lay through such activity. He possessed a remarkable verbal memory and a sweet singing voice. He learned unbelievable stories of mythology, of esoteric ritual, of cult songs. Many hundreds of pages of stories and ritual poetry were taken down from his dictation before he died, and he regarded his songs as much more extensive. He became indispensable in ceremonial life and before he died was the governor of Zuñi. The congenial bent of his personality threw him into irreconcilable conflict with his society, and he solved his dilemma by turning an incidental talent to account. As we might well expect, he was not a happy man. As governor of Zuñi, and high in his cult groups, a marked man in his community, he was obsessed by death. He was a cheated man in the midst of a mildly happy populace.

It is easy to imagine the life he might have lived among the Plains Indians, where every institution favoured the traits that were native to him. The personal authority, the turbulence, the scorn, would all have been honoured in the career he could have made his own. The unhappiness that was inseparable from his temperament as a successful priest and governor of Zuñi would have had no place as a war chief of the Cheyenne; it was not a function of the traits of his native endowment but of the standards of the culture in which he found no outlet for his native responses.

The individuals we have discussed are not in any sense psychopathic. They illustrate the dilemma of the individual whose congenial drives are not provided for in the institutions of his culture.

SUGGESTIONS FOR STUDY:

1. Does the first sentence express the complete main idea?
2. How many main divisions are there? Could they be arranged in reverse?
3. What is the principal method of development?
4. Is the transition from one paragraph to the next clear? Everywhere?
5. What terms suggest that Miss Benedict is a scientist engaged in technical exposition?
6. What is the meaning of *ethnologist,* different *facets, paramount* sin, constantly *reiterated,* sufficient *motivation, potentially* vicious, *asocial* situation, *dilemma, pliant* personality, *esoteric* ritual?
7. Write a theme developing an idea through a series of examples.

THEY DIDN'T CONFORM
by Peg Sonenfeldt

ALMOST from the beginning, Frank and Theo DeFebio were considered "strange folk" here.

Theo, a graduate of Smith College, drove a taxi—something few women do in this tight-knit, southern community. Frank had a beard, was a pacifist, and had served a jail sentence as a conscientious objector.

Frank and Theo and their boys, Teddy, 9, Denny (a foster child), also 9; and Nicky, 5, settled in an abandoned Coast Guard Station, 50 feet from the ocean. At first, they tried to "farm" the sandy soil—a back-breaking task.

They lived quietly and alone on their beach until Theo sought a permit to educate her own children. "Frank and I

From Parade, May 25, 1952.

believe that parents who have the ability and desire to teach their children should be allowed to do so," she said.

State school authorities denied her request. But the DeFebios refused to send the children to public schools. Soon after (in December, 1950), Frank was arrested for breaking the compulsory school law.

There followed seven court actions. The highlights:

The three boys were taken from the DeFebios and assigned to foster parents under the Dare County Welfare Dept.

Frank was sentenced to 30 days in prison. Theo picketed the courthouse, sleeping night after night on its steps.

Frank, arrested again in April, 1951, for "parental incompetency," attempted suicide. He recovered, but a month later was sentenced again to 30 days for keeping his children out of school.

In a tempestuous scene, the three boys were torn away from Theo as she stood on the courthouse steps.

What about the DeFebios themselves? What are they like? Opinions are mixed. Some Manteo people speak hotly against Frank and Theo:

"They're screwball," said the editor of the local paper, Victor Meekins. "When you deal with crazy people, you have to deal with them differently than normal people. . . ."

Chief of Police Chester Mitchell said: "Right from the beginning, I thought they were sort of queer. There's just something wrong with people that want to get off by themselves. . . ."

Lloyd Midgett, one of Manteo's three taxi drivers, said he was afraid of Frank. "I wouldn't like to be with him while I was by myself," he said. "A man who tries to kill himself—there's no telling what he might do to somebody else."

Frank DeFebio's reply to such charges is a quotation from William James: "We have grown afraid to be poor," he recites. "We despise anyone who elects to be poor in order to simplify and save his inner life."

But the DeFebios have friends, too.

"People here gave them plenty of our traditional southern hospitality when they first came," says editor Meekins.

"I liked Theo and Frank," said David Stick, an ex-

Marine who runs a craft shop near Manteo. "But early in our friendship I had qualms about their living in Dare County.

"Theo's hair was unfashionably long (it falls to her waist), and Frank had a beard. The DeFebio's were very different, and in Manteo one has to be rich to be eccentric."

And their children?

The foster parents assigned by the Dare County court liked them.

"I often wondered how such strange people could have such nice children," said Mrs. Mary Burrus. "They wouldn't fight—wouldn't strike a lick at each other—and they always seemed happy together."

"They were fine children," added Mrs. Dora Hazen, another foster mother. "They were truthful, obedient and kind, and I never knew youngsters who shared as they did. Just this spring, Teddy found his first ripe strawberry, and he divided it three ways with his brothers."

Early this month, the children had not been returned. The parents have appealed to the Superior Court, but hearings have been delayed.

Meanwhile, the three boys seem quite happy. Their mother pilots "Flag Me," Cab #44 in Washington, and their father labors on a construction project. Manteo still simmers over the case.

And happiness? The DeFebios haven't found it.

SUGGESTIONS FOR STUDY:

1. What is the main idea, and where is it expressed?
2. How many main divisions are there?
3. Could this essay fit into the previous essay? In what relationship?
4. Write a theme using an incident to develop an idea.

The Mecca Building in Chicago is a symbol of one of America's most critical problems.

THE STRANGEST PLACE IN CHICAGO
by John Bartlow Martin

FROM THE Chicago Loop, where sunlight off the lakefront strikes the shining towers, State Street runs straight south, wide, busy with streetcars and heavy trucks. Quickly the buildings get shabby—little stores selling auto parts, a junkyard crammed with rusting wreckage. The city is harsh: concrete streets, brick building walls, black steel viaducts. Beyond 22nd Street the faces of the people are black. This is the South Side Negro section. Here the street is quieter, the sun is hazy and dirty and pale, the sky is a network of trolley wires. Across an expanse of new-turned earth stretches a new public housing project, with a playyard for the children, and at 32nd Street begins the new campus of the Illinois Institute of Technology, sleek brick-and-glass buildings surrounded by new trees and new grass. And just beyond the Institute rises a great gray hulk of brick, four stories high, topped by an ungainly smokestack, ancient and enormous, filling half the block north of 34th Street between State and Dearborn. It is the Mecca Building.

Let us note its setting. Across State Street are a cleaning shop, a barber shop, a grocery, the Railroad Men's Social

Copyright 1950, by Harper and Bros. Reprinted by permission of Harold Ober Associates.

Club, McClain's Hair Goods, a Bar-B-Q, the office of H. Young the Icer, the Church of God & Saints of Christ in an old storefront. An old man pulls a handcart filled with junk across an empty lot. From a deep hole tunneled under the sidewalk emerges the head of a little Negro boy, playing. The sidewalk is cracked and broken. Nearby are rickety wooden tenements.

The Mecca Building is U-shaped. The dirt courtyard is littered with newspapers and tin cans, milk cartons and broken glass. Pigeons roost on a car on blocks. A skinny white dog huddles in a doorway. Iron fire escapes run up the building's face and ladders reach from them to the roof. There are four main entrances, two on Dearborn and two on State Street. At each is a gray stone threshold and over each is carved "The Mecca." The Mecca was constructed as an apartment building in 1891, a splendid palace, a showplace of Chicago. Today it is still an apartment building and a showplace but of a very different sort. It has become one of the most remarkable Negro slum exhibits in the world. Let us pass through the arched doorway of the Mecca; let us see what the Mecca looks like inside, see who the people in it are and how they live, whence they came and why they stay.

Inside, a powerful odor assails the visitor at once, musty, heavy, a smell compounded of urine and stale cooking and of age, not necessarily an unpleasant odor but a close powerful one, which, like that of marijuana, once smelled is never forgotten. The stone slab step is hollowed. The lower part of the walls of the vestibule once was covered with marble but now the marble has been stripped away in ragged patches, revealing naked brick and mortar. It is dark here. Ahead stretches a corridor; it is like a tunnel, it seems endless and it is indeed a block long, running all the way to the Dearborn Street entrance; down its whole length hang only five light bulbs, glowing feebly in the gloom. Tan paint is peeling from the wall, the doors of apartments open into the corridor. This is the base of the U in the U-shaped building.

The arms of the U are identical. They are great halls, each lit by a skylight four stories overhead which, because of the dirt that has accumulated on the glass through years of neglect, admits the kind of unreal light found underseas. This light slants down in great long angling shafts filled with floating dust, shifting as the sun moves across the sky, falling in fitful patches on the floor. Around the walls run three balconies guarded by ornate wrought-iron grillwork, and off these balconies open the doors to the apartments, like tiers of cells in a prison cellblock. The floor in the center of the well is of hardwood, splintered now, and beneath the balconies it is of tile, broken in many places. A janitor with a wheelbarrow is slowly patching the tile with concrete; his shovel makes a rasping, scraping sound. From somewhere in the building comes always the sound of distant human voices—women talking, a baby squalling, children screaming, men muttering, no words distinguishable. Spittle splats flatly on the tile floor, falling from a great height, spat by a man or a woman standing on an upper balcony. All day long people stand at the balconies, leaning on the wrought-iron railings with hands clasped out over them, gazing out at other people facing them across the well in silence, gazing down at the floor far below, spitting, small human figures in a vast place, two or three on each of the four floors, occasionally calling back and forth to one another but most of the time just standing silent. The building is never entirely quiet, not even very late at night, since so many people live here; but it is so vast that it seems quiet, even amid uproar.

In the shadows against a pillar marked with matchstrikes leans a man, his shirt-collar buttoned but without a necktie, his hat-brim slanting low over his scarred face, a cigarette slanting from his mouth; he is just standing there watching. How many people live here? He laughs. "I don't know." Two thousand? "Oh, more than that. There's 176 apartments and some of 'em's got seven rooms and they're all full." A heavy round-faced man in a long white apron holding a ball-peen hammer approaches: "You are visiting some of the historic sites of the city? You found one all right. If it don't fall in on you while you're lookin'." How many people live here? "That," he says, "is a mystery. You'll find them sleeping in bathtubs, sleeping in the kitchen under the sink, anywhere they can sleep." Nobody, in truth, knows how many people inhabit the Mecca Building. The janitor, Jimmy Sanders, estimates 2,300; the Democratic precinct captain, William Patrick Fitzgerald, who has lived here eighteen years, estimates 1,400; the owner doesn't know. All the inhabitants except one woman are Negroes. The Mecca Building contains more people than most Chicago precincts; indeed, it constitutes a precinct in itself, the 27th Precinct of the 2nd Ward.

II

On the third floor an old woman stands by the railing, a towel wound round her head, a big gold ring on her finger. Watching dispassionately as children run in from school for lunch, their screams ringing piercingly through the building, she says judiciously, "That size runs to roller skates," and then, "When I first came here they used to control the children. White people hadn't been gone so long, 1917 it was. They used to have a policeman here nights, you could hear a needle drop. Now they's shooting here five times a night. Them young men and the young girls is the worst. I'd move out tonight if they'd find me a house. I moved out for a while once but I came back to have company, my daughter lives here and my granddaughter was born here," and she turns and shuffles into her flat.

In the long first-floor corridor the janitor passes, Jimmy, a short squat man in a leather cap and jacket, ambling along with a Yankee drill in his hand. "I'm the maintenance man," he says. "I do a little of everything—work a little, fight a little, sleep a little, play a little." Right now he is accompanying the rent collector, a white man, a wiry Scot named John. "I go around with him," Jimmy says, shifting the stub of his dead cigar to the other corner of his mouth, "because the young fellas in the building think he's got money with him." About a year ago the young fellows robbed an insurance collector of $17. The rent collector, John, says, "I lost all my hair fighting with these people," and laughs. Actually, he has little trouble collecting rents, which are cheap. His troubles are of a different sort: he and Jimmy fight a hopeless rearguard action against decay and vandalism. "Last night they shot out the light bulbs," says Jimmy. "And the windows—in the last year I bet I put in over two hundred windows. They break 'em fast as you put 'em in." Who does it? "Outsiders, most of it. And the kids here. The kids gets to playin' and throwin' at one another and first thing you know they break the glass. There's nothin' you can do about it. You can't kill one 'cause he broke the glass."

As the rent collector walks along, a woman calls from the third-floor balcony, "Hold your head up, John, John, hold your head up, I want to talk to you," but John plods on, grinning secretly. A sign by the basement stairs reads, "Put All Complaints in Mail Box." Near the State Street entrance another janitor has temporarily left his job of cementing a broken place in the floor and is stooping over at an apartment door, digging with a knife at something in the door. He gets it out: a bullet. "That's a thirty-eight," he says, turning it over in his hand, shiny and twisted. Then, to a woman who has come to the door, "They try to shoot you out last night?" She laughs. "Yeh, try to kill me. Like shootin' rabbits in a swamp down yonder." He says, "They was really shootin' here last night. Some of 'em shootin' for fun, some of 'em fightin'. That's every night around here. Couple of 'em got shot the other night." Any ever killed? "Oh, yes, one got killed summer before last up there in that corner," pointing upward. Why? "I don't know."

Down the stairs comes a man on crutches, his left leg off above the knee, his pants leg pinned up, coming down the steps, the crutch and his good leg visible first, then the man, thin, wearing white pants and a brown coat and hat; he walks diagonally past the mailboxes to the grocery, pausing to adjust his pipe.

High on the fourth west gallery, close up under the skylight, the balcony seems narrow. Two boys wrestle on it, and one falls heavily against the iron railing, which trembles but holds firm. It is four stories down to the ground floor; nobody ever heard of a child falling. An old woman is sweeping the floor. High up here at the north end a dozen young men and women are congregated, well-dressed, two of the men off to one side leaning idle on the railing and peering sullenly down, the others close together, laughing, fooling around with each other, the girls in tight white sweaters, the young men in snap-brim hats and suitcoats over sweaters.

III

High on the fourth floor dwells George Kinchlow, an old man. He is seventy-seven. He is sitting on a daybed in the dark. Saving electricity. He rises, a frail white-haired little man in cracked cheap slippers, and turns on a small dangling light for his visitor. The living room is nine feet by six. Against faded wallpaper hang publicity photographs of Irene Castle and of Velez and Yolanda and an old gold-framed photograph of a little boy in a sailor suit, his son. Clothing, rumpled and dirty, hangs on the chairbacks. Kinchlow apologizes for the way things look. "I been sick with high blood pressure, can't do much. That's why I got this towel around my neck to keep warmed up. Sometimes I sit in front by the window." The window is in the bedroom; it offers a view of the trolley wires on State Street and, in the distance, a dim grayness, perhaps Lake Michigan, far away. On the walls are more fan pictures and also pictures of the Pope and Franklin D. Roosevelt. On a dresser stand family photos and over the bed is a figure of Christ on a crucifix beneath a picture of the Boswell sisters.

Kinchlow was a porter all his working days. He left Indianapolis because "my hopes died out." He married, moved into this flat in 1915, and stayed. They raised their son here. The son has proved a disappointment to Kinchlow. "He does very little work of no kind." Mrs. Kinchlow died, "different ailments, locked bowels, the doctor said can't do nothin', they took her to county hospital and that night they called me up and told me she had died."

On the wall above the daybed are a picture of an Indian on a horse, and a cloth motto, "Father and Son." The steam in the radiator hisses; the apartment is hot but Kinchlow wraps the towel more closely about his thin throat. His fingers are long and skinny. Does he like living in the Mecca Building now? "God no! There ain't nothing here to like. But it's been awful hard to get a flat. Even hard to find a room. So, I just stuck on anyhow. It gets worse all the time. And for one thing, if there was flats to rent, my money's too thin. I only get the old-age assistance and that was cut last month—they chopped $4 off of that, I was getting $62. I was already livin' from hand to mouth, I didn't dare to buy myself a pair of pants or I'd be good and hungry for a few days before that next month come around. When they cut that, they said the cost of living come down. I wonder O my God, on what? 'Cause all kinds of staple foods that you've got to have, they've got me so I'm scared to go into a butcher shop and order a decent piece of meat, oh my, it's terrible high." He gets his check monthly. "My check day is for tomorrow, get my little $58, go pay $20 rent right away, I wouldn't take no chances on getting held up or being wild or nothing, I take it right over. Or send my son over with it. Then starts my hustling and scrabbling for another month. I have to be awful careful how I buy. I used to go downtown to Goldblatt's and Hillman's, buy my stuff on Saturday, I could get it so much cheaper, half-way decent roast of beef. Then the carfare went up to fifteen cents and I walked. I enjoyed it, too. But since I gotten old it look like walkin' is mean to me."

Presently he shuffles out to the tiny kitchen. "Supper last night," and he touches a pot of spareribs and lima beans on the stove, "it won't be throwed out, warm it up, *eat it*, all I can do is just look at those nice chops and roasts."

Now near dusk, the fourth-floor balcony is wrapped in gloom, and young men congregate, lounging, smoking cigarettes, they are not talking; and down on the ground floor beneath the balcony a wiry girl of twelve wrestles with a smaller, prettier girl in a new blue snowsuit, throwing her to the floor, rolling over and over with her in the dirt by the fresh cement the janitor poured. And whooping from the darkness in the far recess of the well comes a rushing crowd of boys and girls, flowing past the iceman, who is still at work, and the din grows louder, screams and cries, loud thumps and thunderous footsteps as the crowd swirls on around the corner into the dark then back, ten children, perhaps ten or twelve years old, armed with spears and bows and arrows, running, screaming, whooping. A man says, "That's all day. And all night too." They are dark leaning shadows racing around a pillar; they have upset and plundered a garbage can and now they throw applecores and onions at each other across the well, the air is filled with flying applecores and onions, and a boy of sixteen armed with a whiskey bottle chases a girl on roller skates, at whom another boy shoots an arrow.

In a corner a small child sits on the floor, playing a mouth organ, and a boy about ten with a long-bladed knife lurks behind a post. Near the doorway two boys of nine or ten detach themselves from the rest and fight, fight in earnest, biting, kicking, hitting, swearing, then silently fighting, not talking, just breathing heavily, until a man comes in off the street and stops them, a tenant with a briefcase home from the office, taking one boy with him as he ascends into the upper reaches of the building.

IV

When the Mecca Building was constructed it was considered one of the largest and finest apartment buildings in Chicago if not in America. It catered (almost needless to say) to a white clientele. But after 1900 the Negro migration to Chicago forced the black belt to expand, and by 1912 the Mecca Building was the home of the Negro elite—doctors, lawyers, business men.

A woman who lives there still, Mrs. Florence Clayton, arrived in 1916, and she remembers, "There were carpets on the stairs and halls. There were goldfish in the fountain. On the first floor there were lounge chairs and outdoors we had a flower garden and beautiful trees and green grass, you could go out there, oh, it was lovely. The courtyard was all fenced in and there was a lovely walk through the flowers."

The building started to deteriorate during the 1917-18 war. So did the whole neighborhood. Booming war industries pulled thousands of Negroes to Chicago. The luckier ones abandoned the region of 35th and State to the poor and the wicked. The black-and-tans where Chicago jazz flowered were right here. Jimmy, the janitor, recalls, "There were lots of fights and cuttings. Building was full of prostitutes. I saw a man throw a prostitute over the third floor railing—from the third floor to the first floor. Didn't hurt her much. She only weighed ninety pounds, kind of light. Finally one of the pimps killed the building watchman. Did it over a woman. And she wasn't even living with him." Jimmy pushes his leather cap back off his forehead. "That about ended it, though. They got a new watchman and he was a killer. He was just a little man but he had great big eyes and he'd shoot you with either hand. He had a cemetery of his own before he died. He only killed nine people—between the basement here and that wire fence. The building got kind of decent after that—families, working people."

And then the Depression came along, and the wicked left, and almost none but the poor remained. The Depression was awful in the black belt. About 1932 the bottom fell out. One woman who lived here then recalls, "The building was partly empty. One lady told me she was sitting down on the curb and the police passed and it was cold and they asked her what was the matter and she said she'd been set out and they told her to come on in here and the first flat she'd find, sit down. They carried her to court later but they didn't make her get out, they couldn't, people had no work to do then. It was always warm and nice in here during the Depression."

The Depression accounts for the presence today of the building's only white tenant, a heavy, soft-faced, white-haired woman of sixty-six. "I'd been a housekeeper at a hotel and one of my maids, a colored girl, she was married to a white doctor and they lived here in the Mecca Building. I couldn't find a job, I just got stuck, I couldn't make it, and they took me in." Some of the Mecca inhabitants who moved in while they were on relief are now earning good money in the steel mills or on Pullman cars and one or two earn upward of $5,000 a year, but they are imprisoned here by the scarcity of dwellings for Negroes. A few of the long-time tenants remain by choice, oddly proud of the building. A few earn money by living there—they sublet rooms in their apartments for as much as $12 a week. The janitor Jimmy says, "Every day people come in, many as ten or twelve a day, lookin' for a place, they been walkin' the street, lookin' for some place to go, say, 'Janitor, if you can get me an apartment in here I'll give you $100,' but there ain't none."

There are several women's clubs in the building, such as the Old-Age Pensioners Club and the Twelve Tribes. Fitzgerald, the Democratic precinct captain, has been elected sweetheart of these. Fitzgerald, a neat, well-dressed, youngish man, has said, "If there's a weddin' I'm there, if there's a death I'm there, if there's a birth I'm there. I had a baby born in my car a while back, trying to get the mother to the hospital." Fitzgerald is a court bailiff by day. The Mecca precinct has voted Democratic since 1932. Like the other tenants, Fitzgerald worries about the children. "In summertime the police chase them off the street. One day I come home and the police had backed up a wagon ready to take a whole load to the station for standing in front of the building. I had to put a stop to it. I had three ball clubs last summer and got uniforms for 'em all."

In a vacant store on the ground floor is the Mecca Center, for children. Nobody knows how many children are being raised in the Mecca Building but most people guess five hundred, and now at 4:30 P.M. on a Thursday fifteen of the five hundred are in the Mecca Center. The Center is a big square bare room, a dais at one side, a great clutter of dusty newspapers behind a desk, a piano and a windup Victrola against one wall, a tom-tom and Indian heads in the display window. Two older boys are playing Ping-pong and at a small table two younger ones are playing checkers but the rest of the younger ones, probably from nine to twelve years old, are chasing each other around the room, snapping cap-guns at each other, and soon the checker game stops and all thirteen of the younger ones are chasing each other, climbing over tables and chairs, leaping through the air onto each others' backs, screaming wildly; the Ping-pong players, older, proceed with their game, each with an arm outstretched to fend off the littler kids, occasionally pausing to take a cut at a near one's head; a dozen chairs stacked against a wall collapse as a boy's body crashes into them. A man in a hat is standing in a corner watching, saying vaguely, "She was supposed to come and be a musical program but I ain't seen her come in."

On the wall is a program schedule allotting various hours of the week to such activities as "Teen-Age Club," "Children's Story-Telling Hour," "Parents' Club Meeting." Right now, it is "Children's Game Period." The man watching says sharply, "You—let that Victrola alone," to a boy climbing onto it in order to leap onto another boy's back. A woman arrives bustling in. "I teach music and dramatics and folk dancing. I have about sixty enrolled. From six to eight we have singing and at nine physical culture and clubs." She is taking off her gloves, as unmindful of the children as they are of her; the children are growing more serious in their play, the temper has changed, ugliness has crept in, they battle silently, not laughing or screaming, only panting hard. The man is making plans to take some of them to the circus.

In one apartment in the building a woman and her husband are raising nine children, raising them in one room. This summer afternoon she is sitting in a chair by the door of the one room, her baby on the bed, evidently asleep but looking dead it is so thin and still, and the mother is saying, "It is hot at night, at night you burn up. My husband and I sleep in the bed. The kids sleep on the cot." The nine kids. They are from nine months to fifteen years in age. The room is eight feet by eleven. In it are one bed, one davenport, one radio, one light bulb, one picture, two straight wood chairs, one wicker table (on which stand a seashell, a jar of deodorant, and a can of face powder), one calendar. Back of the bed is a closet curtained with a rag. One necktie hangs on a nail in the wall. The plaster is broken. Her husband earns $45 a week as a machine operator. They pay $6 a week for this room. They have lived in this room four years.

The mother is twenty-nine years old. When she and her husband first came to Chicago they lived in one room on Wentworth Avenue, then in three rooms on Prairie Avenue until "the lady sold the building," then in five rooms elsewhere on Prairie Avenue again "till the lady sold the building," then in four rooms elsewhere on Prairie "till the man sold the building," then here. They came here on August 6,

1946. "My husband knew the man that had this apartment so he let us have a place in it that same evening. We were out on the street." They can find no other place to live. "I looked so much that I'm just disgusted about it. They say you're a citizen of Chicago and on votin' day they're right up to your door to vote. My husband, he wrote to the Mayor of Chicago and everyone else and I don't see no results," and she rises and fumbles behind a curtain on the window ledge and finds two letters. She is young, quick-moving, pretty; her teeth flash and she wears big gold earrings and she appears about the age of her oldest daughter, fifteen, who now comes in and stands in the doorway looking reproachful. One letter is a long form letter from the Chicago Housing Authority:

"Dear Friend,
". . . The housing projects now in operation have such lengthy waiting lists that no additional applications are being taken at this time. . . ." The other is a personal letter from a Housing Authority official: "Mayor Kennelly has referred to us for reply your letter of March 2, concerning your need for adequate housing. We are very sorry."

"All this stuff's just a racket," says the mother of nine. "They ain't doing nothing about it. Makes me sick." She hitches her chair around to face the wall. "After all, my husband works and makes an honest livin' and he do support his family the best that a workin' man can. His children do get clothes, the onliest kick that they can have is that they don't have no place to live. And that's not his fault." The baby on the bed stirs a little, then lies still again.

V

Until 1941 the Mecca Building was owned by a New York estate. The janitor Jimmy only once saw a representative of the estate. In 1941 the estate sold the Mecca to its next-door neighbor, the Illinois Institute of Technology. The Institute bought the building for only one purpose: to tear it down. The Institute was expanding its campus in accordance with a neat plan integrated with the neat plans of numerous other agencies for clearing the South Side slums. It wanted to replace the Mecca Building with a laboratory. But its plans ran head-on into an important need of the people who dwelt in the Mecca Building, the need for a place to live.

For nine years it has tried to evict them, taking them to court and warning them the Mecca is a firetrap. Thus far the tenants have managed to generate enough political pressure to stay. Recently, when the Institute again started eviction proceedings, State Senator C. C. Wimbish, a lawyer who has represented the tenants in court, said, "If they try to put these people out, they'll have a race riot down there on State Street and I intend to make it as tense as possible. Any roof is better than no roof."

It is quiet in the building on a summer morning, quiet as a tomb. Spit falls flatly on the ground floor, spat by a silent watcher high on the balcony, and in a dark corner recess on the topmost floor a young girl, pretty, wearing a tight white sweater, strains against a young man leaning on the wall. An old man in blue pajamas, his eyes wild and staring, his body very thin, totters along, clutching at the railing, saying in a high, cracked voice, to a visitor, "Call me a telephone number please, mister, will you call me a telephone number," but a large woman steps from a doorway and shakes her head at the visitor, making circling motions beside her temple, and moves to take the old man's arm, and seeing her he starts, as though to run, then weeps, and she leads him away. A puff of blue smoke hangs in the dead air on the second balcony where a man is leaning on the railing, smoking. A janitor collects garbage in a cart that rumbles on the broken tile like a tumbril. Everything echoes in the halls, voices are hard to comprehend, are confused with distant sounds.

A visitor twists the bell on Mrs. Corene Griffin's apartment and she calls, "Who is it?" then unfastens the chain. Her mother is sitting by the window in the sun, as always. Mrs. Griffin says that when she got the most recent notice to vacate, she went house-hunting: "I found a place to buy at a real estate office way up on the North Side but no other collored people live right there, and I don't want to get bombed on," as indeed many Chicago Negroes have been when they tried to leave the black belt. She goes over beside her mother, who is rocking. "I think this housing situation is terrible, it's all politics, that's all. I'm not mad at the school. It's their property, we know that. I'm mad 'cause all this politics. Put 'em in office and they didn't did nothin'. They build streets and superhighways and recreation—not houses. They should turn that money loose and stop it—people has got to have some place to live. They gonna do *anything* if they don't."

She laughs, but does not sound amused: "They say they gonna place us somewhere. *Place* us! I don't wanta be placed anywhere myself. They might place me in some mudhole somewhere and I never did live in that," and she laughs again. Her mother mutters something. "I don't know what they going to do with us. After all, there's no use in pushing us around from one place to another, that's no way to live." And then, after a pause, "It's all so mean."

Her mother, rocking, has started muttering steadily; she is looking out the window, her head in its white lace cap bobbing gently up and down. What is Mrs. Griffin going to do?

"I don't know. I'll have to have a place for my mother. I couldn't tell you what I'm going to do, to save my neck." Her mother, rocking, begins to mutter louder, but her words are not intelligible, it is just a human voice, muttering, and it is impossible to tell whether in anger or in joy, it is only sound.

SUGGESTIONS FOR STUDY:

1. Is the purpose of the essay descriptive or expository?
2. Is Martin careful to maintain a physical point of view throughout the description?
3. Do "The city is harsh" and "the sun is hazy and dirty" help to fix a mental point of view?
4. Does Martin depend on labeling adjectives or on concrete detail to develop this point of view?
5. Does Martin use a dominant image for the building and for each wing? What?
6. Is there an appeal to more than sight in the hollowed stone slab step?
7. To what other senses does Martin appeal?

8. Is Martin's presentation of the social dilemma by means of quotations effective? Why?
9. What is the meaning of *marijuana, vandalism?*
10. Write a description of a place that differs markedly from other places or that has a wider significance than its physical being.

* * *

Almost one hundred years ago a distinguished historian and Member of the British Parliament predicted disastrous results for the American democratic system.

A LETTER TO AN AMERICAN
by *Thomas Babington Macaulay*

SIR: The four volumes of the *Colonial History of New York* reached me safely. I assure you that I shall value them highly. They contain much to interest an English as well as an American reader. Pray, accept my thanks, and convey them to the Regents of the University.

You are surprised to learn that I have not a high opinion of Mr. Jefferson, and I am surprised at your surprise. I am certain that I never wrote a line, and that I never in Parliament, in conversation or even on the hustings—a place where it is the fashion to court the populace—uttered a word indicating an opinion that the supreme authority in a State ought to be entrusted to the majority of citizens, in other words, to the poorest and most ignorant part of society. I have long been convinced that institutions purely democratic must, sooner or later, destroy liberty or civilization, or both.

In Europe, where the population is dense, the effect of such institutions would be almost instantaneous. What happened lately in France is an example. In 1848 a pure democracy was established there. During a short time there was reason to expect a general spoliation, a national bankruptcy, a new partition of the soil, a maximum of prices, a ruinous load of taxation laid on the rich for the purpose of supporting the poor in idleness. Such a system would, in twenty years, have made France as poor and barbarous as the France of the Carlovingians. Happily, the danger was averted; and now there is a despotism, a silent tribune, an enslaved press. Liberty is gone, but civilization has been saved.

I have not the smallest doubt that, if we had a purely democratic government here, the effect would be the same. Either the poor would plunder the rich and civilization would perish, or order and property would be saved by a strong military government, and liberty would perish. You may think that your country enjoys an exemption from these evils. I will frankly own to you that I am of a very different opinion. Your fate I believe to be certain, though it is deferred by a physical cause. As long as you have a boundless extent of fertile and unoccupied land, your laboring population will be far more at ease than the laboring population of the old world, and, while that is the case, the Jeffersonian polity may continue to exist without causing any fatal calamity. But the time will come when New England will be as thickly populated as Old England. Wages will be as low, and will fluctuate as much with you as with us. You will have your Manchesters and Birminghams, and in those Manchesters and Birminghams hundreds of thousands of artisans will assuredly be sometimes out of work. Then your institutions will be fairly brought to the test. Distress everywhere makes the laborer mutinous and discontented, and inclines him to listen with eagerness to agitators who tell him that it is a monstrous iniquity that one man should have a million while another cannot get a full meal.

In bad years there is plenty of grumbling here, and sometimes a little rioting. But it matters little, for here the sufferers are not the rulers. The supreme power is in the hands of a class, numerous indeed, but select; of an educated class; of a class which is, and knows itself to be, deeply interested in the security of property and maintenance of order. Accordingly, the malcontents are firmly yet gently restrained. The bad time is got over without robbing the wealthy to relieve the indigent. The springs of national prosperity soon begin to flow again; work is plentiful, wages rise, and all is tranquillity and cheerfulness. I have seen England pass three or four times through such critical seasons as I have described.

Through such seasons, the United States will have to pass in the course of the next century, if not of this. How will you pass through them? I heartily wish you a good deliverance. But my reason and my wishes are at war, and I cannot help foreboding the worst. It is quite plain that your government will never be able to restrain a distressed and discontented majority. For with you the majority is the government, and has the rich, who are always a minority, absolutely at its mercy.

The day will come when, in the State of New York, a multitude of people, none of whom has had more than half a breakfast, or expects to have more than half a dinner, will choose a Legislature. Is it possible to doubt what sort of Legislature will be chosen? On one side is a statesman preaching patience, respect for vested rights, strict observance of public faith. On the other is a demagogue ranting about the tyranny of capitalists and usurers, and asking why anybody should be permitted to drink champagne and to ride in a carriage, while thousands of honest folks are in want of necessaries. Which of the two candidates is likely to be preferred by a workingman who hears his children cry for more bread? I seriously apprehend that you will in some such season of adversity as I have described, do things which will prevent prosperity from returning; that you will act like people who should in a year of scarcity devour all the seed corn, and thus make the next year a year not of scarcity, but of absolute famine. There will be, I fear, spoliation. There is nothing to stop you. Your Constitution is all sail and no anchor.

As I said before, when a society has entered on this downward progress, either civilization or liberty must perish. Either some Caesar or Napoleon will seize the reins of government with a strong hand, or your Republic will be as fearfully plundered and laid waste by barbarians in the 20th

Century as the Roman Empire was in the fifth—with this difference, that the Huns and Vandals who ravaged the Roman Empire came from without, and that your Huns and Vandals will have been engendered within your own country by your own institutions.

Thinking thus, of course, I cannot reckon Jefferson among the benefactors of mankind. I readily admit that his intentions were good and his abilities considerable. Odious stories have been circulated about his private life; but I do not know on what evidence those stories rest, and I think it probable that they are false or monstrously exaggerated. I have no doubt that I shall derive both pleasure and information from your account of him.

T. B. MACAULAY

Holly Lodge
May 23, 1857

SUGGESTIONS FOR STUDY:

1. What purpose do the first and last paragraphs serve?
2. Is the rest of the letter an opinion supported by reasons and illustrations? What is this opinion—or main idea?
3. Would you agree that the essay consists of two main divisions—democracy in Europe and democracy in America?
4. Would you include the English experience with economic depressions in this second division?
5. Contrast paragraphs 3 and 7 regarding the arrangement of the parts.
6. What is the purpose of the first sentence in paragraph 5? of the second sentence?
7. What is the principal method of development in paragraph 5?
8. Does the writer use antithesis and balance? Where?
9. Are his prophecies vague, or is he as specific here as elsewhere in the letter?
10. What is the meaning of *artisans, demagogue ranting, engendered, odious?*
11. Write a theme in which you discuss an arbitrary action by local political bosses, campus leaders, college authorities; a specific example of the good or evil accomplished by a specific law; an example of the majority being demonstrably wrong; false prophets; or write a letter in which you develop a single opinion within a specific occasion.

284 Current Prose

······························

When Daisy Mae finally captured Li'l Abner, nobody, Al Capp tells us here, was more surprised than the cartoonist himself. Perhaps. Li'l Abner fans, accustomed to last-minute escapes, can assure Capp he had plenty of company. But the reasons he finally let her catch Li'l Abner may seem as surprising as the fact itself, and they provide a commentary on twentieth-century America as provocative as Macaulay's in the preceding selection.

IT'S HIDEOUSLY TRUE
by Al Capp

YOU MAY, unless you had something better to do, have been reading my comic strip *Li'l Abner* this week. If so, you are probably startled to see that my hero is apparently being married to one Daisy Mae Scragg. This time it's the real thing. Yes, after 18 years the poor lout is finally, hopelessly married, and in one of Marryin' Sam's cheapest, most humiliating weddings.

I never intended to do this. My comic-strip characters are not the kind who grow through boyhood and adolescence, get married and raise their own kids. The Yokums of Dogpatch are the same sweet and brainless characters they always were. And the fact that Abner always managed somehow to escape Daisy Mae's warm, eager arms provided me with a story that I could tell whenever I couldn't think of

················

From Life, March 31, 1952. Copyright Time Inc.

anything better. Frankly I intended to go through life happily and heartlessly betraying you decent, hopeful people who want to see things come out right. I never intended to have Li'l Abner marry Daisy Mae because your pathetic hope that I would was one of the main reasons you 50 million romance lovers read my strip.

For the first few years it was easy to fool you; you didn't know me well then. You followed developments eagerly, trustfully. When I met any of you, I was asked, "When will Li'l Abner marry Daisy Mae?" in a friendly, hopeful tone. Later, as I betrayed your hopes in more and more outrageous ways, your tone became a little bitter. One year I had Daisy Mae marry a tree trunk, thinking that Abner was hiding inside it. Next day, naturally, it turned out that the contents were an old pair of socks, but that Daisy's marriage to them was irrevocably legal. That was a pretty problem. Your tone became threatening. Later on I poisoned her, and Abner consented to marry her because it was her dying wish (Why not? She would be safely dead in a minute anyway); but just as you thought the wedding had finally taken place, I let her drink some of Dogpatch's sizzling superfluid, "Kickapoo Joy Juice," which instantly restored her to life, so Abner was no longer bound by his promise. You still asked me when they would *really* marry, but your tone was a little more threatening. Then I let Daisy ecstatically marry a boy who not only turned out to be merely Abner's double but a bigamist too, so even that marriage didn't count. Now your tone was downright mutinous, and your question went something like: "For God's sake, will Abner EVER marry Daisy Mae?" Just the same, I knew you would still keep watching and waiting. This was the kind of suspense I needed to keep you reading my comic strip, so, no matter how impatient or indignant you got, I never intended to let your foolish, romantic dreams come true.

So why did I do it this week? Why, after all these years of tricking you, did I finally trick myself? Well, the real reason isn't as simple as Abner, Daisy or even suspense. To understand why I have done this awful thing you will have to bear with me while I explain how and why I created them in the first place.

When I was in my early 20s and about to start a comic strip, I found myself in a terrible dilemma. The funny comic strip, the kind I wanted to do, was vanishing from the funny page. A frightening new thing had been discovered: namely, that you could sell more papers by worrying people than by amusing them. Comic strips which had no value except that they were comic were beginning to vanish from the funny papers. Rube Goldberg's dazed *Mike and Ike,* Fred Opper's *Happy Hooligan,* who wore a tomato can on his head, Milt Gross's *Count Screwloose,* who regularly escaped from the booby hatch only to return to it because things were more normal there—this beloved procession of clowns, innocents and cheerful imbeciles—slowly faded. In their place came a sobbing, screaming, shooting parade of the new "comic"-strip characters: an orphan who talked like the Republican platform of 1920; a prizefighter who advised children that brains were better than brawn while beating the brains out of his physically inferior opponents; detectives who explored and explained every sordid and sickening byway of crime and then made it all okay by concluding that these attractively blueprinted crimes didn't really pay; and girl reporters who were daily threatened with rape and mutilation.

Don't get me wrong. I was terrified by the emergence of this new kind of comic strip 18 years ago only because I didn't have the special qualities they required—not because they didn't have quality. *Dick Tracy* is a magnificently drawn, exquisitely written shocker comparable, in its own terms, with Poe. But "suspense" strips, though enormously effective, disdain fun and fantasy. Suspense was what editors wanted when I was ready to create my own comic strip—but all I could do was fun and fantasy.

So I tried to draw straight-faced suspense comic strips. I tried to create smart and superior heroes, and submerged them in blood-curdling tragedies, increasing in complexity, hopelessness and horror and there by creating reader anxiety, nausea and terror—*i.e.,* suspense. But I couldn't do it. I just couldn't believe in them. The suspense strips require one-dimensional characters: good guys and bad guys, and no fooling around with anything in between. I simply couldn't believe in my one-dimensional good guys and bad guys—as I drew them. I discovered good things in the bad guys, and vice versa. So my hero turned out to be big and strong like the suspense-strip heroes, but he also turned out to be stupid, as big, strong heroes sometimes are. His mammy, like mine, and possibly yours, turned out to be a miracle of goodness, but at the same time she was kind of bossy, quite self-righteous and sweetly ridiculous. His girl, although wildly beautiful, is vaguely sloppy and, although infinitely virtuous, pursues him like the most unprincipled seductress.

The good people in my hero's town, possibly like those in your town, often are a pain in the neck. And the bad 'uns, like some bad 'uns in real life, are often more attractive than the good 'uns. The Scragg Boys, Lem and Luke, are fiendish when they are snatching milk from whimpering babies or burning down orphan asylums to get some light to read comic books by (only to realize that they can't read, anyway); but even the most horrified reader can't help being touched by their respectfully asking their pappy's permission to commit all this manslaughter and mayhem. Monsters they certainly are, but they are dutiful children too.

The society people in *Li'l Abner* always have impressive names, but there is always something a little wrong with them too—like Henry Cabbage Cod, Daphne Degradingham, Sir Cecil Cesspool (he's deep), Peabody Fleabody and Basil Bassoon. Dumpington Van Lump seemed a harmless, hospitable kid until it developed that his favorite book was *How to Make Lampshades Out of Your Friends*. Colossal McGenius was so brilliant in giving business advice that he seemed to be justified in charging $1,000 a word for talking to worried tycoons; but it turned out that his weakness was telling long, involved jokes (at $1,000 a word) about three Bulgarians, whereupon he remembered, much too late, that they were actually three *Persians,* and so he had to start the story all over again. When he finally got to the advice it was great, but by that time the tycoon had gone bankrupt.

When I introduced a mythical country, Lower Slobbovia, I was as technical as the straightest suspense-strip creator, and gave readers a map. The map was perfectly reasonable except that the names of its parts created some distrust and disrespect for the country. The oceans were the Hotlantic and Pitziffic, and there was another body of water called the Gulf of Pincus. The capital, Ceaser Siddy, home of Good King Nogoodnik, was flanked by the twin cities of Tsk-Tsk and Tch-Tch. Its leading citizens had familiar and famous, but somehow embarrassing, names like Douglas Snowbanks, Jr., Harry S. Rasputintruman and Clark Bagle. Everything in *Li'l Abner* was my effort to be as straight as the straight strips, but colored, however, with my conviction that nothing is ever entirely straight, entirely good, entirely bad, and that everything is a little ridiculous. As in the straight suspense strips, I dutifully created the standard, popular suspense situations, but something forced me to carry them so far that terror became absurdity.

For instance, when the Yokums make gigantic sacrifices for what they are convinced is a noble and beneficial cause, the reader knows they are swindling themselves; even victory will benefit only the enemy. When the Yokums are being heroes they are being not only heroes—they are being damned fools at the same time. When their adversaries are being villainous, they are not only vile, they are also confused and frightened.

Li'l Abner had to come out that way, because that's the way things seem to me. Well, it happened to make a big hit. It was a success because it was something I hadn't thought much about as such. It was a satire. Nobody had done one quite in these terms before. I was delighted that I had. I was exhilarated by the privilege this gave me to kid hell out of everything.

It was wonderful while it lasted; and I had no reason for marrying Abner off to Daisy Mae. But then something happened that threatens to shackle me and my kind of comic strip. It is what I call the gradual loss of our fifth freedom. Without it, the other four freedoms aren't much fun, because the fifth is the freedom to laugh at each other.

My kind of comic strip finds its fun wherever there is lunacy, and American life is rich in lunacy everywhere you look. I created labor-hating labor leaders, money-foolish financiers, and Senator Jack S. ("Good old Jack S.") Phogbound. When highway billboard advertising threatened to create a coast-to-coast iron curtain between the American motorist and the beautiful American countryside, I got some humorous situations out of that too. Race-hate peddlers gave me some of my juiciest comedy characters, and I had the Yokums tell them what I know is true, that all races are God's children, equally beloved by their Father. For the first 14 years I reveled in the freedom to laugh at America. But now America has changed. The humorist feels the change more, perhaps, than anyone. Now there are things about America we can't kid.

I realized it first when four years ago I created the Shmoo. You remember the Shmoo? It was a totally boneless and wildly affectionate little animal which, when broiled, came out steak and, when fried, tasted like chicken. It also laid neatly packaged and bottled eggs and milk, all carefully labeled "Grade A." It multiplied without the slightest effort. It loved to be eaten, and would drop dead, out of sheer joy, when you looked at it hungrily. Having created the animal, I let it run wild in the world of my cartoon strip. It was simply a fairy tale and all I had to say was wouldn't it be wonderful if there were such an animal and, if there were, how idiotically some people might behave. Mainly, the response to the Shmoo was delight. But there were also some disturbing letters. Some writers wanted to know what was the idea of kidding big business, by creating the Shmoo (which had *become* big business). Other writers wanted to know what was the idea of criticizing labor, by creating the Shmoo, which made labor unnecessary.

It was disturbing, but I didn't let it bother me too much. Then a year later, I created the Kigmy, an animal that loved to be kicked around, thus making it unnecessary for people to kick each other around. This time a lot more letters came. Their tone was angrier, more suspicious. They asked the craziest questions, like: Was I, in creating the Kigmy, trying to create pacifism and thus, secretly, nonresistance to Communism? Were the Kigmy kickers secretly the big bosses kicking the workers around? Were the Kigmy kickers secretly the labor unions kicking capital around? And finally, what in hell was the idea of creating the Kigmy anyhow, because it implied some criticism of some kinds of Americans and any criticism of anything American was (now) un-American? I was astounded to find it had become unpopular to laugh at any fellow Americans. In fact, when I looked around, I realized that a new kind of humorist had taken over, the humorist who kidded nothing but himself. That was the only thing left. Hollywood had stopped making ain't-America-wonderful-and-ridiculous movies, and was making ain't-America-wonderful-but-anyone-who-says-it's-ridiculous-too-deserves-to-be-picketed movies. Radio, the most instantly obedient to pressure of all media, has sensed the atmosphere, an atmosphere in which Jack Benny is magnificent but in which Will Rogers would have suffocated.

So that was when I decided to go back to fairy tales until the atmosphere is gone. That is the real reason why Li'l Abner married Daisy Mae. At least for the time being, I can't create any more Shmoos, any more Kigmies; and when Senator Phogbound turns up now, I have to explain carefully that, heavens-to-Betsy, goodness-no, he's not typical; nobody like THAT ever holds public office. After a decade and a half of using my characters as merely reasons to swing my searchlight on America, I began all over again to examine them, as people. Frankly, I was delighted with them. (Frankly, I'm delighted with nearly everything I do. The one in the room who laughs loudest at my own jokes or my own comic strip is me.) I became reacquainted with Li'l Abner as a human being, with Daisy Mae as an agonizingly frustrated girl. I began to wonder myself what it would be like if they were ever married. The more I thought about it, the more complicated and disastrous and, therefore, irresistible, the idea became.

For instance, Li'l Abner has never willingly kissed any female except his mother and a pig. Well—if he got married, he'd *have* to. Even he couldn't avoid it for more than a month or so. What would happen? Would he approve of kissing? Would he say anything good about it? (And thus make it popular with millions of red-blooded young Americans whose "ideel" he is.) Would he do it again? As a bachelor he is frankly a bum. He just sleeps, eats and goes catfishing. As a married man he would have to support his own household. How would he do it? Is there anybody stupid enough to hire someone as stupid as he is? Is there *any* profession that requires as litle intelligence as he has? And how about Mammy Yokum? She has always ruled Abner with an iron fist. Would she continue to after he has his own home? And how would Daisy Mae take this? Sure, she's been sweet and docile with Mammy Yokum all these years, but that might only have been because she needed her help in trapping Abner. Now that he's her'n, will she show her true colors and tangle with Mammy for the lightweight championship of the new Yokum home? How about babies? Married people frequently have babies. Would *they* have a baby? Will he really be born on the Fourth of July? Is it possible that they'd name him Yankee Doodle Yokum? Babies have uncles. Could I freeze the blood of the entire nation by having Mammy Yokum (who can accomplish anything, even singlehanded) produce a baby of her own, five minutes after Li'l Yankee Doodle Yokum was born? Would this child be known as Oncle Yokum?

And how about Sadie Hawkins Day? It has become a national holiday. It's my responsibility. It doesn't happen on any set day in November; it happens on the day I say it happens. I get tens of thousands of letters from colleges, communities and church groups, starting around July, asking me *what* day, so they can make plans. Well, Sadie Hawkins Day has always revolved around Li'l Abner fearing marriage to Daisy Mae. Now that his worst fears have come hideously true, what will he and Daisy Mae do on Sadie Hawkins Day? Will Lower Slobbovia inaugurate its own "Sadie Huckins Day" and import Li'l Abner and Daisy Mae as technical advisers? In short, once Abner and Daisy Mae are married, do they live happily forever after like other people, or is this just the beginning of even more complicated disasters, more unbearable miseries? They are married, all right. But if you think the future is serene for them, you're ("Haw! Haw!") living in a fool's paradise.

SUGGESTIONS FOR STUDY:

1. What is the main idea, and where is it expressed?
2. Would you say the essay has two main divisions—I did not intend . . . ; I have done so because . . . ?
3. Does Capp cite specific detail from his creations to support his points? For example?
4. What tone does this detail give the essay? Does the essay end with this tone? Does this tone harmonize or contrast with Capp's serious purpose?
5. Do you find Capp's analysis a better explanation of the popularity of comic strips than the thesis that the world is going to the dogs?
6. Can you identify the comic strips that replaced *Happy Hooligan* and *Count Screwloose?*
7. How does Capp show that his characters are not one-dimensional?
8. Is the comparison between Jack Benny and Will Rogers effective?
9. What is the meaning of *irrevocably, dilemma, manslaughter and mayhem?*
10. Write a theme on comic strips or a comic strip; or discuss the reasons for a decision.

Here an unreconstructed Democrat, a Hollywood writer and producer, pursues a point similar to Capp's in the previous essay.

CONFESSION OF A CONFEDERATE
by Nunnally Johnson

MY NAME is Nunnally Johnson. N-u-n-n-a-l-l-y, Nunnally. I was born Dec. 5, 1897, in Columbus, Ga., of white Methodist parents. I am married to another white Methodist and have, all told, four children, all of them white Methodists, too.

I am not a member of the Screen Writers Guild.
I am not a Communist.
I am not a Republican.

The only organization that I belong to is the Limited Editions Club, which I am assured is as clean as a hound's tooth.

I have not attended a meeting or gathering of any sort where anyone was scheduled to rise and speak on any subject whatever, political, educational, or just entertaining, for twenty-five years, or since I was a cub reporter and had to cover such enlightening exhibitions nightly.

As for contributing money to causes, once in Dave Chasen's Restaurant I slipped ten bucks to a girl in a low-cut blouse who turned out to be collecting for the Abraham Lin-

Reprinted by permission from The New York Times, December 28, 1947.

coln Brigade (and me a Confederate!), but the accepted view about town is that politically I am a tightwad from way back and would not give 85 cents to see Henry Wallace walk on water. I bat and throw right-handed.

The explanation for this unsolicited autobiographical information is that I am a Hollywood producer with a picture recently released.

Nobody seems to want to know what frats a book publisher belongs to, to make sure he isn't running around with the Wrong Crowd. Nobody hauls a radio producer up on the carpet and says, "You did a bad t'ing in one of your broadcasts, but if you think we're going to tell you which one it was you're crazy." Nobody subpoenas a stage producer and warns him to watch his step if he doesn't want to get a horn on the next play. And nobody, but nobody, drags a newspaper or magazine publisher down to Washington and pokes around in his political background and associations by way of seeing to it that he isn't sneaking a subversive line or two across in his How-to-Cook-a-Pot-Roast column.

But with a moving picture producer it's different. Either he unbosoms himself at once these days, to be measured by the New Standards, or the next thing he knows the Man is around from the Committee. Or worse still, he becomes subject to the attentions of the Committee's volunteer field workers. If he gets past the first of these, the Smeller, an operative who claims to function like a dog, he has still to face the Reader, an actor-scholar so transported by his ability to read books with no pictures that he is said to have devoured $458\frac{3}{4}$ volumes on the suburbs of Leningrad alone. And if not yet down, he has then to deal with the Mother, a human Geiger counter who apparently vibrates with a low hum at the merest suggestion of subversiveness.

If he fails even one of the ghostly tests set by these unofficial agents, the air is suddenly full of yells and screams and charges of treason and the whole pack is off for Washington with a bale of short-hand notes showing that a bit player in the third reel said: "Well, my goodness, that is some mighty red blood on Bickerstaff's left hand." And sure enough, even before breakfast the Man is around to git him.

Recently, to give some semblance of form and definition to this high-minded hobby, certain members of the group descended from the mount with two tablets of stone tersely graven: Screen Guide for Americans—A List of the More Common Devices Used to Turn Non-Political Pictures Into Carriers of Political Propaganda, including thirteen flat orders to the rest of Hollywood on how pictures are to be made from now on.

This development has made it doubly necessary for me to open the books but immediately on myself and everyone else connected with this picture, "The Senator Was Indiscreet," for what have we done, first crack out of the box, but busted wide open the very first of these commandments, the one forbidding any light treatment of politics! I couldn't be more embarrassed.

And yet none of us should have been altogether surprised by this particular fiat. In the whole history of our country nobody had ever before treated politics lightly. Nobody had ever used politics and politicians as material for comedy. Oh well, a few perhaps, yes, if you want to count Reds like Mark Twain, Will Rogers and Irvin Cobb. But I mean real Americans, true blue and loyal to their country. Who today ever speaks lightly of politics and politicians with the sole exception of newspaper cartoonists, editorial writers and radio comedians?

It was an absolutely fresh subject that we had hit on, a virgin field for comedy, and we should have expected some totalitarian objection to its use in a picture.

As a matter of fact, we were not altogether negligent in our preparations for this courageous venture into the unknown. We took certain precautions.

For one thing, it was agreed among us at the studio that it might be a wise move for me to drop my subscription to PM temporarily and take a whack at reading a column by George Sokolsky, whoever he is. For another, it was suggested that I should stop going around telling people that an expression like "We disaffiliate" clearly indicated that John L. Lewis must have studied English under Amos and Andy. Too frivolous. And for still another, it was thought just as well to begin soft-pedaling the fact that I once produced a poor-folks picture called "The Grapes of Wrath" and to concentrate instead on my sponsorship of "Dimples," an early Shirley Temple masterpiece.

The same carefulness went also into the casting of the picture. But since in those days we didn't know it was okay to inquire into a player's private beliefs, we were forced to resort to a secret process of testing William Powell, Ella Raines, Peter Lind Hayes and the others for Americanization, and all, I am happy to report, came through with flying colors. For example, when we suddenly played "O Chichornia" on the set to note involuntary reactions of joy and homesickness, they hissed it, the whole company.

But our most masterly stroke, really a matter of sheer inspiration, was in the selection of a writer. Since George S. Kaufman, the director, and I were not only Democrats but Roosevelt Democrats at that, the smartest move we figured we could possibly make would be to suck a Republican in on the deal. In any business at all these days and in particular the movie business, it does a Democrat no harm whatever to be seen as much as possible in public with a certified GOPster, and if necessary, give him a piece of the business itself, just as a few years ago the crafty Republican contemplating negotiations in Washington quickly provided himself with an old line Democrat to stand up front.

The Republican pillar of respectability we took in was named Charles MacArthur and while he didn't look the part and God knows didn't act it, he had the papers to prove himself a registered paid-up GOP card-toter and so we wasted no time in tying him up. When presently it turned out that he could also write and was, in fact, the possessor of a distinguished record of achievement both in the movies and on the stage, one can imagine our pleasure and satisfaction. Personally, I hadn't even known there was such a thing as a witty Republican. Live and learn, though, live and learn.

It is still possible, of course, that the Man will be around anyway, in spite of all our precautions, but somehow I doubt it. I put a lot of faith in old Charlie's presence in our line-up. Because the way I figure it, a Congressional committee will think a long, long time before finding anything questionable in a picture written by a good, solid, substantial, high-tariff Republican. MacArthur, I mean.

SUGGESTIONS FOR STUDY:

1. What is the purpose of the opening paragraphs?
2. Is Johnson's apparent purpose his real purpose?
3. What details, witticisms, or absurdities make clear that Johnson is writing satire?
4. This essay was written in 1947. Is it dated?
5. What is the meaning of *subpoenas, negligent, card-toter?*
6. Write a theme attacking some current attitude with which you disagree. Use satire if you feel at home in it; if not, don't.

John Allan May, a staff writer for the American newspaper, The Christian Science Monitor, *reports an Englishman's reactions to the 1952 Republican convention. He finds it surprising—and far more impressive than he had expected.*

AN ENGLISHMAN VIEWS THE REPUBLICAN CONVENTION
by John Allan May

AN ENGLISHMAN getting his first view of an American political convention on television is likely to feel as if he were a man either from Mars or in Mars.

Reprinted from The Christian Science Monitor, July 14, 1952.

This is something he never has known but has only imagined. And whatever he imagined, it wasn't this.

After looking in at odd moments over a period of many hours, even days, this viewer had not even seen a steam roller.

Speaking personally and frankly I found this especially surprising. I had expected to be struck by the thought that the atmosphere was as artificial as it was colorful, but instead I have found it a great deal of the time remarkably natural and about as colorful as a committee meeting in the Old Kent Road.

I had expected a great deal of uninhibited noise and dressing-up and emotion, with parades and war whoops and brass bands and orchestrated cheers and always a prance or two of drum majorettes in the lead.

Well, people in the streets of Chicago, or in the hotel lobbies, may have been struck by the oddities and eccentricities but I have been surprised at their scarcity.

It is possible, of course, that television has brought big changes to the art of politics. Now that politicians realize they live in glass houses maybe they have drawn the proverbial conclusions.

On the other hand it is possible that in the role of wise onlooker one too often prepares himself to see everything but the obvious and to expect everything but that which is to be expected.

Perhaps it simply is that one has heard the words "grass-roots democracy" so often recently that they have become parched and withered as a phrase and lost their meaning. That certainly could be the reason why the moment was startling when one seemed actually to hear the grass growing.

One had seen and heard, at odd moments, hour after hour, so many fragments of speeches that it was difficult to know who was speaking, and on what topic, and for what faction, and not always easy to care. One had noted the inevitable fascination that a good gavel holds for even the best chairman (and especially a gavel made from a rail split by Abraham Lincoln).

One had watched the cameras again and again play over the huge picture of Lincoln behind the rostrum and had heard speaker after speaker linger over resounding words spoken first by that first Republican President.

One had seen serried ranks of people in the great hall, sometimes seeming to shelter quietly in a forest of banners, sometimes seething and swaying before a wind of oratory. One had noticed a few balloons, a few eccentric costumes, a little "mugging" in front of television cameras. One had wondered irrelevantly at how odd a close-up picture can look, full of disconnected background motion and murmurings, comings and goings and standings and sittings and apparently aimless wanderings, the whole effect curiously like a magnified microscopic picture of a particle of sea water.

One had heard religious and patriotic songs sung splendidly by great singers like James Melton and had watched the "colors" presented by an American Legion guard of honor. Now and again one had heard familiar local tunes struck up by an orchestra or an organ and had then watched temporary pandemonium.

One had heard strong talk and listened once to encomiums that must have established a new altitude record for high-flown words.

One had heard a great deal of noise. But I for one could not detect the crunch of public opinion giving under the heavy weight of "steam rollers" or even just the weight of confusion, which some suggested might at times be plainly audible.

Indeed one had heard individual delegates stoutly refusing to accept their own delegation leader's count and demanding an immediate open poll of individual views. And had chuckled at the one-man delegation from the Virgin Islands speaking up loudly and with sonorous pride as well as humor: "The entire Virgin Islands delegation votes 'No'!"

Then somewhere along the line, I don't quite know when or why, there began quite suddenly to well up the tide of the obvious. The obvious simply was that these people were sincere.

They weren't people just going through the motions. They were not a mob but 1206 individuals. And they knew it —they were people, folk of every kind and of every physical and mental shape; folk with ideas, folk with prejudices; good speakers, bad speakers, many who wouldn't get a chance to speak at all; business folk, insurance salesmen, businessmen, lawyers, politicians, men and women—every one of them somehow plainly exuding a strong conviction that the great hall where a political leader was being chosen was just exactly as full of meaning as it was of individuals. Out of tedium came excitement; out of muddle clarity; out of turbulence dignity.

Nothing quite like this happens anywhere else in the world, one knows that. Many peoples elect their leaders but relatively few select the contestants for leadership; sometimes one forgets that.

It is hard for a phlegmatic Englishman to admit it, but around this time there was a lump in my throat.

SUGGESTIONS FOR STUDY:

1. What is the main idea?
2. Could you divide the essay into three parts—what May expected but did not see, what he did see, and what he finally understood as really significant?
3. Does he obviously repeat a word to indicate he has come to this understanding?
4. In the paragraph on "grass-roots democracy," what is May referring to in "the moment . . . when one seemed actually to hear the grass growing"?
5. What is the meaning of *uninhibited* noise, *eccentricities, serried* ranks, wondered *irrelevantly, pandemonium, encomiums, sonorous* pride, *exuding* a conviction, *phlegmatic* Englishman?
6. Write a theme commenting on some public event you have personally witnessed.

A great and always newsworthy congressman and mayor, an avowed foe of the bosses, describes his entry into politics.

from THE MAKING OF AN INSURGENT
by Fiorello H. La Guardia

I PRACTICED law actively from 1910 to 1915 and sporadically in later years when my political activity permitted. I did not accumulate much money, but I managed to live, found time for study and research and certainly learned a great deal about the political and economic conditions in my city.

On several occasions I was offered appointments to the magistrates' bench in New York, which I refused. I was also offered nominations for the higher courts and turned those down. An independent group once offered me the nomination for justice of the Supreme Court of the State of New York. That independent nomination together with the regular party nomination would have meant certain election. By that time I had served two terms in Congress and had been President of the Board of Aldermen in New York. But I had no ambition to be a Supreme Court justice, and I declined. William Randolph Hearst, who was keeping alive his Independence League, by use of which he had sought several times to be

From *THE MAKING OF AN INSURGENT* by Fiorello La Guardia, Copyright, 1948 by J. B. Lippincott Company, published by J. B. Lippincott Company.

Mayor of New York and Governor of the State, asked me to come to see him during the nineteen twenties about my nomination for justice of the Supreme Court. I told him that I was not interested in becoming a judge and wanted to return to Congress. I wanted to make law and not merely to construe it. Also, I did not have the high regard for the courts of our State that a lawyer with judicial ambitions ought to have. Mr. Hearst told me that in all his thirty years' experience in politics up to that time, it was the first instance he had ever encountered of anyone refusing the nomination for Supreme Court justice. He could hardly believe that I meant what I said.

As I have already stated, I joined the Republican Party because I could not stomach Tammany Hall. Again, let it be understood, that when I say Tammany Hall I mean the Democratic political machine in all five boroughs of Greater New York. They are all alike.

I lived in a district in Greenwich Village where the Republican organization was exceptionally clean. It produced such fine men as Herbert Parsons, Fred Tanner, Henry H. Curran and Frank Stoddard. However, we were a regular political club. History will bear me out when I say that the minority party in any large city can afford to be somewhat virtuous. However, if it happens to get control of the city government, it will resort to the very same activities and indulge in the same bad habits as its rival, assuming it can control the elective officials.

I had been storing up knowledge, and I was eager to bring about better conditions, particularly a more equitable economic situation and less favoritism to special interests in the administration of the law. That was why I was determined to become a Congressman. From the time that I returned to New York after my experience abroad in the Consular Service, I read the *Congressional Record* and kept abreast of activities in Congress. I also made myself familiar with the legislative history of that period. Somehow—I did not know how—I had a feeling that some day I would get into Congress. I kept my eyes open, but I felt that my chances in New York City were very slight. The Republican districts had their Congressmen, but it required a great deal more political influence than I had to obtain a nomination in one of those districts, where nomination meant almost certain election. It was hard to break down the Democratic majorities in their districts. For a time I thought I might go West to a younger state, where the chances were better.

One night I happened to be in the club rooms of the 25th Assembly District, my own district, where I was an election district captain for a time, when the boys were filing in petitions for the nomination for Congress. It was in the late summer of 1914. The petitions were printed, and the names of State and county candidates appeared on them. There were blanks left for the local candidates for the State Senate and Assembly and for representatives in Congress.

Someone hollered out, "Who is the candidate for Congress?" The leader of the district—I think it was Clarence Fay—came from his backroom office. He shouted out, "Who wants to run for Congress?" That was my chance. "I do," I said. "OK, put La Guardia down," Clarence said. That was all there was to it. But I darn near missed out even so. One of the men asked, "Hey, La Guardia, what's your first name?" I said, "Fiorello." "Oh, hell," he said, "let's get someone whose name we can spell." I spelled the name carefully and slowly and had to argue hard to get it on the petitions.

I took my nomination seriously. I soon learned that I was not supposed to take it seriously. When September came along, I attended my first political meeting. It was in one of the district club houses. Pamphlets were distributed throughout the district announcing the meeting, and stating that all the prominent candidates would talk. I was there bright and early. The meeting started. Candidate after candidate spoke. The State candidates came in, and they had the right of way. I waited and waited for my turn. Two or three times in the course of the evening I was sure that I was next when the chairman would say, "And now we will hear from a young and promising candidate." I would get up each time, only to see that someone else was being introduced. The meeting ended around 11:30 that night. I had not been called on. I protested to the chairman, who was talking to the district leader. "How come?" I asked. Everybody had a good laugh. "Why, Fiorello, you haven't a chance of winning," they told me. "We've never elected a Republican to Congress from this district. Now, what you should do is go out and campaign for the State Senator and Assemblyman, help elect the ticket. That is all you can do." "Could I try?" I pleaded. "Oh, no, don't be foolish. You just go out now and help the others, and some day you may get a nomination for an office you can win."

I didn't think that was quite on the level. A few of the boys in the district agreed with me, among them Harry Andrews, who was district secretary, Louis Espresso and old Mike Kehoe. Kehoe, who was in his late seventies, was a master mind and a good political strategist. He was very much amused at my predicament. "Kid, don't be discouraged," he said, "but go out and try."

I discovered that the procedure at that first meeting was repeated at all the regular party meetings. I was not to get a chance to speak at any of them. I went out and bought a secondhand Ford. Harry Andrews and I plastered it with signs, and I started out on my own private, individual campaign. We went from corner to corner every night in that district, and we never missed a wedding, a funeral, a christening or any other kind of a gathering we could get into.

The 14th Congressional District ran from the Hudson River clear across Manhattan to the East River. It included some of the tenement sections of the lower East Side, teeming with Italian and Jewish immigrants. My knowledge of Italian and Yiddish came in handy. I rang doorbells and talked to the immigrant families. At outdoor meetings I would wait until the regular political rally had ended, pull up in my Ford as the people were leaving, gather a crowd and do my talking.

My opponent was Congressman Michael Farley, a saloonkeeper and president of the National Liquor Dealers' Association. He had been the regular Tammany representative in Congress from that district for some time. I was called down once or twice for being "too rough" on him. Distinguished and serious gentlemen in the community pointed out to me that the retail liquor business was a lawful occupation and urged me not to disparage the Congressman who was in that business. I did not disparage him. I merely pointed out that he was not a good Congressman and wasn't even a good bartender.

When the votes were counted that November 1914, Congressman Farley was re-elected by the small margin of 1,700 votes. Never before had the Democratic majority in that district been less than 16,000 votes. Both my Republican colleagues and my Democratic opponents began to take notice of me. The Republicans began to think that maybe I had a future in politics because I could put on a campaign that got the public interested and therefore it would be wise to keep me in the political family. The showing I made attracted enough attention among the politicians to make them think it worth while to give me the appointment of Deputy Attorney General of the State of New York.

The Republicans that year had elected Charles S. Whitman Governor and carried the State, as they usually did in those days, permitting Tammany the rich plunder in the city, by tacit agreement between the bosses of both parties.

* * *

I kept pretty busy in 1915 and 1916, what with my work in the Attorney General's office, learning to fly, and building my fences for the 1916 Congressional campaign. I had my heart still set on going to Congress, and my first defeat did not discourage me. Once when I was in Washington, a member of Congress gave me a card to the "family" gallery. I would not go. I did not want to enter the House of Representatives until I could go on the floor as a member. But I read the *Congressional Record* religiously. That was the easiest part of my preliminary training. The big job was making friends, so that I could win the election.

I knew that I could not depend much on the Republican organization, because of my first experience with it in 1914. It was pretty clear to me that the seat in Congress from my district appeared to belong to the National Liquor Dealers' Association in the name of Michael Farley, the Democratic incumbent, by tacit agreement with the Republicans. But I kept building up my contacts. My law office was a regular Legal Aid Society, and after office hours at the Attorney General's office I made many friends useful to me in politics by going to clambakes, balls, weddings and funerals—functions inseparable from the life of a man in politics. I got to know a great many people in my district.

When the time came for the Congressional nomination in 1916, I was surprised, shocked and hurt to learn that I was not slated for the place on the Republican ticket. I felt I was entitled to it because of the run I had made in the previous election two years before. But that run had attracted a great deal of interest in the nomination. Everybody was nice, giving me good advice about not taking another licking. I was destined, they said, to be a judge or something big like that. "Just be a good boy, go along with the organization, help wherever you can," they told me. That didn't register very well with me.

I got my petitions printed. I was told that was not in the books, that recognition had been given me by my appointment as Deputy Attorney General; I must not hurt my own interest, but just go along and be a good soldier. I insisted that I would contest any nomination made by the party and run in the primaries against another Republican organization choice.

Finally, I made an appointment to see Fred Tanner, who was then Republican State Chairman. He had been leader of my home district. Fred Tanner was a prominent lawyer, scholarly and gentlemanly, who was interested in politics. He had had a meteoric rise in the Republican Party, but he was far too refined and clean to make a success as boss of the New York State Republicans. Naturally, Tanner was greatly occupied, as it was a Presidential year. New York State was going to the Republican convention in Chicago with its Governor, Charles S. Whitman, as its favorite son. I do not believe Fred Tanner was very hot about Whitman.

I had an interesting talk with the State Chairman. He repeated the old gaff about my future in politics, and he tried to convince me that it was to my interest to stay put that year. I was not a bit impressed. He was frank enough to tell me that a young outsider wanted the Congressional nomination badly that year. And this young man's friends had promised to make a substantial contribution to the Republican Party, if he got the nomination. The outsider's name was Hamilton Fish. There is no doubt that he wanted to go to Congress, and he succeeded after World War I. But he was elected to Congress from Dutchess County, a long way from 14th Street in Manhattan.

Fred Tanner made one blunder in his effort to talk me out of running that year. He said that if I had gone to any expense, such as printing my petitions, or anything else, he would see that I was reimbursed. Well, I just hit the ceiling. I don't think Fred meant it the way I took it. But I blew up, and that just about ended our talk. As I started out of his office, Fred shouted to me, "Fiorello, hold your horses. Damn it, if you want to run, go ahead and do it. Don't blame me if you're licked again."

Harry Andrews was a very useful man around our district. He was young, a good stenographer, did most of the clerical work, and acted as secretary to the district leader. He had a job as a secretary to a judge. In 1914 he was in my corner, and he was very helpful to me in both the primary stage of the 1916 campaign as well as in the election. I got him to study law and had the pleasure of seeing him grow and develop to the point where I appointed him a magistrate when I was Mayor. I learned a great deal about politics from Harry, and he, in turn, I believe, learned some things about government from me.

We got my petitions signed and filed. Though I never got a nod or a word from the Republican Party officials, no opposition developed, much to my surprise, and I entered the primaries unopposed. I did have opposition for the Progressive Party nomination. My friend Ben Marsh, a real liberal and a true progressive, who has been on the right side of many losing causes, was my opponent. I won the Progressive nomination, too, and always had a sort of feeling that Ben voted for me.

The campaign was hot. I got a tremendous start on my

opponent, the sitting Congressman. His office-holding had gone to his head, and he was terribly inflated. He seldom showed up at his saloon, and when he did, forgot to treat the boys. He had become a "big shot," and was seldom seen in the district. That would not have been so bad if he had ever done anything in Washington. So I had plenty of material to work on.

This time I did not wait for the party leaders to get me started. I was 'way ahead of them. The campaign was difficult because my district had such varied interests. The East Side section was interested in economics and the future of Europe; Washington Square, before Greenwich Village had become The Village, was most conservative—for higher tariffs, lower taxes, big business stuff; and the West Side Irish were anti-British and completely Tammanyized.

While I had many friends in the Socialist Party, they waged their fight against me on the East Side. It was their tactics to accept an ultra-conservative rather than a progressive. Tammany was counting on a heavy vote in the West Side section of the district and the solid Little Tim Sullivan Third District on the East Side.

This time my candidacy was not taken by Tammany Hall as the joke it had been to its henchmen two years before. They were in a dilemma. They didn't dare put Mike Farley, their candidate, on the stump. So all sorts of stump speakers were imported into the district. We had a great time with them. I covered every corner in that district, I think. We would start early in the evening, on the West Side, keep going east, and it was not unusual for the last street meeting to end 'way past one o'clock in the morning. Then, to Stuyvesant Hall or some coffee house on the East Side for another hour or two of campaigning.

Tammany was not really worried. They depended on two things: on the Democratic majority usual in that Congressional district, which they considered overwhelming, and on the count. Republican leaders in the West Side districts and in some of the East Side districts were not only weak but untrustworthy and venal. The Republican leader in Little Tim Sullivan's East Side district was an Italian who had made a fortune as a padrone for the Erie Railroad. He worked very closely with Tammany Hall and would do nothing to incur its displeasure. He always got advice, protection and help from the national Republican administration. He was illiterate, ignorant and arrogant. He didn't even treat his family well. The Tammany leader in the same district was one of the Sullivan clan. Little Tim Sullivan was personally a nice fellow, but as tough a Tammany leader as they came. We prepared for fraud by organizing in this district a corps of volunteer watchers for the count, a precaution I have always taken in my subsequent campaigns.

The fighting Irish were helpful to me in that campaign. I knew more about the history of Ireland than Mike Farley did, and some of the Irish thought Mike Farley had not been anti-English enough. I was greatly aided by a corps of volunteers headed by one who became known as the Irish Joan of Arc. She was a real spellbinder; she was not particularly supporting me; but she was certainly opposing Mike Farley.

In my talks on the East Side I dismembered the Hapsburg Empire and liberated all the subjugated countries under that dynasty almost every night. The funny part of it is that I was not fooling and happened to guess future history correctly.

Charles Evans Hughes was the Republican candidate for President against Woodrow Wilson, running for re-election. Naturally, the interest in the campaign was focussed on the Presidential election, which was a tense and close struggle. In the Republican part of the district, which constituted only a small percentage of the total vote, I had the advanage of the fact that they were all for Hughes and would vote the straight Republican ticket, including me. Hughes was very popular as a former Governor of New York and a Justice of the United States Supreme Court. We were certain of getting a big vote in that "blue stocking" section of my district, and, in fact, we did very little campaigning there.

We were all pretty tired that last Monday night before election day. We stuck it out at meetings until two o'clock in the morning. We had to get up very early on election day, for we had a job to do. After about three hours' sleep, we covered the two or three lodging houses in the district, flop houses. At five o'clock we visited these, for we knew that Tammany planned to vote the inhabitants in a pack between eight and nine that morning. Our boys were ready with coffee and rolls and doughnuts, so that by the time the Tammany men came around, the flop house inhabitants had already voted. It was the first time in years, some of the old timers remarked, that the guests of these flop houses had voted sober.

We had a little trouble early in the morning when word was spread, allegedly by one of the Republican leaders, "La Guardia hasn't got a chance, so trade votes for Congress for a Republican Assemblyman." We got hold of that leader quickly, took him in the car with us and went from polling place to polling place straightening out that one.

Our real trouble started when the polls closed and the count began. In those days we still had paper ballots. The count was long and tedious. There was ample time and opportunity for marking ballots so that they would be disqualified, for substituting ballots, and every other kind of dirty, dishonest political trick.

I took the toughest district on the waterfront to watch. This attracted a lot of attention, and finally Charles Culkin, one of the top men in Tammany Hall, who held high office from time to time, and was the Tammany leader of that district, came to the polling place. He gently told me, "Why La Guardia, what are you doing here? You shouldn't be here. Everything is all right." "Everything is not all right," I said, "and what is more, Charlie, you sit here and help me watch this count. There is going to be an honest count, and, if not, someone is going to go to jail, and I mean you, Charlie. You stay here and protect your own district." He did. I took a few precincts even in Charlie Murphy's own home district, although he was then the strong boss of Tammany Hall.

I had all sorts of people watching that district of Charlie Culkin's as well as the other districts. There were school teachers, doctors, business men, longshoremen and some tough guys on our side. In the final count in the district where I was helping to watch, I defeated my Tammany opponent by a very small margin. The Democratic vote in that district was usually five to one against the Republican. Charlie Culkin's jaw dropped. He shook his head and asked me if I was satisfied with the count. "Yes," I said, "as soon as the certificate is signed and turned over to the police." It was.

All through the Democratic districts on the West Side riverfront I was running 'way ahead of the ticket. We knew then that if we could keep up that lead, we would overcome the normal majority for the Democrats. We were going well on the East Side. It, too, was well organized. All of our watchers were instructed to remain on duty until the count was entirely completed, the returns officially signed, and the ballot boxes sealed.

It was about four in the morning before we could get a final count. I had won the election. But it was a good thing we had watched that count carefully, for I won by 357 votes—7,272 for me, 6,915 for Farley.

I got quite a reception on the East Side. Sam Koenig, who was the Republican county chairman, was genuinely elated at my victory. There is one thing I could always say about Sam Koenig then and during the many years following: if he gave you his word about something, he kept it. I anticipated an enthusiastic reception in other parts of the 14th Congressional District. After all, it was the first time a Republican had been elected to Congress below 14th Street since the foundation of the Republican Party. I particularly thought I would get a riotous reception in my own home district. I never saw such gloom anywhere. The hangers-on at the club hardly nodded to me. Someone was on the telephone in the rear office, assuring the Democratic leader of the district, who was supposed to be his rival, "No, Joe, we didn't double-cross you; we didn't do anything for this fellow. You just can't control him." An apology for my victory is what I heard instead of congratulations! Those are just some of the little things that have made me an incurable insurgent.

SUGGESTIONS FOR STUDY:

1. Does this personal-experience narrative give considerable information about the ways of American politics? For example?

2. What tone do you find in the paragraph beginning, "Someone hollered out"?
3. Does La Guardia use informal diction elsewhere? Is it effective? What idea about La Guardia do you get from it?
4. Is the paragraph beginning, "I took my nomination seriously," unified, coherent, fully developed?
5. Does the paragraph beginning, "My opponent was Congressman Michael Farley," suggest that La Guardia may have been "too rough" on Farley?
6. Does the apology at the end of the selection bear on La Guardia's earlier statement about a tacit agreement between Republicans and Democrats?
7. According to La Guardia, what functions are inseparable from the life of a man in politics?
8. What caused La Guardia to "hit the ceiling" in his talk with the state chairman?
9. What is the meaning of *sporadically, tenement, tacit, henchmen, venal, padrone, subjugated, insurgent*?
10. What, besides active campaigning, was necessary to La Guardia's winning the election?
11. Write a theme about local, campus, or fraternity or sorority politics, or about your political knowledge, or ignorance, or education; or write a theme using an autobiographical incident to develop an idea.

With politics as with cars, if you want to know how a machine operates, ask the man who owns one. Edward J. Flynn, long a political boss in the Bronx, gives some firsthand comments on the nature of politics.

BOSSES AND MACHINES
by Edward J. Flynn

AS LONG as we have a two-party system of government, we will have machines. Whether they will be good or bad depends upon the interest of citizens in their party government, upon whether that interest is just as strong and unflagging as their interest in their local, state, and federal government. A whole can never be bigger than the sum of its parts.

The reason more people do not accept the inevitability of machine politics is that whenever they think of machines and bosses, they seem to think only of the successful ones. In every county in New York City there is, and always has been, a Republican organization. To be sure, they even call themselves "organizations," although they are as truly machines as their Democratic counterparts in every respect save that of success at the polls. The nominations for the various offices in the Republican party are dictated by the Republican County Leaders, who are, of course, the Republican county bosses.

From *YOU'RE THE BOSS*, by Edward J. Flynn. Copyright 1947 by The Viking Press, Inc. Reprinted by permission of The Viking Press, Inc., New York.

The present Governor of New York, Thomas E. Dewey, accepts advice and even dictation from the Republican bosses in the various counties throughout the state. The newspapers favorable to Dewey (or to the Republican party generally) describe this as "receiving suggestions from the leaders of the party." It is only the "leader" you don't like who is a "boss," and the "organization" you don't like that is a "machine."

This is equally true throughout the United States. In practically every state and every city there is a Republican machine and a Democratic machine, and there is always one man who is the boss of each machine. The final responsibility for nominations is wholly in his hands. Thus, when you condemn the "boss system" you condemn both major parties, and indeed all political parties, because all operate in exactly the same way.

This system is a direct result of the election laws not only in the State of New York but in every state of the Union. The election laws provide the method under which parties are organized. Those laws apply to the Democratic party and to the Republican party alike.

If this is true, then what can be done and what should be done? One must work with the tools at hand. If a machine is bad, it can be reformed only by the members of the party concerned. Many people criticize government, and then announce that they are not affiliated with either of the major parties. This is ridiculous. They can never hope, through unorganized mass, to accomplish anything. If they wish to cure a situation, they must do it through the machinery that is set up by the election laws.

I do not want to minimize how difficult a job this is. It is difficult because in a successful machine the leaders have so well fortified themselves that it takes time to upset them. It cannot be done in a year. In some cases it cannot be done for many years. But if the start is made, eventually the vicious element in an organization can be removed. Those who have the courage and persistence to survive early discouragements win out in the end.

An instance of this that probably is fresh in the minds of most is the so-called "Pendergast machine" in Kansas City,

Missouri. This organization got so bad that Pendergast and others connected with it went to prison. This did not mean the end of Democratic organizations in Kansas City. There is still a machine there. It is a better machine because of the exposures that purged it, but it is still a machine. Its legal structure is exactly the same as before. But because the decent Democrats of Kansas City finally became sufficiently aroused to take part in the primaries and in the selection of County Committeemen and District Leaders, the Pendergast machine, as such, was destroyed.

There is no use periodically electing "Fusion" or "Good Government" candidates. They will either stay in power a short time, or they will set up their own machines, or, what is far more likely, they will merge back into one or the other of the two major parties. The Republican and Democratic parties have survived a good many "reform" movements in the form of third parties, the one over a period of ninety years, the other over a period of nearly a century and a half. Third-party movements have never succeeded nationally. They have succeeded about once in fifty times in the states. They have succeeded, all too briefly, about once in twenty times in the cities. These figures speak for themselves.

If we are to have uniformly good government, local, state, and national, I am afraid a lot of men and women will have to get down off their high-horses and grub around in practical politics as active members of a party. I wish we had in our school systems required courses of training in citizenship, which would send forth graduates by the hundreds of thousands who would assume such responsibilities as readily and as naturally as they assume the responsibility of earning a living. So far as I can see, the emphasis in whatever practical politics is taught is placed upon general elections rather than primaries. The so-called "independent" voter is all but deified, when he ought to be condemned as a shirker.

Waiting until after the candidates are nominated is waiting until you have missed the boat. Whatever is to be done must be done before the nominations are made. There is no machine—I do not care how powerful and well entrenched it appears to be—that would dare to nominate a candidate for office it knew its own people did not want. Many poor candidates are named because of the fact that the so-called boss of the organization knows that the great majority of the members of his party would take no interest in the primary election anyway. Bosses get away with a good deal by default —your default.

SUGGESTIONS FOR STUDY:

1. Does the clause "If they wish to cure a situation" suggest the basic organization of the selection?
2. What kind of sentence is used at the beginning of the second main division?
3. Is the first division organized geographically?
4. Does Flynn concede that his cure isn't easy? Is this sound argument?
5. What does Flynn say is the difference between *organization* and *machine, leader* and *boss?*
6. Can you think of other word pairs in which the denotation is very similar, the connotation very different?
7. In the previous selection did La Guardia, in effect, take the advice Flynn offers here?
8. Does Flynn use informal language more than La Guardia or less?
9. What is the meaning of *unflagging, fusion, shirker?*
10. Write a reply based on personal experience to some essay in this book with which you disagree.

Woman's world, advertising version, features a short life but a merry one.

IS IT ANYONE WE KNOW?
by Agnes Rogers

ACCORDING to the advertisements which liberally adorn and, to a large extent, support the numerous newspapers and magazines of the United States, the typical American woman is young, beautiful, well dressed, beloved, and very, very happy. Statistics, or a look at your friends, do not bear out this radiant picture, but the picture remains, and with good reason. The men who plan and produce the ads are a highly intelligent and skillful lot and they are, after all, in business. The women they present are what American women like to think they are, or could be; otherwise the products wouldn't sell.

The illusions of a society are often contradicted by cold figures, but the illusions have their own reality which, in a way, complements the statistical tables, and you need to look at both to round out the scene. The world of ads may be a dream world, but it's been concocted with the eager endorsement of the women who read the ads—and act on them. For example, the census reports tell us what occupations American women are engaged in. The advertisements reveal which of these occupations American women approve of. A vast number of women work in factories, but you never find them in the ads. (During the war, to be sure, women in war plants

Copyright June 1946, Harper and Brothers.

were much in evidence, but after victory was won they retired from the scene, presumably to go back home where they belong.) There are some two million domestic servants in the United States, but you will look in vain for an advertisement that shows one. Shopgirls, beauty parlor operators, elevator operators, seamstresses, waitresses—none of these occupations is considered fit. Apparently nobody wants to be identified with these useful but unglamorous jobs. Of the service occupations, that of air-transport hostess is admitted, and occasionally a switchboard operator is shown—that noble girl whose vision of her high duty makes her look a little over your head; but that is about all.

The office worker, however, belongs to an approved group and is well represented in the advertisements. She is about twenty years old, rather small, brunette, and dressed well but modestly in a neat suit or shirtwaist type of dress. Her hair is perfect, her complexion flawless, her stocking seams straight, her blouse immaculate. A very lovely girl and definitely wholesome. She is very happy indeed. And why shouldn't she be? Doesn't her boss provide the finest and newest office equipment? What more could a worker want when typewriters, carbon paper, water cooler—even the paper towels in the washrooms—are of the finest quality? No wonder she smiles all day long. No dissatisfaction over salary, hours, or overtime mars the cheerful efficiency of advertisement office life, where all the girls are the same age and all are equally contented.

Nor does sex rear its pretty head here. In those parts of the magazine devoted to editorial matter, you will find plenty of stories about the "office wife" who is a formidable rival to the legal one, and about the secretary who marries her boss; but nothing of the sort is permitted in the advertising sections, where the relationship between management and labor is innocent of such goings on. The American business man (in the ads) is a family man of impeccable personal habits, sometimes a card, but never predatory, and the business girl knows her place—and his—you may be sure.

Occasionally a career woman appears. Her occupation is not defined but she has an air of command and you can tell from her clothes that she must receive a high salary. She is older than the office worker—an elderly twenty-seven possibly—and sits at a handsome desk and telephones. She dresses very smartly and may even wear a hat in the office. (In real life, this is the mark of an editor of a fashion magazine or a wealthy volunteer worker for a worthy charity.)

Certain professions are on the preferred list. The movies, of course. Photographs of real movie stars appear frequently, with noted actresses endorsing this article and that, which by inference is responsible for their beauty, art, popularity, earning power, or whatever stellar quality the reader would like to possess.

The trained nurse (imaginary, not actual) is another familiar figure. She is a little older than the office worker, and, if possible, even more wholesome. She too smiles, but not so widely as to show her lower teeth. This is natural since she represents hygienic satisfaction in the purity of the product recommended, which is, after all, a more sober reaction than the pure thrill of handling that wonderful carbon paper. The nurse has also an air of experience (no, not worldly) that is lacking in the stenographer.

Of late, the woman doctor has begun to be recognized. She is not on a par with men doctors and so far has been entrusted only with baby cases in families too poor to consult a real doctor, but she has a solid, substantial look and obviously knows what she's about. She is not beautiful, not even pretty—an exception to the rule that all American women are beautiful. This shortcoming is permitted because she has character, which, though of limited value, is clearly OK in a woman doctor.

Curiously enough the largest professional group—the teachers—is not represented at all. Nor will you find any librarians, social workers, or researchers in the advertisements. Too bookish, no doubt. For the women in the ads do not read. They take a book (and a box of candy) when they travel, but they don't open the book. Newspapers are for men; and magazines, to which these women owe their existence, are read in secret if at all.

The professional model, on the other hand, gets a fair

amount of attention and appears to be catching up with the movie star as the embodiment of charm. These girls have a lot more than pretty faces and figures. One current campaign is built around actual models who are also mothers, and thus combine the best features of glamorous professional life and devoted motherhood. They have talents to spare. Not only are they models, mothers, wives, housekeepers; they are also skilled at ballet dancing and music or dress design.

A few other living people are admitted to the world of advertisements. Besides movie stars and models, certain photogenic young women whose names are listed in the *Social Register* are seen from time to time in the ads. They are either engaged to be married or are young matrons, famous for gracious entertaining. It is comforting to see that these well-placed young women are marked by a sense of *noblesse oblige* as well as faultless taste in face creams, cigarettes, coffee, or whatever. They do their duty to society by serving on charitable committees, and during the war they contributed to the morale of the armed forces by working in canteens and in other ways devised by the Red Cross.

But the occupation most frequently portrayed (and in this the advertisements and the census concur) is that of housewife, and it is here that the American woman is at her most radiant, most healthy, most energetic. The number of things she manages to pack into a morning! Getting the breakfast, washing the dishes, making the beds, cleaning the house, marketing—all of these chores she tosses off in the twinkling of an eye. Of course she has all that household machinery, and occasionally the children lend a hand. Her eight-year-old daughter *likes* to help make the beds and dry the dishes, and if the playful scottie runs off with a pillow case or grabs one end of the dish towel it's that much more fun for everybody.

She has no servants, not even an occasional cleaning woman or laundress. She does the family washing, to the envy of the neighbors who lean over the fence and cry out in wonder at the snowy sheets flapping on the line. She cleans and waxes the floors, pausing at times to explain to a friend how *easy* it is with this wonderful new polish. She even makes professional-looking curtains and slip covers and occasionally paints furniture. (Her husband does the larger pieces.) She does all this with her hair arranged as for a party, dressed in the freshest of house dresses, over which she wears a wholly unnecessary apron without so much as one spot on it; and she frisks about tirelessly on very high heels.

Her reward is the fond admiration of her devoted husband, the envy of her neighbors, and the boasting of her children, who lisp their praises of Mom's cooking and other accomplishments to anybody who will listen.

The housewife smiles even more than the office worker. After all, there are more things in a house than in an office. All that household equipment, all those new sheets, towels, soaps, lotions, waxes, polishing agents, her own clothes—every item in the inventory gives her rapturous pleasure whenever she uses it. And if this weren't enough, there are countless brands of food, each one of which sends her into ecstasies as she sees the pleasure—and health—they bring to the members of her family.

II

The diversions and recreations of the women of the advertisements are varied and apparently very good fun. American women appear to have a good deal of leisure which they employ happily. Shopping or strolling along city streets takes up a good deal of their time. Alone or with a friend, or a dog or two, they stroll gracefully about, attracting admiring but respectful glances from male passers-by. Sometimes they wander through a park, pausing at times to lean against a tree—or if it's a street without any trees, an unexplained pillar.

Bridge is popular. In the afternoon, the American woman plays bridge with three other American women, to the accompaniment of fairly elaborate (non-alcoholic) refreshments; in the evening, she and her husband play with another married couple. She's fond of dancing, either in night clubs or at a friend's house. Sometimes she and her husband in the privacy of their bedroom break into an impromptu dance at the beauty of his unshrinkable shirt, and she's been known to execute a few steps out of pure happiness in her new slip that doesn't twist or ride up.

She very occasionally visits an art gallery, but her taste in pictures is better expressed in home movies or snapshots that commemorate sweet moments of the past when the children were smaller. Sometimes she listens to music via the radio or phonograph. On the creative side, she plays the piano. That is, if someone's listening. Little girls may play the piano with no one else in the room, but as the girls grow older, they play only when admiring young men are leaning over their shoulders.

Male companionship is also an agreeable phase of all outdoor activities. At first blush, the woman in the ads appears to be pretty much of a sportswoman, but if you look more closely you will see that she is more likely to be looking at games than playing them. She spends more time on the sand or at the edge of the pool than she does in the water, more time patting the horse than riding it. And she is always accompanied by a devoted masculine friend.

An unimportant but piquant note is struck in the number of things she does in her underwear that other women do fully dressed—if, indeed, they do them at all. Clad in a nightgown or slip or, quite simply, in girdle and brassiere, the ad-girl plays with her dog, arranges flowers, plays the phonograph, telephones, admires her pearls, and stands on tip-toe while the wind blows through her hair. Singing during this exercise is optional.

The ad-girl also travels. Planes, trains, and buses have their complement of feminine passengers. The most elegant of the travelers go by train in a private room. These women are the best dressed, the most aristocratic looking and, true to their class, unsmiling. (A nice point to be remembered is that the more sophisticated she is, the less our heroine smiles. Perhaps the wealthy are not so easily satisfied.) Travel is no novelty to them and a certain languid acceptance of luxury is to be expected. Not so well dressed but more cheerful are the plane passengers who chat and play games with their flight companions while hurtling through perpetually smooth and sunlit space. But happiest of all are the fortunate people who go by bus. There's a dream quality to the ad-buses seldom approached in real life. No crying children, no stale air, no crowding, no oversize people in the next seat mar the gaiety of the occasion. Small wonder the younger women bubble over with delight and even the older couples (for this is one place the older woman is allowed in) smile contentedly as the picturesque landscape glides by.

Unusual, too, is the air of eager anticipation and serenity that marks the family about to go on an advertising-journey. There is no trace of the tension, frayed temper, preoccupation with bags, worry about what's been left behind, and general breathlessness that charge the atmosphere when regular families start on a trip.

III

According to the ads, love plays an important part in the daily lives of American women. The men in this country must be highly inflammable (after office hours, that is) since the least thing sets them off. A woman has only to apply a particular kind of face powder, hand lotion, tooth paste, nail polish (the list could be continued indefinitely) to be the center of masculine attention—and more too. The dazzled man takes one look (or sniff) and instantly offers romantic adoration, gay comradeship, or awed devotion coupled with the most honorable intentions. To be sure there are one or two perfumes so heady that they lead inevitably and rapidly to a frankly passionate embrace. (Until fairly recently this scene was played in the costume of the '90's and the man was a violinist and therefore emotionally unstable, but today the performers wear modern dress and the man has discarded his violin.) However, the woman who deliberately uses these perfumes knows what she's in for—and, of course, he may propose marriage as soon as he gets his breath.

The low boiling point of American men has another aspect. They marry readily, it would seem, but their wives have to be constantly on the alert to keep love's fires burning—or even to keep their husbands. Nothing kills married love as quickly as dishpan hands or dull, stringy hair. More perfume, more hand cream, more lipstick, more brilliantine are needed to retain the husband's admiration. Such a thing is never suggested, but one wonders if the reason why the wife can never relax in her perfection of grooming—she wears lipstick even when she's asleep—may not be that her husband will suddenly succumb to the rosy brilliance of the next door neighbor's fingernails if her own polish shows so much as one chip.

He never does, however, and family life in the ads flows along untroubled by misunderstandings, quarrels, infidelities, divorce, or even those small stresses and strains of married life that most people know. (The stresses and strains threaten, but they're immediately dispelled by the wife's prompt action with cosmetics, vitamin-enriched food, or some sort of pill.)

The pattern of American family life is firmly fixed. The young couple live with their two children in a suburban house that looks like a cottage outside and reveals unexpected spaciousness within. The living room is well furnished in what might be termed modified modern style, the dining room is more likely to be Georgian, and the bedrooms, with the exception of Junior's—which is manly and simple—are surprisingly fancy. Such details as white fur rugs, pale satin draperies, white telephones, French figurine lamps, which are the usual decor for the woman engaged in the rites of good grooming or enjoying her underwear, might suggest a lady's maid somewhere in the offing, but we know that American homes are servantless. Bathrooms and kitchens gleam with the newest and sleekest machinery. Throughout the house, the floors, rugs, walls, curtains, furniture are in perfect condition. Nothing needs painting, papering, cleaning, or repairing.

The husband leaves the house in the morning and the children depart for school after a harmonious and health-building breakfast. The wife then whips through the work of the house with enormous speed and efficiency and is free for those manifold diversions already mentioned. But she's at home to welcome the rest of the family. She is a watchful and devoted mother, it is true, but she doesn't get to play with the children. That is father's job. He is the one who teaches Junior to play ball or goes skating with Sister. And when they return to the house after these exertions all hot and breathless—or all cold and breathless, depending on the time of year—there is mother, ready with ice-cold fruit juice or piping hot cocoa.

Dinner is the evening meal and this is the high point of the day, as well as triumphant proof of America's abundant food supply. Roast chicken (big as a turkey), vegetables galore, stacks of bread, jellies and pickles, salads, and cakes are heaped on the dining-room table each evening. There's hardly room on the table for some of the original containers in which the food was packed, but mother manages to get them on. These containers or the new pressure cooker on the table may strike some critics as questionable form, but she knows better. And anyhow, when our young couple give a dinner party or celebrate some tender anniversary—just the two of them—the appointments of the dinner table are strictly correct and very grand. Then the table gleams with candles and silver; flowers and lace, china and crystal are displayed in profusion; and wine is served. And this brings up the interesting fact that women in the ads do not drink spirits. Wine, yes, and very rarely one cocktail is permitted a very stylish woman, but at those bright parties where fun and games and dancing go on among the young marrieds, soft drinks are the rule. Beer is allowed occasionally, but no woman in the ads ever takes whisky. (And no young man, either. Years of discretion, if not distinction, are needed before an ad-man may have a highball.)

A few sidelights on man's place in the home may be added. The American husband, besides providing generously for his family's comfort and his wife's efficiency, occasionally assists in the actual work of the establishment. His traditional job of tending the furnace disappeared long ago when the oil burner became universal, but he still cuts the grass and puts the screens in and out of the windows spring and autumn. When there's furniture to be painted, he does the big pieces, and he has been seen washing the windows.

From time to time, for the fun of it, he tries his hand at cooking. Rarely will he exercise this talent in the kitchen but you can't keep him away from an outdoor grill. He puts on a chef's cap and an apron with comical remarks on it and everybody has an immoderately good time.

A small point is the husband's habit of taking off his coat as soon as he gets in the house. This is not a hot-weather custom, but an all-year-round one, as if his vitamin diet produced in him such abounding vitality that even a light jacket would be unbearably confining. It may be that extra good health has some drawbacks. Perhaps the American family is getting to be too strong for its own comfort. Certainly the families of the ads are exceedingly robust. Sometimes, to be sure, the common cold attacks, but it lacks its most annoying property—the damage to the sufferer's looks. No woman in the advertisements ever looks as if she had a cold, even when the copy says plainly that she has. She takes a whiff of something and experiences instant relief. She does, to be sure, go to pieces when she gets a pain. Lines of agony are written on her face if her shoes don't fit properly. A headache twists her features into a mask of tragedy. Fortunately, however, these ills are short lived. There's always a remedy that acts promptly and safely. Many a girl who wakes at seven-thirty with a blinding headache is winning the tennis tournament at eleven.

Is there no serpent in this Eden? There is indeed, and it is revealed by its absence rather than its presence. The plight of the older woman is so bad it doesn't bear thinking about.

The grim fact is that all women between the ages of twenty-seven and sixty are exiled from the advertising scene. (There is, strictly speaking, one rare exception—a comedy part played by a fat woman.) What the others do in those dark years we do not know, but their lives must be miserable.

And when at last the poor old soul is permitted to return, she has a wretched time. No more admiration (except once a year on Mother's Day, when she is the recipient of some rather stuffy presents), no more parties, no more bridge, no more strolling in the park. In fact, she almost never gets out of doors at all, except for that bus trip. She still cooks pies and knits and helps with the mending. In the evenings she can listen to the radio and catch up on the reading she didn't do when she was young enough to have fun. Very, very rarely she is permitted to be a wise old aunt who whispers the secret in her niece's ear that saves the latter's marriage. Usually she is crabbed, reactionary, gossipy, and hopelessly out-of-date in dealing with the children. (She still believes in those harsh, old-fashioned remedies.)

The middle-aged and older American man, on the other hand, has a dandy time. He plays golf, goes fishing, drinks all he wants, travels comfortably by plane if he likes, is popular with the younger set, and at fashionable parties he lends an air of distinction (something like a touch of gray at the temples). His poor wife or sister, meanwhile, is sitting drearily at home with her pies and knitting. Occasionally an elderly couple have been prudent enough to take out a particular kind of insurance which permits the husband to retire on $150 a month. When this happens, he makes out pretty well with some mild fishing and frequent naps in a hammock, but his wife doesn't fish. All she does is rock on the porch and wait for the mailman.

One is forced to the conclusion that the American woman —according to the advertisements—has a wonderful life until she's twenty-five. After that she'd better be dead.

SUGGESTIONS FOR STUDY:

1. What is the main idea, and where is it stated?
2. What are the topics of the three main divisions?
3. Are the occupations of the first division arranged climactically?
4. What kind of sentence is used in paragraph 3 to vary the development?
5. Do you agree with the observation that women in advertisements don't read? Is the writer's inference from this observation just?
6. Does the impromptu dance at the beauty of an unshrinkable shirt indicate the tone the writer wants? Are there other equally striking examples? Where?
7. What has the writer used as the basis of her statements throughout?
8. Are the paragraphs definite units in the structure of the essay?

9. What is the meaning of *impeccable, noblesse oblige, decor, galore?*
10. Write a theme about advertising, satiric or serious, in which you look more closely at some specific examples than you have been accustomed to do.

••

Man fashions institutions, and institutions fashion men—and women.

THE WIFE PROBLEM
by *William H. Whyte, Jr.*

IN PRAISE OF ORNERY WIVES

Looking over its survey on the corporation and the wife, Fortune confessed it found the results "a little frightening. Conformity, it would appear, is being elevated into something akin to a religion . . . Perhaps Americans will arrive at an ant society, not through fiat of a dictator, but through unbridled desire to get along with one another . . .

"This devotion to group values is by no means peculiar to the corporation way of life. But how much more are we to adapt? In many modern American environments . . . real advances are going to bring the individual into conflict with the status quo. And unless Americans temper their worship of environment they may well evolve a society so well adapted that no one would be able—or willing—to give it the sort of hotfoot it regularly needs.

••••••••••••••••••
Reprinted by Special Permission of the Editors of FORTUNE; Copyright 1951 Time Inc.

The Wife Problem 329

"Several months ago a top official of one of the most group-integrating of corporations fell to musing over the death of a wise and valuable fellow executive. It made him think a lot, he told one of his associates, of the drift of the company's personnel policy. 'You know, he was a terrifically stimulating person,' he said. 'He was the last character I ever knew.'

" 'I sometimes wonder,' he added thoughtfully, 'whether we'll ever get any more.'

"It's not a trivial question."

OVER THE LAST few decades American corporations have been evolving a pattern of social community able to provide their members with more and more of their basic social wants. Yet, the corporation now concedes, one of the principal members of its community remains officially almost unnoticed—to wit, the Wife. For the good of the corporation, many executives believe, it is time the matter was remedied. "We control a man's environment in business and we lose it entirely when he crosses the threshold of his home," one executive says mournfully. "Management, therefore, has a challenge and an obligation to deliberately plan and create a favorable, constructive attitude on the part of the wife that will liberate her husband's total energies for the job." Others, though they might not put it quite so badly, agree that the step is logical.

Just how to do this is a problem that has many a management understandably baffled. On one very basic matter, however, management is not in the slightest baffled. It knows exactly what kind of wife it wants. With a remarkable uniformity of phrasing, corporation officials all over the country sketch the ideal. In her simplest terms she is a wife who 1) is highly adaptable, 2) is highly gregarious, 3) realizes her husband belongs to the corporation.

Are the corporation specifications presumptuous? It would appear not. The fact is that this kind of wife is precisely what our schools and colleges—and U.S. society in general—seem to be giving the corporation.

Let us define terms: we are discussing the wives of the

coming generation of management, whose husbands are between 25 and 40, and in junior or middle echelons of management or with logical aspirations of getting there. There is, of course, no sharp dividing line between age groups, but among older executives there is a strong feeling that this younger generation of wives is the most cooperative the corporation has ever enlisted. "Somehow," says one executive, "they seem to give us so much less trouble than the older ones." "Either the girls are better or the men are marrying better," says another. "But whatever it is with these people, *they get along.*"

Perhaps it is merely that this generation of wives has not yet grown older and more cantankerous. Perhaps. But there is evidence that this group-mindedness is the result of a shift in values more profound than one might suppose. The change is by no means peculiar to the corporation wife but by the nature of her job she may be the outstanding manifestation of it. And a preview, perhaps, of what is to come.

First, how do the wives conceive their own role? Critical literature has been answering the question rather forcefully, with the result that many Americans (and practically all Europeans) assume that the wife of the American businessman not only is the power behind the scenes but wants to become more so. The picture needs considerable revision. For the striking thing that emerges from wives' comments is the negativeness of the role they sketch. As they explain it, the good wife is good by *not* doing things—by *not* complaining when her husband works late; by *not* fussing when a transfer is coming up; by *not* engaging in any controversial activity. Moreover they agree heartily that a good wife can't help a husband as much as a bad wife can hurt one. And the bad wife, clearly, is one who obtrudes too much, whether as a "meddler," a "climber," a "fixer" or, simply, someone who "pushes" her man around.

Resolutely antifeminist, the executive wife conceives her role to be that of a "stabilizer"—the keeper of the retreat, the one who rests and rejuvenates the man for the next day's battle.

This stabilizing calls for more than good homemaking and training the kids not to bother daddy before dinner.

Above all, wives emphasize, they have to be good listeners. They describe the job somewhat wryly. They must be "sounding boards," "refueling stations," "wailing walls." But they speak without resentment. Nurturing the male ego, they seem to feel, is not only a pretty good fulfillment of their own ego but a form of therapy made increasingly necessary by the corporation way of life. Management psychologists couldn't agree more. "Most top executives are very lonely people," as one puts it. "The greatest thing a man's wife can do is to let him unburden the worries he can't confess to in the office."

In addition to listening she can do some judicious talking. If she is careful about it she can be a valuable publicity agent for the husband. "In a subtle way," says one executive, "they put in a plug for the husband. They tell things he wouldn't dare tell for fear of seeming immodest." In similar fashion they can humanize him if he's a boss. "About the time I get fed up with the bastard," says a junior executive, "here I am, going over to dinner at his house. And she's so nice. She jokes about him, kids him to his face. I figure he can't be so bad after all."

Low-key "stabilizing," then, the wife sees as her main task. There is another aspect to her role, however, and it is considerably less passive. For the good corporation wife must also be a social operator, and when husbands and wives sketch out the personal characteristics of the ideal wife it is the equipment for this role that comes first to their minds. What they ask for, more than any other quality, is gregariousness, or a reasonable facsimile. Here are some of the ways in which they spell it out.

EXECUTIVE: "She should do enough reading to be a good conversationalist. . . . Even if she doesn't like opera she should know something about it so if the conversation goes that way she can hold her own. She has to be able to go with you if you're going to make a speech or get an award, and not be ill at ease."

EXECUTIVE: "The hallmark of the good wife is the ability to put people at their ease."

WIFE: "The most important thing for an executive's wife is to know everybody's name and something about their family so you can talk to them—also, you've got to be able to put people at their ease."

EXECUTIVE: "Keeping herself so she is comfortable with people on the boss's level is important. I don't think reading and music and that kind of stuff are vital."

EXECUTIVE: "The kind you want is the kind that can have people drop in any time and make a good show of it even if the baby's diapers are lying around."

WIFE: "It's a very worthwhile bunch we have here. Edith Sampson down on Follansbee Road is sort of the intellectual type, but most of the gang are real people."

For the corporation wife, in short, being "sociable" is as important as stabilizing. Like the army wife, an analogy she detests, she must be a highly adaptable "mixer." In fact, she needs to be even more adaptable than the army wife, for the social conditions she meets are more varied. One year she may be a member of a company community, another year a branch manager's wife, expected to integrate with the local community—or, in some cases, to become a civic leader, and frequently, as the wife of the company representative, to provide a way station on the route of touring company brass.

As a rule, she is inextricably bound up in the corporation "family," often so much so that her entire behavior—including what and where she drinks—is subtly conditioned by the corporation. "It makes me laugh," says one wife in an eastern city dominated by one corporation. "If we were the kind to follow the Pattern, I'll tell you just what we would do. First, in a couple of years, we'd move out of Ferncrest Village (it's really pretty tacky there, you know). We wouldn't go straight to Eastmere Hills—that would look pushy at this stage of the game; we'd go to the hilly section off Scrubbs Mill Pike. About that time, we'd change from Christ Church to St. Edwards, and we'd start going to the Fortnightlys—it would be a different group entirely. Then, about 10 years later, we'd finally build in Eastmere Hills." It makes her laugh, she says, because that would be the signal to everybody that she had become a wife of the top-brass bracket. Which she probably will.

Few wives are as articulate as that on the social role, but

intuitively they are generally superb at it; their antennae are sensitive, and they know the rules of the game by heart. Second nature to the seasoned wife, for example, are the following:

> Don't talk shop gossip with the Girls, particularly those who have husbands in the same department.
> Don't invite superiors in rank; let them make the first bid.
> Don't turn up at the office unless you absolutely have to.
> Don't get too chummy with the wives of associates your husband might soon pass on the way up.
> Don't be disagreeable to any company people you meet. You never know . . .
> Be attractive. There is a strong correlation between executive success and the wife's appearance. Particularly so in the case of the sales wife.
> Be a phone pal of your husband's secretary.
> Never—repeat, never—get tight at a company party (it may go down in a dossier).

One rule transcends all others: *Don't be too good.* Keeping up with the Joneses is still important. But where in pushier and more primitive times it implied going substantially ahead of the Joneses, today keeping up means just that: keeping up. One can move ahead, yes—but slightly, and the timing must be exquisite. Whatever the move, it must never be openly invidious.

Perhaps it is for this reason that, when it comes to buying an auto, the Buick is so much preferred: it envelops the whole executive spectrum and the jump from a Special to a Super, and from a Super to a Roadmaster, can be handled with tact. Not always, though. In one eastern steel town, where cars have always been the accepted symbol of rank, the chairman of the board has a Cadillac—certainly a high enough ceiling. The president, however, has taken to buying Buick Supers, with the result that people in the upper brackets are chafing because it would be unseemly to go higher. Except for the chairman, accordingly, only the local tradespeople drive Cadillacs and Roadmasters.

The good corporation wife, the rules continue, does not make friends uncomfortable by clothes too blatantly chic, by references to illustrious forebears or by excessive good breeding. And she avoids intellectual pretensions like the plague.

Are these rules of the game merely the old fact of conformity? In part, yes. But something new has been added. What was once a fact has now become a philosophy. Today's young couples not only concede their group-mindedness; they are outspokenly in favor of it. They blend with the group not because they fear to do otherwise but because they approve of it.

While few young wives are aware of the sacrifice involved, the role of the boss's wife is one that they very much covet. In talking about the qualities of the ideal wife—a subject they evidently had thought over long and often—they were at no loss. In one third of the cases the American woman's favorite cliché "gracious" came instantly to them, and in nearly all the others the descriptions spelled out the same thing. Theirs is a sort of First Lady ideal, a woman who takes things as they come with grace and poise, and a measure of *noblesse oblige;* in short, the perfect boss's wife. But how near do they come to the ideal?

What, for example, of the listening job that wives take such pride in? How well can they listen? Consensus of a cross section of U.S. executives: not very well. ("And for God's sake, don't quote me.") There are excuses aplenty. "If he has had a rough day," says one wife, "I don't want to hear about it. He'd only get mad and say things the children shouldn't hear." The husband, however, may be the one chiefly to blame. He asks for active, intelligent listening, yet seldom wants advice ("Women just don't understand").

And how well does she handle the special social problem? In advancing the husband in the office, the corporation is quite likely to advance him socially as well. There is no easy out for the couple in such cases, and for the wife the inward tug of war between the social *status quo* and the prospect of advancement can be extremely poignant. "I must have made some terrible mistakes," laments one wife now in mid-passage. "I love people and I've made many intimate friends in the company, but since Charlie got his new job it's just been hell on us. He has so much control over their lives, and it's all gotten so complicated."

The fact that the office can spell sanctuary for the husband does not go unresented. Perhaps this is why the Christmas office party provokes such surprisingly bitter, if concealed, feeling from many wives. It dramatizes the wife's exclusion. Here, on this appointed day, is the world she can never share, and for all her brave little chuckles at the standing jokes of the office gang, she comes face to face with the fact. That is, if she's allowed to attend.

Burning though this exclusion may be to the wives, it is a topic they dislike intensely to talk about or to think about. And for them, indeed, the waters may well be better left muddy: to peer too deeply is to uncover an underlying point even more provoking. Where, the awful question comes up, does the man find his major satisfactions?

A common feminine observation is that a man's major satisfactions come from the home. If he's happy there, he can be happy in his work, and vice versa. The belief is probably necessary. Is it correct as well?

Item: As management psychologists note, the average executive shows a remarkable ability to repress his home worries while on the job; rarely, however, can he shut out office worries at home.

Item: The reaction to this Hobson's-choice question: "If you had to make the choice, which would you take: an increasingly satisfying work life and a proportionately souring home life—or the opposite?" The answers would surprise wives. "This business of doing it all for the family," as one husband confesses, "it's just a rationalization. If I got a windfall today I'd still knock myself out."

"Man's love is of man's life a thing apart," Byron once observed. " 'Tis woman's whole existence." So, for all the group integration and communication skills she can muster, it will probably remain.

The schism between Home and Office has been even more accentuated recently. Thanks, in part, to the way the tax structure has accumulated, the corporation now provides the man with a higher standard of living in his work than in his home—and, it might be added, a higher one than his wife enjoys. From 9 to 5 he may be a minor satrap, guiding the destiny of thousands, waited on by secretaries and subordinates; back in his servantless home he washes the dishes. Nor is it merely the fact of his satrapy; the corporation virtually rigs it so that he can have more fun away from home.

The expense account has become a way of life. There is not only travel. There are also luncheon clubs, company retreats, special conventions, parties and perquisites, and, though the wife may be thrown an occasional convention as a crumb, the expense-account world rarely encompasses her. It is primarily a man's world—and if the man is at a low salary, he is likely to find the pattern of life at 7118 Crestmere Road dull in comparison.

"The company has spoiled Jim terribly," says one wife. "Even when he was only earning $7,500 a year he used to be sent to Washington all the time. He'd go down in a Pullman drawing room and as J. R. Robinson of the General Company, take a two-room suite. Then he used to be asked by some of the company officers to a hunting and fishing lodge that the company kept in the north woods. When he went to New York, he'd entertain at 21, the Barberry Room and the Chambord. Me, meanwhile, I'd be eating a 30¢ hamburger and, when we went away together on vacation, we would have to go in our beat-up old car or borrow my sister's husband's. This taste of high life gives some of these characters delusions of grandeur. Small wonder that they get to fidgeting after they have been home a couple of weeks."

"What the hell can you say?" says one executive. "Here I am eating high off the hog, meeting interesting people, while Jo is slaving back home. I get a big bang out of all this, but I also have a sort of guilty feeling, so I say to her, 'Gee, honey, I hate all this traveling, but I just have to do it.'" Of the wives *Fortune* interviewed, many mentioned, commiseratingly, how their husbands looked forward to coming home, how awful it was sleeping in hotel beds, rattling around on trains and eating bum food.

There are some things, however, that cannot be explained away. For more than sirloins and drawing rooms are at issue; over the long pull this disparity aggravates perhaps the most subtle problem of marriage: equality of growth. If marriage, as Sociologist Everett Hughes puts it, is a "mutual mobility bet," for whom are the cards stacked?

Growth can mean many things. To the younger generation of executives it seems to mean an increasing ability to handle and mix with people. And the terms are the same for the wife. "The wife who is not very sociable," goes a highly typical male observation, "might not affect the husband directly, but she can hurt him just the same. A lot of business is done weekends. If she doesn't go for this, her lack of growth can hold the man back." "I have seen it happen so many times," says another executive sadly. "He marries the kid sweetheart, the girl next door or a girl from the jerkwater college he went to. They start off with a lot in common. Then he starts going up. Fifteen years later he is a different guy entirely. But she's stayed home, literally and figuratively." Even the old idea of a wife as a sort of culture carrier is virtually dead; she is still expected to read and things like that, but for functional reasons. "Sure I want her to read good books and magazines," as one executive puts it. "I don't want her to make a fool of herself in conversation."

Fundamentally, of course, the problem goes back to whom the executive chooses in the first place. Is the moral that he should marry a girl "superior" to him? Thanks to the commonly accepted saw that a woman can pull a man up, but not vice versa, there are many who think he should. ("My best executives," remarks one boss, "are the ones who 'outmarried' themselves.") But the pitfalls are many. Her qualities may drive the man to preoccupation with office prestige in order to prove himself to her; furthermore, unless she is excellent at hiding her superiority—or lets it rest fallow—she can hurt his chances in a close "family" community. The Bryn Mawr accent can be absolute death for a career in some Midwestern corporations.

What kind of background for the woman, then, is the optimum? A serious career can be dismissed easily; there is almost universal agreement among wives, husbands and corporations on this score. Work before marriage, however, is generally approved. "I feel the fact that I worked before marriage," says one wife, "is a help. I know what goes on in an office and can understand what Charles is up against."

College? Here is the *summum bonum*. There are some obvious reasons; because virtually all executives now go to college, the couple in such cases starts off with shared values. But corporation people mention a reverse factor almost as much. It is not so important for the wife, they say, to have gone to college, but it is very important not to have *not* gone to college. If she hasn't, corporation people warn, she is prey to an inferiority complex that makes it difficult for her to achieve real poise. Some corporations, accordingly, make it their business to find out whether or not the wife has a degree.

More and more corporations these days are interviewing the wife before hiring an executive, and some are not uninterested in fiancées. There are many holdouts ("This railroad picks its executives and lets its executives pick their wives and so far it's been okay"), but roughly half of the companies on which *Fortune* has data have made wife-screening a regular practice and many of the others seem about ready to do so. And the look-see is not academic. About 20% of its otherwise acceptable trainee applicants, one large company estimates, are turned down because of their wives.

Ordinarily the screening is accomplished via "informal" social visits. Many executives, for example, make it a point to call on the wife in her own home. Louis Ruthenburg, board chairman of Servel (which never hires an executive without a look at the wife), likes to recall how one college president used to insist on eating breakfast with a candidate's family; the wife who didn't fix her husband a good breakfast, he used to say, wasn't a good risk. To help them spot such key indicators many executives rely heavily on their own wives. "My wife is very, very keen on this," says one president. "She can spot things I might miss. And if the gal isn't up to par with her, it's no go."

But the initial screening is only the beginning of the corporation's interest. In one way or another the corporation manages to keep an eye on the wife, and more and more the surveillance is deliberately planned. At the Container Corp. of America, for example, it is the duty of all vice presidents to get acquainted with their subordinates' wives, and on their travels they are expected to meet the wives of executives in the field. Thus, when a man's name comes up for promotion the company has the answers to these questions: What is the health of the family? What is their attitude toward parenthood? How does the wife run her home? Does she dress with taste?

The effect of all this surveillance on the husband's career is substantial. In the home office of an insurance company, to cite one not untypical example, the president is now sidetracking one of his top men in favor of a less able one; the former's wife "has absolutely no sense of public relations." In another company a very promising executive's career is being similarly checked; his wife, the boss explains, is "negative in her attitude toward the company. She feels that business is her husband's life and no part of hers." Wives who have donated income of their own to raise the family living standard may also call down sanctions on the husband. Says one president, "When a man buys a home he can't afford on his salary alone, we either question his judgment or feel that the wife wears the pants." In either case his career is not likely to profit.

So with alcohol. The little woman who gets tipsy in front of the boss is not quite the joke her celebration in cartoon and anecdote would indicate; indeed, it is almost frightening to find out to what degree executive futures have been irretrievably influenced by that fourth Martini. And it need happen only once. Recently the president of a large utility felt it necessary to revise his former estimate of two executives. At the last company dinner their wives drank too many glasses of champagne. "They disported themselves," he says regretfully, "with utter lack of propriety."

Interestingly, divorce rarely disqualifies a man. Because of the phenomenon of the outgrown wife, the regret of most companies is tempered by the thought that the executive's next and, presumably more mobile, wife will be better for all concerned; one company, as a matter of fact, has a policy of sending executives away on extended trips if they need separating from nagging or retrograde wives.

One company has arranged for the team of consulting psychologists it retains to help out in delicate situations (currently they are making progress with an alcoholic wife). In most cases, however, the salvage task is up to the top man himself. "A lot of the 'company business' that presidents do," says one of them, "covers this sort of work. Take a situation I've got to wrestle with now. In one of our branch plants the wives of two vice presidents have started a feud. The men get along fine, but one of the wives is a real troublemaker. So I guess it's up to me to take a trip halfway across the continent —for other reasons, of course—and try and see what I can do about it."

Important as the wife-screening process may be, most executives realize that it is, at best, only a negative measure. For even with the most cooperative wives there can be much misunderstanding over such topics as travel and long hours. Therefore it is the company's duty, they argue, to *sell* the wife on the corporation's point of view. The result is an increasing use of such media as films, brochures and special mailings to drive home, in effect, the idea that the corporation isn't stealing her husband from her.

But something far more important is being brewed for the wife. It is not enough, in the view of many companies, that she merely be "sold" on the company; she should, they believe, now be integrated *into* it. "When a man comes to work for us," says William Given, chairman, American Brake Shoe Co., "we think of the company as employing the family, for it will be supporting the entire family, not merely the breadwinner." "The days of the strictly home wife," says a bank president, "are gone. She has become indispensable to our entire scheme of business." Among U.S. corporations, easily the most conspicuous and successful example of this kind of integration has been Thomas J. Watson's International Business Machines Corp. "Our wives," Watson explains, "are all part of the business. We started with just a few hundred people in 1914 and decided that no matter how large we grew we would carry it on in the family spirit. We always refer to our people as the 'I.B.M. Family' and we mean the wives and children as well as the men."

As a result the company can correctly claim that it makes available "complete social satisfactions." For $1 a year I.B.M. people enjoy a country club with swimming pool, bowling, 18-hole golf course, softball, tennis, picnics and parties of all kinds. Even the children are integrated. At the age of 3 they may be enrolled in a special children's club, and at 8 go on to become junior members of the big club.

In keeping with the family spirit Mrs. Watson, a very gracious, modest woman, sets an example for other wives. "She's made my work play," her husband explains. "She has a great gift for human relations. I confer with her about personnel because she knows all the people. She has met them at luncheons where we hold a regular receiving line, and every year she goes to the 100-Percenter Club meetings." In addition to this Mrs. Watson travels with her husband all over the world and keeps in touch with I.B.M. people; last year she traveled 38,046 miles and met 11,845 I.B.M. men and their wives.

Social integration, however, does not mean that the corporation necessarily *likes* the wife. A great many, as we have seen, do. But in some cases the corporation welcomes her largely as a means of defending itself against her. Amiable as it may be about it, the corporation is aware that the relationship is still triangular—or, to put it another way, if you can't beat 'em, join 'em. "Successes here," says one official, "are guys who eat and sleep the company. If a man's first interest is his wife and family, more power to him—but we don't want him." "We've got quite an equity in the man," another explains, "and it's only prudence to protect it by bringing the wife into the picture."

In fairness to the corporation wife, she must be recompensed somehow for the amount of time the company demands from her husband. Companies recognize the fact and are consequently more and more providing social facilities—from ladies' nights to special clubs—to hypo the sense of identification.

One corporation has gone considerably further. Via the

wife of the heir apparent to the presidency, there has been set up, in effect, a finishing school so that the wives can be brought up to the same high standards. As soon as the husband reaches the $8,000-to-$10,000 bracket the wife becomes eligible for the grooming. It is all done very subtly: the group leader drops helpful advice on which are the preferred shops, where to dine, what to wear when doing it and, somewhat like a good cruise director, has a way of introducing newcomers to congenial people. "Her supervision is so clever and indirect," says one wife, "that the other wives appreciate it probably."

When the corporation turns to the Sales Wife, its attention becomes even more intense. As an economic lever on the salesman, companies have learned, there is no stimulus quite so effective as the wife, if properly handled. Some sales executives make a habit of writing provocative letters to the wife, reminding her of the sales-contest prizes her husband could win for her and how he is doing at the moment (not so well as he should be).

As an extra employe, the wife's potential is so great that with some concerns the "husband and wife team" is not only desirable but mandatory. And the wife is not always merely the junior member. "Wives can do a lot on their own," explains the president of a large paper-box company. "A lot of important business connections have grown from friendships between our wives and wives of executives of other companies. One of our executives' wives recently was down at Miami for two weeks, and a friendship she struck up with a woman there resulted in a big order from an account we hadn't been able to crack in 15 years."

Insurance companies, among the first to exploit this "team" potential, bear down heavily on the theme through a constant stream of literature addressed to wives. Through magazine articles penned by veteran wives they are told of the psychological requirements ("Earl Made a Believer of Me," Mrs. Earl Benton explains to wives in a typical article).

The question of integration is by no means simple. What we have been talking about so far is the kind of integration deliberately planned by companies. But there is another kind. Quite beyond the immediate control of the corporation there are forces at work to draw the bonds between wife and corporation even tighter.

Paradoxically, perhaps the greatest of these is the very decentralization of industry. Thanks to this growing trend, it is now a commonplace that the road to advancement is through transfer to the different seats of the corporation empire.

With their talent for adaptability, the younger generation of wives is in most respects well prepared for this new way of life. Most accept it philosophically, and a good many actually prefer it to staying put in one place. "Any time the curtains get dirty," says one wife, "I'm ready to move. I enjoy meeting new people and seeing new places. And it's kind of a vacation sometimes."

There are, nevertheless, some very real tensions produced. And for no one more than the wife. It is she, who has only one life in contrast to her husband's two, who is called upon to do most of the adjusting. The move at once breaks up most of her community friendships, severs her local business relationships with the bank and the stores, takes her from the house and the garden on which she worked so long, and if the move takes her to a large city it probably drops her living standards also.

But it is the effect on the children that concerns wives most. While the children are very young, most wives agree, the effect is not harmful; they make and forget friends easily. As they reach junior-high age, however, a transfer can become a crisis. Recalls one wife: "Every time my daughter made a place for herself at school with the other kids, we'd move, and she'd spend the next year trying to break in at another school. Last year, when she was a senior in high school, she had a nervous breakdown. She was sure she was an outsider." The effect is not often this drastic but, while most children sweat out their adjustment without overt pain, the process is one parents find vicariously wrenching. One executive who recently changed to a nontransferring company has no trouble recalling the exact moment of his decision. One night at dinner his little boy turned to him, "Daddy," he said, "where do you really live?"

While constant transfer exposes the couple to many environments, it is, nevertheless, one of the most powerful of all the forces for integration. Because moving makes their other roots so shallow and transitory, the couple instinctively clings all the harder to the corporation.

What are the wife's basic unadjusted feelings about all this? The answer is clear: she likes the way of life. To picture her as a helpless sort of being pushed around by the corporation would be to attribute to her a sense of plight she does not feel; she must be considered not only an object of the integration but a force for it in her own right. She has become such an ally of the corporation, in fact, that on several matters it would almost appear that she and the corporation are ganging up on the husband.

Whatever else she may think of the corporation, on three main points she and her sisters agree:

The corporation means opportunity. The big company, wives explain, plays fair. "We went over all the pros and cons of bigness before Jim joined Du Pont," says one wife, "and we've never regretted joining. The bigness holds out a challenge for you."

The corporation means benefits. "Eastman Kodak has wonderful goodwill policies," a wife explains. "I used to have to attend to all the home details like insurance and bills. Now the company has someone who does those things for you—they even plan vacations for you."

The corporation means security. "Some companies may pay more at the start, but employment is not so secure. Here they never fire anybody, they just transfer you to another department."

Few wives go on to articulate their image of "the Company." But there is an image, nonetheless, that of a beneficent "system," at once impersonal and warm—in a nice kind of way, Big Brother.

There is, of course, another side to the picture. Many companies that have extensive wife programs do not attempt

The Wife Problem 345

social integration, and some not only look on the wife—to borrow one executive's explanation—as none of their damn business, but take active steps to see that she *doesn't* get close to them. A sampling of executive views—oil company: "We are just as happy if we never see her at all." Tool company: "If wives get too close to management they always get too status-minded. That means trouble." Motor company: "Wives' activities are their own business. What do some of these companies want for their $10,000? Slavery too?"

SUGGESTIONS FOR STUDY:

1. What is the source of the many quotations used?
2. What is the main idea, and where is it expressed?
3. How does the executive wife see her role? Is this a major division of the essay?
4. What elements does the essay discuss in the special social problem of the wife?
5. What specific steps are the corporations taking to solve this problem?
6. Is there a force beyond the company's conscious planning that makes the wife cling to the company?
7. Does management everywhere agree that the wife is the company's concern?
8. What is "the Pattern"?
9. Is the rule "Don't be too good" ambiguous?
10. What can you tell of the meaning of the following from the context in which they are used: *gregarious* wives, middle *echelons*, reasonable *facsimile*, *hallmark* of a good wife, *analogy*, *articulate* wife, are *intuitively* superb, executive *spectrum*, *consensus*, *status quo*, *poignant* struggle, find *sanctuary*, *Hobson's choice*, *schism*, minor *satrap*, *disparity aggravates*, *preoccupation*, *prestige*, *optimum*, *summum bonum*, *surveillance*, call down *sanctions* on, *irretrievably* influenced, such *media*, an *equity* in, *mandatory*, *paradoxically*, *overt* pain, *beneficent* system, *transitory* roots?
11. Write a theme discussing the general pattern of some institution with which you are familiar and the way you fit into it. This calls for thinking the pattern through.

> Whatever your attitude toward our national passion for sports—and attitudes vary—it is impossible to deny that the world of sports has developed some of the most colorful characters to appear on the American scene. Here is a lively portrait of one of the liveliest persons in modern baseball.

LEND AN EAR TO OLD CASE
by Clay Felker and Ernest Havemann

THE FINEST theatrical performance in America, bar none, is put on absolutely free of charge by a gray-haired, weather-beaten old gentleman with the appropriately histrionic name of Charles Dillon Stengel. It can be seen any night from March to early October, in whatever part of the country the New York Yankees happen to be training or playing. All you have to do is wander casually into the lobby of the Yankees' hotel—or, if the Yankees happen to be on a losing streak, into a nearby saloon. The locale does not matter at all; the act requires no props and no costumes except the one worn by the old gentleman, and the only requirements are adequate floor space and a reasonably silent and attentive audience. Given these modest requisites, he can spring into action anywhere, with a repertory that seems to be inexhaustible. For the elderly gentleman, besides working as the fabulously successful manager of the Yankees under the *nom de dugout* of Casey Stengel, is also a monologist, mimic, dia-

From Life, Sept. 29, 1952. Copyright Time Inc.

lectician, pantomimist and acrobat of remarkable talent. As a manager he has no equal today; as of this moment he has the Yankees there or thereabouts, and if he takes the pennant[1] he will equal the four-in-a-row record of such other legendary managers as John McGraw and Joe McCarthy. But he is gifted with a marvelously elastic and outlandish face, a propensity for eloquent gestures, and is even better as an entertainer.

A typical performance this year was presented in the lobby of the Sheraton-Cadillac Hotel in Detroit, a setting of such quiet comfort and splendor that it helped inspire Old Case to new heights. As soon as a sufficient crowd of newsmen and players had gathered in the cool of the evening, he was off like a whirling dervish. Artfully dodging bellboys and more inhibited patrons, he flew from wall to wall catching imaginary fly balls. He clutched his stomach, fell down and was Phil Rizzuto blocked by a runner at second base. He leaned into an imaginary dugout and caught a foul for Catcher Yogi Berra. He climbed a wall and made a great catch by Center Fielder Mickey Mantle. He thrust out his chin, which juts two inches in front of all the rest of him in repose and a good five inches in action, and took a cut at the ball with his long apelike arms. The ball sailed for a towering homer that carried far over the heads of the astonished clerks at the reservations desk. Then, after jogging around the bases with the winning run, he tired of reconstructing the day's game and turned to imitating the windup and hesitation pitch of the Browns' Satchel Paige. Beyond doubt it was one of the finest Stengel performances since the younger days when he could re-enact an entire double play, including the parts of the two base runners.

The night was warm and the illustrated lecture strenuous; there was a brief pause while Casey removed his jacket of tan, green and orange plaid and folded it neatly over the bell captain's stand. The bell captain did not mind at all but continued to watch with open mouth, doubtless neglecting several urgent phone calls from patrons with luggage to be moved, while the next phase began. "Best man I ever had on

---

[1] He did.

tag plays," said Casey while suddenly turning into an infielder, "was an athalete I had at Boston. Never saw anything like him. Put the ball on you fast and never got it kicked out of his hands."

Whang. The ball flew into second base. Casey caught it and leaned down for the tag. Runner out.

"He didn't bring the ball down on the runner and leave it like a mustard plaster hoping to stick there."

With a snort of contempt Casey made a sloppy tag. A spectral foot came out of nowhere and kicked his arm. With sad eyes he followed the ball up and away, apparently into a chandelier. Runner safe.

"No, sir. He used a sweeping motion and got that ball away as soon as he tagged him."

Clumping around the sofas on his stumpy legs, Casey snagged throws from the catcher and from the outfield, slapping the ball on imaginary runners who came hurtling into second. You could almost see the spikes fly.

"Yes, sir, I never saw anything like him." A grunt, and another runner bit the dust. "That guy done that to my man in the series, you know." (This was Stengelese for "Getting back to how a runner can kick the ball out of a fielder's hand, Eddie Stanky did it to Phil Rizzuto in the 1951 World Series.") "Pretty good on tags, but come to hitting or fielding he was in trouble." (Stengelese for "Now I'm talking about this Boston player again. He was terrific on tags, even though he couldn't do anything else.")

"Here we go again. Whoops." The ball flew into second. Casey grabbed it, swept his glove across the runner's foot for one graceful instant, and then lifted it quickly out of the way. "Let's see you kick that one!" The ball flew in again. "Gotcha!"

Finally Casey stopped, bowed to the bell captain and put his tan, green and orange jacket back on. "Goodnight, gentlemen."

As he departed toward the elevators, a sports reporter remarked, to no one in particular, "I don't know why a man in his position wears suits like that. Sometimes he looks like a burlesque comedian—but if you listen to him long enough, you'll learn a lot about baseball. I learned things tonight about tag plays that I never heard of before." The bell captain nodded and seemed to be repressing an almost irresistible urge to applaud.

The only trouble with listening to Stengel is that it requires a great deal of endurance. Stengel loves to talk; indeed he is probably the most indefatigable talker in the world, at least of the male sex. He can hardly stand to remain silent even for a minute. When someone interrupts to ask him a question, he is so impatient to reply that the bloodless lips of his seamy face work in and out; his jaw muscles twitch, and the wrinkles from the collar of his uniform to his jutting jaw jump in anticipation of the restless flow of words that will soon be tumbling forth. At the left side of his mouth, running almost to his chin, is a line as deep as a canyon. It has been worn there, through the years, by the relentless rumble and roar of words pouring out of the side of his mouth like an eternal waterfall. When the sides of the canyon begin to quiver with the vibration of the flood, watch out. The filibuster is on and will continue far into the night, interrupted only by an occasional vast face-squeezing wink, to punctuate a joke, or by Casey's disturbing habit of now and again running a huge paw across his mouth, wiping out entire words, phrases and sentences.

It requires a good deal of linguistic talent to understand the flood of words, even when all of them can be heard clearly. Casey's agile tongue skips from subject to subject with the bewildering speed of a *jai alai* ball. He hates grammar, transitions, references, unnecessary explanations and simple logic. He disdains to use names and even avoids pronouns except when mingled with such complete lack of continuity as to confuse the issue altogether. To comprehend Casey's remarks about the Yankees, for example, you have to know that "the little feller," is Phil Rizzuto and that "the chief" is Pitcher Allie Reynolds. "The kid" is Mickey Mantle, except when it is Infielder Billy Martin. When talking about Yogi Berra, Stengel says merely, "my catcher." The other players are known, interchangeably, as "my man," or simply "the guy out there." The opposition team is "them"—and often in the middle of everything there suddenly appears an anonymous "him" which is impossible to pin down and perhaps has no meaning whatever. Casey apparently uses "him" as a sort of utility infielder, to throw in whenever a gap appears in his eccentric syntax.

Stengel's busy and unpredictable tongue has provided sportswriters with some of their happiest moments for many years. This year at spring training Casey was asked who he figured would be his regular third baseman. "Well," he said, "the feller I got on there is hitting pret-ty good and I know he can make that throw, and if he don't make it that other feller I got coming up has shown me a lot, and if he can't I have my guy and I know what he can do. On the other hand the guy's not around now. And, well, this guy may be able to do it against left-handers if my guy ain't strong enough. But I know one of my guys is going to do it."

To translate this speech, it was necessary to know that Stengel was using "feller" to refer to two separate and distinct players, and "guy" to three. What he meant was this: "Well, I'm playing Gil McDougald at third in spring training; he's hitting all right and has a good peg from third to first. But if he slumps, I've got Rookie Andy Carey, who has shown a lot of promise. If neither McDougald nor Carey works out, I've got Bobby Brown reporting to the camp as soon as he finishes his winter medical studies, and we've used Brown at third with good success in the past. On the other hand Brown isn't here yet and we don't know how he'll be this year. And, well, maybe McDougald can hit left-handers if Brown doesn't come through. But I know one of the three will be all right on any given day."

Casey himself sometimes gets tangled in his own tangents and loses the path. Frequently he begins to tell a story at the start of the evening, gets sidetracked into footnotes and that-reminds-me's and is still approaching the point by way of interminable circumlocution some five or six hours later. The audience remains fascinated, although wondering when he will get there. Suddenly the bartender steps up, points to the clock and says, "The bar is closing." "Gentlemen," says Casey, rising from his chair and smoothing his plaid coat, "there is much more which could be said but my man here in the white jacket has said it all. Goodnight."

In the course of a season he leaves a staggering number of anecdotal men on base; he is probably the greatest teller of unfinished stories since Scheherazade. Once a reporter left the ball-park press box to go down and ask Casey a simple question: who was going to pitch the next day's game? An hour later he returned to the press box, somewhat dazed. "Well," asked a colleague, "did Casey tell you his pitcher?" "He started to," said the reporter, "but then he began talking about playing under John McGraw and that reminded him of the time he was managing Toledo and from there we went to the Pacific Coast League. The way I get it, tomorrow's pitcher is Christy Mathewson."

Another reporter once called Stengel in his hotel room to talk about a big trade between the Red Sox and White Sox which had just been announced on the news ticker. "It goes this way, Case," said the reporter. "The Red Sox get Ray Scarborough and Bill Wight from the White Sox for Al Zarilla, Joe Dobson and Dick Littlefield. What do you think of the trade?" There was a long pause and then from Casey's end came the edifying comment: "Well, the feller ought to help them."

Because of his rambling monologues, his disheveled face and his belligerent anthropoid walk, Stengel was for years known in the baseball world chiefly as a clown. The reputation started when he was a 20-year-old rookie outfielder in the Blue Grass League, playing for Maysville, Ky. As he tells it now, "There was a lunatic asylum across from the centerfield fence, and the inmates made me their favorite ballplayer. I was having trouble learning to slide so I used to throw my glove down on the ground and slide into it going to and from my position. Them nuts in the loony bin always cheered when they saw that, but my manager use to tap his forehead and point at the asylum and say it's only a matter of time Stengel."

Up in the majors with Brooklyn two years later, Stengel got more laughs than base hits. Once it was arranged for Wilbert Robinson, the Brooklyn manager, to settle the old argument by trying to catch a baseball dropped from an airplane. Stengel was selected to drop the ball. Characteristically—and with terribly messy results—he dropped a ripe grapefruit instead. He was traded to Pittsburgh and was roundly booed the first time he reappeared in visitor's uniform in the Dodger ball park—whereupon he performed the famous stunt that everybody remembers from his playing days. He bowed low to the Brooklyn crowd and removed his cap, letting a sparrow fly out. With Pittsburgh he lasted only until he stood statue-still in the outfield one day, complaining that he was too weak to move because he wasn't paid enough to eat.

Stengel brought his baseball career to a climax, however, in something of a blaze of glory. He played for the Giants under tough old John McGraw, who knew how to handle young cutups, and batted .368 one year. When the Giants played the Yankees in the 1923 World Series, Stengel gave the Giants their only two victories by hitting two crucial home runs. (McGraw had not completely stifled his spirit—after the second homer he thumbed his nose at all the Yankees he passed on his way around the bases.)

In 1926—when he was 36 and through as a player—he started as a manager at Toledo, in the American Association. There then began a long series of ups and downs, mostly downs. He won the pennant at Toledo one year, eventually went up to the majors to manage the impossible Brooklyn team of the early 1930s, failed as everyone else had done and was fired while his contract still had a year to run. After the year of idleness he caught on with the Boston Braves, who were, if anything, more impossible than the Dodgers. He stayed there six years, badly mired near the bottom of the second division, and seemed destined to wind up as a manager whose only claim to fame was a minor league pennant won in the dim and distant past.

In those melancholy days at Boston, Stengel's humor turned sour and he was hardly the best-loved manager in the game. For example he had a player named Max West, a pretty fair hitter but a dub in the outfield. One day while lumbering vainly after a fly, West crashed into a wall and split his scalp. As he left the field for a doctor's help, Stengel said bitterly,

"You got a great pair of hands, Max." Once his third baseman let an easy grounder bounce off his glove for a two-base error. When the third baseman got back to the bench Casey said, "Next time a ball is hit toward you please don't touch it, because then my left fielder can come in and hold it to a single."

Partly because of such sarcasms, partly because of his team's dismal record, Stengel was himself subjected to one of baseball's historic indignities. In the spring of 1943 he was hit by an automobile and suffered a broken leg that kept him from actively managing the team for two months. Sportswriter Dave Egan of the Boston *Record* promptly nominated the motorist as "the man who has done the most for Boston baseball." A year later Casey, by then 54, was back in the minors and apparently through forever.

What the critics did not realize, however, was that Casey had been saddled for most of his managerial life with teams so hopeless that no one could have been good humored around them, much less successful. In the minors Stengel caught on by luck with the Milwaukee team of the American Association, which was just getting good under the active player-procurement policies of Owner Bill Veeck, the man who later ran the Cleveland club and is now trying to resurrect the Browns. This time Stengel had some real material—and besides he was older and wiser. He led his youngsters right up to the pennant—his first in 17 long and discouraging years. Later on he moved on to Oakland in the Pacific Coast League, pushed his team into the play-offs for three years in a row and finally won a pennant there too in his third try. By the time the Yankees needed a new manager in 1949, Stengel had metamorphosed from a has-been clown and scold into the man most likely to succeed.

The rest has been history. Stengel inherited a pretty good team: Tommy Henrich and Joe DiMaggio were still slugging the ball; a young catcher named Yogi Berra bade fair to take his place beside them, and Joe Page was the best relief pitcher in baseball, practically untouchable. But there were weak spots too—an almost untried rookie at second base, a left fielder who had trouble hitting left-handers and a right fielder who couldn't hit right-handers. Stengel juggled all these doubtful assets into a pennant and World Series winning balance sheet that looked much better than it really was. He made a fine art of the two-platoon system, fielding one team against left-handed pitching and another one against right-handers. When the team was hitting, he played for the one big booming inning in the oldtime American League slugging tradition. When hits were scarce, he shifted to John McGraw's National League system of stealing, hit-running and squeezing for the single run. Sometimes he almost seemed to be a mystic, with invisible little men perched on his shoulder to whisper strategy into his ear.

At crucial moments he stuck in the unlikeliest pinch hitters, and they delivered. He benched a steady hitter for an erratic one—and the off-and-on hitter caught fire. He juggled his fielders and they came up with game-saving catches; he always had the right man in the right place on the right day. He persuaded the Yankee management to buy him old Johnny Mize—a first baseman who had been considered washed up for years—and Mize began hitting the ball over the fences. Once in the ninth inning of a tight World Series game, when a hit would have beaten the Yankees and the opposition had a power hitter at the plate, Casey motioned one of his outfielders to play in instead of moving out toward the wall. Nobody yet knows what made Casey think it would happen, but the hitter was out on a little Texas Leaguer that would have dropped in for a hit had the outfielder been in his normal position.

In succeeding years Stengel has done an even more remarkable job. He lost Tommy Henrich to Father Time, and then Joe DiMaggio tailed off to a .263 hitter and finally retired too. Joe Page lost his stuff. The Marines took away Second Baseman Jerry Coleman; the Army took away Third Baseman Bobby Brown and Pitchers Whitey Ford and Tom Morgan. This year the once mighty Yankees boast only one man who had hit more than 20 homers by the end of the second week in September. Yet Casey has had them right up there all the way.

How does he do it? Casey sometimes wonders himself.

One night in August, when his team had gone into a slump and dissipated a 7½-game lead, a reporter wandering near the Yankees' hotel found Casey sitting all alone at midnight on a park bench. As usual he was talking, this time to himself. The reporter got out his notebook and took down the words as they flowed down the canyon creased along the left side of Casey's mouth: "I tell you, I don't know what to do. I could take the second baseman out, but then I'm hurt because the other feller don't make the double play like the other feller. Or maybe I could use the new feller at third, but the guy don't hit right-handers. Or I could take out my right fielder because he ain't going well against right-handed pitching either, but I guess I got to stick with what I have even though none of the fellers is doing what I'd like. Well, I guess the trouble is I use to have more pinch hitters on the bench that would scare hell out of you than I have now. We don't hit it often enough when we should hit it often enough and all I can say is it sure would be charming to have a star at every position but I haven't so what am I gonna do?"

Translated, this meant, "I could bench Billy Martin because he isn't hitting, and try Kal Segrist at second base—but the trouble is that Segrist can't handle double plays as well as Martin. Or maybe I could use Carey at third, except that Carey can't hit right-handers. Or I could pull Bauer out of right field, because he hasn't been hitting right-handers either. Well, I guess what I really need is some good pinch hitters to throw in for the big innings, but I haven't got them so what can I do?"

The fact is, however, that Casey seems to have done it, whatever it was. His nightly illustrated lectures, though they sometimes outrage the hotel desk clerks and elderly patrons, have taught his youngsters a lot about baseball. His hunches —which are not really hunches at all but a kind of slide-rule engineering formula—have paid off. His wit, once bitter, has now been turned into a comforting thing that makes rookies feel at home and befathered in the frightening crowd-packed vastness of Yankee Stadium. Casey has no children, and he has seemed to take a special pleasure out of bringing up young players like Yogi Berra, Gil McDougald and, now, Mickey

Mantle and Billy Martin. On the other hand he is still capable of an occasional blast, to keep the players on their toes. One of them burst forth early this month, when a group of Yankees sat around their train gaily playing Twenty Questions after what to Stengel was a particularly humiliating and painful defeat in Philadelphia. Ole Case laid down the law, so publicly that the next day every time a Yankee got into the batting cage the opposition players yelled, "Is it animal?" "Is it mineral?" "Is it alive?" And, by what was surely not complete coincidence, the Yankee play immediately picked up.

The words pour down the canyon, and the Yankees keep winning. They win with or without Henrichs and DiMaggios. In fact, they have been winning with the weakest team—on paper—that the Yankees have had in years. When Casey stomps out of the dugout on those ancient legs, his chin jutting and his oversize ears flapping in the breeze, and the pronouns tumbling over one another in magnificent confusion, the opposition knows that there goes a man—and there, in all likelihood, goes the ball game.

What will Ole Case do when this season's wars are over? Perhaps he will retire; he has been threatening to retire for years. He is 62 years old now and wealthy. He invested his early baseball earnings in land which turned out to have oil under it, and he has a fine home in California where he could sit in his private swimming pool, collect his royalties, clip his coupons and quit worrying about the income taxes on the $80,000 a year in salary and bonuses that the Yankees pay him.

He has earned his rest; his withering neck can hardly afford another wrinkle and his knotty legs may soon find even hotel carpets too much for them. Then, there is also the matter of Mrs. Stengel, a California realtor's daughter to whom he has been married for 28 years. Mrs. Stengel is tall, slim, chic and of the firm opinion that no wife should be forced to listen to nothing but baseball talk for three decades. Indeed she preserves a kind of memento of her martyrdom in the form of a dent in the ceiling of their California living room. The dent marks the spot where Casey's right shoe landed one night while he was demonstrating the fine points of athletics with a little too much enthusiasm; it is a constant reminder to Casey—she hopes—that there are other and less strenuous things in life. What Mrs. Stengel would like, after all these years, is for Casey to quit traveling, quit worrying, quit wearing those loud jackets and settle down as a West Coast gentleman of leisure.

So maybe this is Ole Case's last year. On the other hand he may try, like Hemingway's old man of the sea, for one more big one. Not quite for the same reasons, of course. The thing is, how much talking can you do to an oil well—or while coming up from a dive in a private swimming pool?

SUGGESTIONS FOR STUDY:

1. What words in the first two paragraphs show that the writer carries through the notion of a theatrical performance?
2. Do you learn something about playing baseball from the antics at the Sheraton-Cadillac?
3. Is some knowledge of baseball required to get the point of words like ". . . tomorrow's pitcher is Christy Mathewson"?
4. Is a knowledge of baseball required to get the point of words like "Well, the feller ought to help them"?
5. Could the whole article have been written in Stengelese? Why? Why not?
6. How is the article organized after the discussion and illustration of Stengelese?
7. Did Stengel's managerial technique change over the years? How?
8. Is the writer being literal when he says, "Words pour down the canyon"? Does he overdo this fanciful language?
9. Does the end of the essay return in idea to the beginning?
10. What is the meaning of *histrionic* name, wander *casually,* modest *requisites, inexhaustible repertory, indefatigable* talker, *eccentric syntax, anecdotal* men on base, rambling *monologue, disheveled* face, *belligerent anthropoid* walk?
11. Write a character sketch of some interesting or strange person you know, using the person's own speech as much as possible to characterize him. Make your own opinion of the person emerge from the sketch.

Occasionally, as the following two selections demonstrate, the daily sports page may become a forum for much larger issues. Milton Gross is a sports columnist for the New York Post; *this is his daily column, "Speaking Out," for May 9, 1952.*

THERE BUT FOR THE GRACE OF GOD
by Milton Gross

THE YEARS do things to the memory, but the recollection of Midgie Serota is clear because it was the sight of Midgie standing before Judge Saul Streit in General Sessions on Wednesday and pleading guilty to conspiring to fix basketball games that brought it all back.

I knew Jackie Goldsmith, who, after months of saying nothing, also admitted his guilt yesterday, and Eli Kaye and Nat (Lovey) Brown because they were all neighborhood kids with an eye for the quick buck, sharp attire and smart manner. But they were not of my time and Midgie was, although he was Jackie's co-defendant.

We played basketball together at Thomas Jefferson High School and there was none who played it with more heart than the admitted fixer who now faces a term up to three years. But Midgie never could make it big this way because he barely made it over five feet in height, though he tried and

-----

Reproduced from the New York Post of May 9, 1952. Copyright 1952 New York Post Corp.

made a letter which seemed so important to all of us in those years.

Midgie had an accurate set shot; not as good as the one Jackie Goldsmith was to fashion a dozen years later, but enough to make him dangerous when you gave him room. When you came in on him Midgie could go around with a shifty dribble and one day in practice against the varsity team Midgie dribbled so recklessly going in for a shot that he crashed head-on with the wall and gashed his face and head.

I remember the kid lying on the floor, blood gushing from his head, and the stunned look on his face. It seemed to me the same stunned look was there again yesterday as he stood before the bar and I wondered why Midgie had come along the road he did. Who could have stopped him before he had gone so far?

I remembered the night immediately following our graduation from high school. Midgie and some others I knew called at my house to go up to The Bronx for a game at Fordham. Midgie gave me a ticket. He had a pocket full of them and I wondered where they had come from. So many, in fact, that he peddled them outside the gyms, selling them under the set price when the weather was bad, but charging all the traffic would bear when the crowd came in droves.

There was a game at the 106th Regiment Armory. I believe it was between the St. John's Wonder Five and CCNY. The old drill shed held no more than 2500, but there already were that many and more inside and as many more outside with tickets in their hands clamoring for admission. There's a twist here, because one of the reporters covering the game that night was Ned Irish and it was this seeming crowd appeal of college basketball that made him work up courage enough to start promoting.

Then the night came when I knew where Midgie's tickets came from. Midgie and a half dozen others were caught at NYU peddling counterfeits. Among the others were a freshman star of the NYU basketball team; a senior at NYU, whose brother later died a violent death as the most talkative member of Murder, Inc; another teammate of mine at Jefferson, who became an accomplished referee, except that last year there were charges aimed at him in a midwest gambling inquiry as a referee in with the fixers. His name never was mentioned but those of us from around the block knew who it was.

The NYU freshman star was expelled from college. So was the senior. No charges were brought against Midgie or against his compatriot who was to become a big-time referee.

Years passed before I saw Midgie again. It was in front of a pool room on Sutter Av. and the way Midgie lounged in the doorway it was obvious this was his hangout.

I asked Midgie how he was getting along and what he was doing for a living.

His exact words are difficult to recall, but they amounted to the makings of a new badger game with an old twist.

"You know," he said, "I've been thinking there's always a way to make a buck. You're a newspaperman and just reading your paper a guy with a head on him can make a few quick."

"Take the death notices," he said. "A smart guy reads them and, quick, he gets an idea. He makes a note of all the addresses of the stiffs and he gets himself a couple of dozen fountain pens. Then he goes out to the houses, talks very sympathetic to the widows or the stiff's kids.

. . . "He says, 'I'm awful sorry about your husband and I called to pay my respects. I used to do a little business with him and just before he died he bought this fountain pen from me. It's not much but it may have been the last thing he ever purchased. I thought maybe you'd like to have it as a keepsake.'" . . .

"You buy one of the pens for a quarter," Midgie said. "You can get maybe three, four bucks from the widow.

"Not a bad racket if a guy wanted to do it and work it right," Midgie said.

Fixing games wasn't either, but as Midgie stood before Judge Streit I imagine he must have had a change of heart. I walked out of that courtroom free and unimpeded and said a silent prayer that I could.

SUGGESTIONS FOR STUDY:

1. What does Gross accomplish in the first two paragraphs?
2. Is the rest of the article arranged chronologically?
3. Are there major divisions in this chronology? What?
4. Do the first and last paragraphs give the article symmetry?
5. Is Gross's diction frequently colloquial, even hardboiled? Cite some examples. Are they appropriate to the subject?
6. Point out transition between sentences and paragraphs—repetition of key words, pronouns, expressions of time, etc.
7. Does Gross use specific detail? Cite some examples.
8. Does Gross use contrast and comparison? Is there a significant implied comparison in the last paragraph?
9. What tone does Gross's use of the name *Midgie* rather than *Serota* give the essay?
10. Does Gross, unlike many moralists, present a moral issue without antagonizing the reader? How?
11. Write a theme discussing a moral issue, and using a specific incident to illustrate your point.

A sportswriter reports his immediate reactions to the death of Franklin D. Roosevelt.

THE CHAMP IS GONE, BUT . . .
by Joe Cummiskey

THE WAY it was around our office at 5:51 p.m. yesterday was just like it must have been everywhere in the world where free men live and where so many now live only to be free. For he was one of us.

Reprinted from PM, April 13, 1945.

Somehow or other, if you were in sports, you never thought of him so much as connected with the high office which he held. Rather, you remembered him most the way he'd chuckle, getting ready to throw out the first ball to open the baseball season. Or how he'd sit on the 50 at the Army-Navy game, in the days when the Army-Navy game was only as grim as football.

You'd remember his voice when you heard the flash of his death and you'd never forget that night at Chautauqua when you were a city editor, listening to him throw his words against that upstate political sounding-board and hear them come back again and again and again:

"I hate war!"

And that was before the men who hated him turned both those phrases into catchwords and tried to throw them into his face, hoping to blind the people who put him where he was. They didn't fool him—or the people.

You remember how only as far back as Washington's Birthday you were on the platform with Mrs. Roosevelt and you still feel the warmth of her handshake and the sincerity with which she offered that same hand to Joe Louis, the one-time cotton picker.

You remembered how, with The Champ showing the way at Casablanca, Teheran, and Yalta, you felt awfully silly punching at these same keys about Branch Rickey's latest troubles in Brooklyn. Or Mel Ott's headaches with the Giants. Or all of baseball's gigantic worries about whether they'd get a green light—and have manpower enough, afterwards—to play in '45.

You remembered how, in the twilight at the Polo Grounds, a game was halted while the loud speakers piped his voice to the filled stands, and how matches flickered in the dark and not a sound was heard as he gave one of his reports to the Nation.

You remembered as late as only yesterday, when the Red Cross ambulances wheeled the lame and the halt, carrying their wounds from the far-off battlelines, into the Stadium to see a ball game in the bright afternoon sun. And you realized that The Champ had been that way himself, all through his public life.

You remembered sitting on the stool in the Flatbush coffee pot one night, arguing—or mostly listening, because you were among Dodger fans—about that very day's game. And then the radio came on with his preparedness speech and his warning of the things that were then yet to come. And you suddenly realize now that it was the only time you ever heard any one man's voice stop a baseball argument in Brooklyn.

You remember last Fall, in the drizzle and the rain, how you got yourself all bundled up and gathered up your three kids and perched them along the line of march where his campaign caravan came from Brooklyn to New York.

And how you shivered from the rain and the cold, but he went bareheaded through it all.

And you remember, after that campaign, that you had the first chance to meet Governor Dewey at the Boxing Commission's party where they announced a new State Chairman and the Gov. looked fit and hearty after his long vacation and rest after the strenuous campaign. By that time, The Champ was winging to Yalta, I suppose. Or somewhere such, getting on with the job to be done.

You remember how, when he got back from over there, he took time out to shake hands with Clark Griffith, owner of the Washington Senators, and to accept, for himself and his wife, the gold-edged season passes for 1945 to Griffith Stadium.

"And it isn't beyond the realm of human possibility that I might get out to your opener this year, Griff," he said. And added, "If all goes well."

I know you're not supposed to quote directly the President of the United States, but the hell with press club protocol on that one.

And you remember the faces of your kids when you told them that he was indeed dead and they couldn't say a word. Not even the one who, last election time, explained to some of her playmates what F.D.R. stood for.

"Why everybody knows that," she said, loftily. "Franklin Democracy Roosevelt, of course!"

She wasn't kidding.

SUGGESTIONS FOR STUDY:

1. Is Cummiskey's diction appropriate to his eulogy?
2. Does he bring humor or political partisanship into the eulogy? Are these appropriate? Why?
3. Does Cummiskey use repetition to indicate structure? Would this be as effective in a larger essay?
4. Write a eulogy of someone, dead or alive, whom you admire. Avoid excessive sentimentality. Or write a theme about something using diction appropriate to something else, like a romance in terms of military strategy. Use terminology with which you are familiar.

David E. Lilienthal, a distinguished public servant who has headed such key agencies as the Tennessee Valley Authority and the Atomic Energy Commission, delivered this statement of faith in democracy before a Senate committee.

THIS I BELIEVE
by David E. Lilienthal

THIS I do carry in my head, Senator.

I will do my best to make it clear. My convictions are not so much concerned with what I am against as what I am for; and that excludes a lot of things automatically.

Traditionally, democracy has been an affirmative doctrine rather than merely a negative one.

I believe—and I conceive the Constitution of the United

Reprinted from The Congressional Record.

States to rest upon, as does religion—the fundamental proposition of the integrity of the individual; and that all government and all private institutions must be designed to promote and protect and defend the integrity and the dignity of the individual; that that is the essential meaning of the Constitution and the Bill of Rights, as it is essentially the meaning of religion.

Any form of government, therefore, and any other institutions which make men means rather than ends, which exalt the state or any other institutions above the importance of men, which place arbitrary power over men as a fundamental tenet of government are contrary to that conception, and, therefore, I am deeply opposed to them.

The communistic philosophy as well as the communistic form of government falls within this category, for their fundamental tenet is quite to the contrary. The fundamental tenet of communism is that the state is an end in itself, and that therefore the powers which the state exercises over the individual are without any ethical standard to limit them.

That I deeply disbelieve.

It is very easy simply to say that one is not a Communist. And, of course, if my record requires me to state that very affirmatively, then it is a great disappointment to me.

It is very easy to talk about being against communism. It is equally important to believe those things which provide a satisfying and effective alternative. Democracy is that satisfying, affirmative alternative.

Its hope in the world is that it is an affirmative belief, rather than being simply a belief against something else and nothing more.

One of the tenets of democracy that grows out of this central core of a belief that the individual comes first, that all men are the children of God and that their personalities are therefore sacred, carries with it a great belief in civil liberties and their protection, and a repugnance to anyone who would steal from a human being that which is most precious to him—his good name—either by imputing things to him by innuendo or by insinuation. And it is especially an unhappy circumstance that occasionally that is done in the name of democracy. This, I think, can tear our country apart and destroy it if we carry it further.

I deeply believe in the capacity of democracy to surmount any trials that may lie ahead, provided only that we practice it in our daily lives.

And among the things we must practice is that while we seek fervently to ferret out the subversive and antidemocratic forces in the country, we do not at the same time, by hysteria, by resort to innuendo, and smears, and other unfortunate tactics, besmirch the very cause that we believe in, and cause a separation among our people—cause one group and one individual to hate another, based on mere attacks, mere unsubstantiated attacks upon their loyalty.

I want also to add that part of my conviction is based on my training as an Anglo-American common-law lawyer. It is the very basis and the great heritage of the English people to this country, which we have maintained, that we insist on the strictest rules of credibility of witnesses and on the avoidance of hearsay, and that gossip shall be excluded, in the courts of justice. And that, too, is an essential of our democracy.

Whether by administrative agencies acting arbitrarily against business organizations, or whether by investigating activities of legislative branches, whenever those principles fail, those principles of the protection of an individual and his good name against besmirchment by gossip, hearsay, and the statements of witnesses who are not subject to cross-examination—then, too, we have failed in carrying forward our ideals in respect to democracy.

That I deeply believe.

SUGGESTIONS FOR STUDY:

1. What comparisons and contrasts does Lilienthal make in defining democracy?
2. Is he confident of the power of democracy?
3. Is he aware of dangers to it?
4. What is the meaning of *arbitrary power, tenet, innuendo, besmirch, credibility*?
5. Write a statement of belief of your own on any issue. Or write a theme divided into two parts, the first of which states the negative, the second the positive side of anything.